LEADING PUBLIC ORGANIZATIONS
AN INTERACTIVE APPROACH

LEADING PUBLIC ORGANIZATIONS
AN INTERACTIVE APPROACH

A. CAROL RUSAW
University of Louisiana, Lafayette

HARCOURT COLLEGE PUBLISHERS

Fort Worth   Philadelphia   San Diego   New York   Orlando   Austin   San Antonio
Toronto   Montreal   London   Sydney   Tokyo

PUBLISHER	Earl McPeek
EXECUTIVE EDITOR	David Tatom
MARKET STRATEGIST	Laura Brennan
PROJECT EDITOR	Joyce Fink
ART DIRECTOR	Sue Hart
PRODUCTION MANAGER	Linda McMillan

ISBN: 0-15-508462-3
Library of Congress Catalog Card Number: 00-103173

Address for Domestic Orders
Harcourt College Publishers, 6277 Sea Harbor Drive, Orlando, FL 32887-6777
800-782-4479

Address for International Orders
International Customer Service
Harcourt, Inc., 6277 Sea Harbor Drive, Orlando, FL 32887-6777
407-345-3800
(fax) 407-345-4060
(e-mail) hbintl@harcourt.com

Address for Editorial Correspondence
Harcourt College Publishers, 301 Commerce Street, Suite 3700, Fort Worth, TX 76102

Web Site Address
http://www.harcourtcollege.com

Harcourt College Publishers will provide complimentary supplements or supplement packages to those adopters qualified under our adoption policy. Please contact your sales representative to learn how you qualify. If as an adopter or potential user you receive supplements you do not need, please return them to your sales representative or send them to: Attn: Returns Department, Troy Warehouse, 465 South Lincoln Drive, Troy, MO 63379.

Printed in the United States of America

0 1 2 3 4 5 6 7 8 9   043   9 8 7 6 5 4 3 2 1

Harcourt College Publishers

*This book is dedicated to students
of public administration, who are
and will be the leaders of this
nation and of the increasingly
interconnected global society
of the twenty-first century.*

———————■———————

PREFACE

WHY I WROTE THIS BOOK   I wrote this textbook for three reasons. First, when I taught in the Master's of Public Affairs degree program, I found there were no textbooks that dealt with public leadership. I adapted leadership theories and concepts from books written for business students. Although there are some similarities, I found many more differences in the two sectors. Even as government has adopted private sector methods for becoming economically efficient and sensitive to customer demands for accountability, government lacks many conditions that allow it to be fully competitive with businesses. For instance, the legal and political framework, proscribing justice and equity, means that no matter how cost-effective public organizations may become, some clients', and customers', demands cannot be met at a level of service they expect. Prisons, for instance, may not be able to accommodate inmates' needs for total comfort and pleasure. The qualitative differences between public and private sector "businesses" made the need for a tailored textbook on leadership compelling.

The second reason comes from the first. If there are plenty of private sector leadership texts, but none for public leaders, what does this say about the importance of leadership in the public sector? As I thought about this, it seemed the omission carried a value judgement. This, along with political rhetoric and media that denigrates public service, made me think about how my students thought about themselves and their careers in public employment.

The third reason for writing this book is a response to a question my students kept asking: "How does this theory or this concept apply to 'the real world' of public administration?" If the material I presented from books and journal articles dealing with leadership—even in the public sector—had limited applicability to situations students encountered frequently in their work outside the classroom, how important was it? And how would such knowledge transfer to the situations in which the students needed to apply it?

To deal with this question, I developed experiential learning activities. Through case studies, small group discussions, role plays, and games and simulations, students can learn how to apply abstract material to situations they are likely to meet in public service. Each chapter contains exercises that guide students' thinking and encourages them to use the chapters' content as a tool for solving problems, developing new learning content, changing individual behaviors, and seeing greater relevancy to the work they do.

A WORD ABOUT EXPERIENTIAL LEARNING   Experiential learning is perhaps most like the way students learn outside class. Learning based on context occurs whenever situations captivate attention. These situations often involve something that is unique, something for which there are no obvious answers, something that is novel, or something that is contrary to standard explanations of cause and effect. Such situations freshen thinking by challenging previously held ideas and by strengthening cognitive, affective, and psycho-motor capacities to learn. Each situation, moreover, becomes grist for future learning. Whenever similar situations occur, the mind searches the existing "database" of knowledge and forms connections. Cycles of storage and retrieval go on endlessly, at conscious, pre-conscious, and unconscious levels throughout the lifespan. Learning how experiential learning works and applying it to the classroom allows students to direct their own development.

Experiential learning is lifelike, in addition, because it occurs in the context of social interaction. People learn to define concepts and develop theories about how and why things "are" from association with others in various roles they play. When learning through participation occurs, students can develop a greater reservoir or "database" of knowledge. They can also examine the accuracy and relevance of existing stocks of information through discussion and reflection on the activity. This enables students to gain a better understanding of the contexts in which they are asked to apply knowledge, a greater variety of tools with which to encounter new or problematic situations, and a deeper understanding of human behavior in creating knowledge.

So, writing this text fulfilled the three purposes. The textbook was a beginning in an area that had been largely ignored and which, I believe, was needed to encourage more people to seek out careers as public leaders. In compiling material that would be useful, moreover, I drew deeply on the disciplined research and practical wisdom of others engaged in leadership theory and practice—particularly those who focused on the public sector. I also used exercises I had developed and tested from ten years' experience as a practitioner in government and nearly as many as an academic. Through the text's content and structure, I have attempted to construct a base of knowledge I hope others will build on. The beauty and value of learning is that it goes on in other contexts, particularly outside of academe. From the textbook, I hope students will take responsibility for their own learning, particularly through group participation, reflection, and action. And through increased competence and self-confidence in assuming the challenges of public sector leadership, students as future leaders will gain the recognition and respect the profession has long deserved.

ACKNOWLEDGMENTS

I wish to thank the students and faculty of the Master's of Public and Urban Affairs program at the University of Connecticut, where I taught leadership classes for seven years. Through them, I was able to develop the idea for the textbook as well as many of the interactive activities. I also wish to acknowledge the helpful critiques and advice of the textbook reviewers: Stephen M. Hennessy, Arizona State University; Ethel Williams, University of Nebraska at Omaha; William H. Kraus, American International University; Daniel Barber, California State University, Long Beach; Martha J. Dede, California State University, Long Beach; and Douglas T. Hall, Boston University. Their expertise as experienced teachers and as practitioners in the field of public administration was invaluable in shaping the theoretical content to the needs and interests of students.

BRIEF CONTENTS

CONTENTS

CHAPTER 4
APPROACHES TO LEADERSHIP: NORMATIVE, SITUATIONAL, AND CONTINGENCY 69

PART II   DEVELOPING INTERHUMAN RELATIONSHIPS

CHAPTER 5
BUILDING TRUST 89

OVERVIEW

OBJECTIVES

- *To define key terms and concepts of leadership*
- *To establish the groundwork for building leadership skills*
- *To describe the constitutional basis for public sector leadership*
- *To introduce leadership themes covered in this book*

INTRODUCTION

Public leadership is undergoing a vast change. Instead of being centered in bureaucratic organizations, leadership is now more collaborative, involving new partnerships with businesses and civic groups. Public leaders are becoming more enterprising, taking on the roles of entrepreneurs, innovators, and team facilitators. The new roles of public leaders require not only a thorough understanding of principles of democratic governance, laws, ordinances, and regulations, but also skill in interpersonal relationships and organizational effectiveness.

These changes offer many stimulating challenges as well as unique rewards. Public leaders are at the forefront of governance. They participate in the legal systems and processes that spell out what and how people define, enact, and regulate their rights, interests, needs, and aspirations. The participation involves the give and take of negotiation and policy making, the managerial skills of administration, and the dynamics of incorporating diverse stakeholders in problem solving and decision making. Public leaders are individuals who require high levels of technical knowledge; skills in understanding complex interactions among lawmakers, executive-level politicians, and citizens; business and civic concerns; sensitivity; and personal integrity. The great challenge of public leadership is to develop these competencies simultaneously in a fishbowl-like environment.

The Dallas Morning News ran a series of articles on "The We Decade: Rebirth of a Community," highlighting the renewed collaboration between government and its varied constituents to achieve common purposes. In one article, Tarrant (1996) quoted the director of a citizenship project, who said, "The evolving relationship between government to community really demands a new look at who is going to be working on the local challenges." Tarrant went on to say that

> ...what is spurring all this activity, according to community experts and activists, is a tectonic shift in societal attitudes to a belief that no one institution—particularly government—can solve all our problems. New times require new strategies.

Serving as a public leader, however, brings special rewards. Public leaders find satisfaction in bringing together people from many differing backgrounds and facilitating solving some of the most nettlesome problems facing the social order. In the process of problem solving, public leaders learn how to tap potential talents both in themselves and in others to bring about creative solutions. This promotes self-actualization and the creation of purpose. As catalysts of meaning, public leaders discover new information, create and utilize resources for problem solving, and make decisions through the synergy of group interaction.

WHAT IS LEADERSHIP?

Catalytic, collaborative leadership is necessary in bringing together a wide range of resources and activating talents and interests in achieving a central goal or purpose. The skills of public leaders involve a balance of achieving goals and motivating followers in arenas that are often ill-defined and subject to change. Because of the multiple demands and ambiguity of purposes, defining collaborative public leadership precisely is difficult.

A definition of public leadership needs to take into account the numerous facets of who public leaders are and what they do. The nature of public leadership is, in large part, defined by the constitutional basis of their work. Public service is chartered by legislation, meaning that the content, scope, and relationship of work is related not to enterprise, but to the authority of law.

Public leaders also use interpersonal skills, individual style preferences, and technical expertise to make decisions. They accomplish objectives according to performance standards established by the nature of an organizational mission and operating objectives. But they also achieve "success" according to how their followers perceive their manner of carrying out duties. In the public sector, "followers" include not only subordinates, but also legislators, interest groups, taxpayers, and governmental agencies.

In further examining the legal nature of public leaders' tasks and the relationship qualities that distinguish public leadership performance, four interrelated themes can be observed.

THE FOUR THEMES

1. Public leadership is based on a form of representational governance. Public leaders require openness to debate, toleration of ambiguously

defined laws and regulations, and a willingness to incorporate demo-cratic values and processes in making decisions. In terms of leader-ship, public leaders take their cues from legislation and from popular consent. Public leaders are more servants than initiators of action. Public leaders exercise a great deal of discretion in performing their roles as servants, however. Through their technical expertise, the re-quirements of local conditions, and the particular interests and needs of followers, public leaders develop a sense of how to define and carry out their responsibilities.

2. Public leadership is based on participation and consensus. Public lead-ers make decisions on behalf of others in accordance with what they believe will benefit the majority. To gain an accurate perception of what stakeholders need, desire, and expect, public leaders gather in-formation from a diversity of followers, build common agendas, set broad goals, and achieve results through follower involvement. Public leadership encourages democratic participation in order to achieve constituent satisfaction with and commitment to ends.

3. Public leadership is based on the concept of ultimate resource account-ability to the people. Public leaders are not accountable to a governing board or trustees, as in the private sector. Rather, both their authority to act and the means to do so stem from the legal–representational form of governance. The "public" in general sponsors the work of public servants through elected and appointed officials. This means that stakeholder accountability is indirect, but maintained through elaborate legal checks and balances. To fulfill responsibilities to the public as ultimate "owner," public leaders need a governing set of val-ues that make accountability a high priority.

4. Public leadership is based on the values of administrative effectiveness and efficiency. Because public leaders are servants or trustees of material, financial, human, and technological resources, they must use the re-sources conservatively and wisely. Many of the notions of effectiveness and efficiency of public leaders come from "Scientific Management" con-cepts (Rainey, 1997), which stipulate that leaders create measurable stan-dards for job performance and coordinate resources to achieve quantita-tive and qualitative outcomes. This suggests that public leaders develop abilities not only in administrative management but also in using human resources to promote cooperation, creativity, and compliance.

DEFINITION USED IN THIS BOOK

The four themes suggest that public leadership encompasses a cluster of abilities and relationships that enable individuals to mutually solve prob-lems associated with governance, create and mobilize resources, develop so-lutions by consensus, and make and implement decisions. Public leadership may thus be defined as an interhuman process of identifying, defining, and carrying out goals using democratically sanctioned norms and behaviors. The definition has five major implications:

1. Leadership is based on the development and use of endearing personal characteristics as perceived by followers;

2. Leadership consists of a sequence of interrelated behaviors that others come to expect in solving problems and making decisions;

3. Leadership entails use of power and influence in fulfilling responsibilities;

4. Leadership is a relationship based on preferred communications styles, as well as identified needs, interests, and capabilities of followers, and on situational requirements; and

5. Leadership involves personal integrity in assuming responsibilities and working with diverse stakeholders.

The definition and the five implications are described in greater depth in the book's chapters.

PURPOSE OF THIS BOOK

This textbook was written to provide the knowledge and skills public sector leaders need to perform their multiple responsibilities with confidence and competence. It assumes that public leadership differs substantially from private sector leadership in its relationship structures, its legally based mission, and its technical content. In the many leadership texts that have been published to date, there is little mention of the unique facets of public leadership and no methodology for teaching it. This textbook fills this gap by examining leadership from a theoretical as well as practical view. It is based on research as well as experience in 8 years of teaching leadership to students in a Masters of Public Administration program. The textbook provides foundational theories, examples in the public sector, and experiential learning activities to further develop skills and competencies. The aim of this textbook is to help students understand the phenomena of public sector leadership, including the nature of work, clientele, and environment, as well as to develop skills that will transfer to their particular work settings. By connecting knowledge acquisition, practice, and reflection, students will be prepared to meet the challenges public sector organizations are facing and will continue to face.

PLAN OF THIS BOOK

To achieve its aim, this textbook is divided into three parts:
Part I includes foundational leadership theories with public sector applications. Part I consists of chapters concerned with power and influence in

developing and carrying out public leadership roles, motivating followers, and tailoring leadership styles to both the needs and interests of followers as well as to the situations leaders and followers encounter.

Part II probes the interhuman or relationship aspects of leadership. It describes leadership characteristics, skills for developing effective human relationships, skills for communicating with a variety of followers, techniques for using the uniqueness of diverse followers, and methods for building and maintaining teams.

Part III describes special abilities public leaders need to fulfill their responsibilities. These include competencies in decision making, conflict resolution, transforming follower values and behaviors, innovation, and ethical integrity.

At the end of each chapter are learning activities that enable students to reflect on the concepts in the reading, discuss central content questions, and assess their leadership abilities. This leads to developing a critical capacity to analyze assumptions, values, beliefs, and actions in social settings. Through the applications exercises, students are encouraged to continue to learn beyond the course.

OUTLINE

PART I: FOUNDATIONAL CONCEPTS OF PUBLIC LEADERSHIP

CHAPTER 1: TRANSACTING LEADERSHIP ROLES AND RESPONSIBILITIES This chapter introduces the concepts of roles and relationships as behaviors leaders and followers negotiate in meeting mutual goals and interests. It discusses how ideas of public leadership roles have developed from perspectives of Scientific Management, human relations, and situational management. The chapter describes the organizational and political contributors to the development of public leadership roles. Chapter 1 also discusses common problems public leaders face in defining and acting their roles and responsibilities, such as role credibility and role stress.

CHAPTER 2: LEADERSHIP AUTHORITY, POWER, AND INFLUENCE This chapter defines *authority* as the right to lead. It also discusses formal and informal power as derived from legal as well as ascribed authority. In examining various theories and bases of power, Chapter 2 distinguishes power from influence. Emphasizing influence as a product of follower inferences, the chapter describes some techniques leaders use to create positive impressions. Among the techniques are use of political and shared power strategies.

CHAPTER 3: MOTIVATING OTHERS This chapter explores the uses of values, motives, needs, and organizational processes and arrangements that influence follower compliance with leader requests. The text contends that motives are complex forces within individuals that stem from needs, drives, and socialized learning. Historically, different leadership approaches have specified how to activate motives to achieve leader purposes. The chapter analyzes the approaches and describes applications from Scientific Management, reward-based theories of management, human relations schools of thought, and organizational development models of enriching worker environments and skill development.

CHAPTER 4: APPROACHES TO LEADERSHIP: NORMATIVE AND SITUATIONAL This chapter introduces conditions, such as individual characteristics, culture, types of preferred power and influence strategies, and conditions within environments that make using any particular style of leadership faulty. To examine how situational leadership has evolved and how it is used today, Chapter 4 highlights several prominent theories, including Fiedler, Hersey and Blanchard, Vroom and Yetton, House, and Kerr and Jermier. By knowing individual preferences and readiness for independent decision making, degree of environmental ambiguity, and tasks that do not require leader supervision, availability of leadership substitutes, leaders can attain the results they desire through different followers.

PART II: DEVELOPING INTERHUMAN RELATIONSHIPS

CHAPTER 5: BUILDING TRUST Effective leader–follower relationships are built on mutual trust. To transact roles and responsibilities and achieve ends, leaders must create conditions that followers accept as valid and useful, and followers need to commit their resources fully. The chapter discusses some conditions that facilitate trust building, such as aligning intentions with actions, personal integrity, self-control, degree of perceived similarity of interests and goals, ability to disclose one's personal thoughts and feelings and use information to improve other and self-understanding, and organizational politics and climate. By developing sensitivity to self in relationship to others, leaders can facilitate trust and enhance collaboration among followers.

CHAPTER 6: CREATING MEANING: APPROACHES TO LEADERSHIP COMMUNICATION Based on the works of Jablin and Putnam, Chapter 6 describes four central approaches to analyzing communications relationships: mechanistic, psychological, symbolic interactionist, and systemic. The chapter discusses the formation and use of symbols in creating meaning as well as some common perceptual errors that occur in interpreting verbal and nonverbal language. The chapter depicts key leader roles in producing organizational culture and managing interpersonal communications networks. Describing impediments that occur frequently in hierarchical organizational structures, the chapter points out distortions in conveying and decoding messages.

CHAPTER 7: LEADING DIVERSE FOLLOWERS This chapter contends that there are multiple forms of "diversity" that affect the character of leader–follower relationships. These include not only race, gender, and age, but also socioeconomic background, culture, thinking styles, and viewpoints. Many conditions that stem from a lack of "diversity," as defined here, produce bias that limits effective group performance. Some conditions the chapter highlights include attributions, ideologies, past experiences, lack of direct and continuing contact, authoritarianism and ethnocentrism, and degree of physical attractiveness. Strategies that fail to integrate follower differences may be based in prejudice and may manifest themselves in stereotypical leadership behaviors. These produce low trust, poor individual motivation, reinforcement of existing stereotypes, and creation of sharply defined role behaviors. Leaders can develop more inclusiveness in thoughts and interactions, however, by understanding the importance of critical thinking, self-reflection, discussion, and participation. To foster collaborative work, leaders can also understand and practice sharing power.

CHAPTER 8: TEAM LEADERSHIP IN THE PUBLIC SECTOR This chapter points out that using teams is central to developing collaborative leadership, particularly in view of the growing interest in public sector productivity and competition with private corporations. Following a distinction between teams and groups, Chapter 8 describes common task and interpersonal roles leaders play in collective settings. The chapter also describes stages of team evolution and pitfalls typical at each. Identifying conflict as one of the most pervasive impediments to team development, the chapter describes seven types that frequently disrupt teams. The chapter concludes by discussing skills leaders need to acquire in order to manage conflict and enable team members to produce high-quality results.

CHAPTER 9: LEADING CONFLICT RESOLUTION IN PUBLIC ORGANIZATIONS Expanding on the use of conflict resolution strategies leaders may use in team building, this chapter describes in greater depth the concept of conflict and relates it to establishing collaborative relationships in nonteam settings. Chapter 9 emphasizes the management of conflict among a myriad of external public organizational stakeholders and constituents. In particular, the chapter describes stages and levels of conflict. It also discusses typical responses. Using techniques from Fisher and Ury's principled negotiation strategy, the chapter describes some ways leaders may achieve ends that benefit both their interests and those of stakeholders.

PART III: SPECIAL LEADERSHIP COMPETENCIES

CHAPTER 10: RATIONAL AND NONRATIONAL PROBLEM SOLVING AND DECISION MAKING IN THE PUBLIC SECTOR Asserting that problem solving and decision making are intertwined and occur on a continuum, this chapter examines both rational and nonrational approaches. Rational approaches, which concentrate on purposeful methods to achieve specified ends, are based in economic theories that proscribe one "best" way to manage. Processes include problem identification, developing and weighing alternative solutions, selecting the optimal choice, and implementing the alternative. Nonrational approaches approaches involve factors that depend on individual and group perspectives. The chapter discusses three of the most common nonrational approaches, incrementalism, satisficing, and garbage-can. Chapter 10 cites and assesses examples of each in the public sector. The chapter also discusses techniques that enhance creative thinking.

CHAPTER 11: PUBLIC LEADERSHIP AND INNOVATION In contrast to transactional leadership, which involves exchange of resources to achieve a desired end or payoff, transformational leadership involves changing follower motivations and goals to reach larger purposes. The chapter points out that innovation is more difficult in the public than the private sector, but can be achieved under certain conditions. It defines *innovation* as changes in services or products resulting in something new to industries, organizations, or individuals. This chapter discusses several forms of innovation in the public sector, such as reinvention, reengineering, and Total Quality Management (TQM). It enumerates conditions for successful innovations and depicts skills leaders need.

CHAPTER 12: THE ETHICS OF PUBLIC LEADERSHIP Because roles of public sector leaders have been changing to adapt to a myriad of new demands for innovation, responsiveness, productivity, and accountability, ethical standards for evaluating leadership behavior have become more complex. In this changing context, Chapter 12 examines foundational concepts of ethics and discusses particular implications for public leaders. This chapter also analyzes conditions affecting ethical development, and organizational, social, economic, and political attributes that facilitate ethical climates in public organizations.

CONCLUSION

As you read the text, think about your development as a leader in the public sector. Through the interactive exercises, discussions, and supplemental classwork, you will be able to connect your experiences with theories and practices in the field of public administration. *The combination will enable you to meet the many challenges of public leadership today.* As the public sector integrates more elements of business, nonprofit, and civic interests worldwide, it joins an increasingly complex web of globally connected organizations. Now is the time for public leaders to build capacities through a life-long learning process and, in so doing, shape the character of the now and future public organization.

QUESTIONS FOR THOUGHT AND DISCUSSION

1. What are some key challenges you see facing public leaders today? How are they dealing with difficult challenges? What are some opportunities that encourage personal growth? democratic practices?

2. In your opinion, what qualities are important in leading public employees and organizations today? How do leaders acquire the qualities?

3. Distinctive identities of public and private institutions are changing as a result of more cross-sectoral interaction. What can these two sectors learn from each other to improve service to the public?

4. What are your skills and strengths as a leader? Which would you like to improve as you read through this book?

SUPPLEMENTAL READING

WELCOME TO THE BRAVE NEW WORLD OF THE NEW PUBLIC LEADER: ROLES AND RESPONSIBILITIES FOR THE TWENTY-FIRST CENTURY

DIRECTIONS

As you read the following article, consider the new roles public leaders play in transforming the social order around them. In many ways, the article describes the innovative and collaborative relationships public leaders are forming increasingly. Note particularly how the leader defines his roles and how followers, in turn, define theirs. These skills and strategies are seeds that will burst into bloom in the chapters to come.

CYBER VILLAGES—NEW CITY RECOVERY FORMULA

Neal Peirce, *Washington Post* Writers Group

ST. PAUL, Minn.—As America's cities get ready for the 21st century, Weiming Lu would like to see them building and perfecting "urban villages" that embody the best we've learned through the urban tribulations of the 20th.

Lu's millennial villages would have a mix of tastefully recycled historic buildings and artfully designed new ones. People would flock to them for their varieties of age and ethnic groups, offices, homes and jobs, urban parks, street art, and entertainment.

The villages would be both arts districts and "cyber villages," attracting companies focused on the Internet, new media and telecommunications industries. Indeed, Lu sees a creative combination of artists and computer software designers, working in the same neighborhood and linked globally through extensive fiber optics and satellite uplinks.

The village would have its own shared heating and air conditioning through underground conduits, an environmentally sustainable neighborhood reducing pollution and saving energy. And it would be economically successful—an engine of urban growth.

The fact is that Lu, a Shanghai-born designer–developer–visionary, has already created just such a village. It's in St. Paul; it's called Lowertown. It's become a prime model for merging historic preservation, successful design, economic rejuvenation, and lively street life, even along streets once threatened with abandonment.

Lowertown is situated where St. Paul was born—on the city's "lower" Mississippi River landing. By the late '70s it had declined into a shabby district of mostly abandoned warehouses, railyards, and parking lots. Yet Lowertown had the residual charm of turn-of-the-century buildings, narrow alleys, and tree-lined streets. And it had crucial location—on the Mississippi, close to downtown and the state capital district.

George Latimer, then St. Paul's mayor, decided Lowertown's economic risk might easily frighten off developers. So in 1978 he persuaded the Twin Cities-based McKnight Foundation to put up $10 million, not in a grant but in a "program-related investment" for Lowertown.

Weiming Lu, former urban design chief for Minneapolis and Dallas—he's been called "the Zen master of urban design and administration"—took over and still heads the Lowertown Redevelopment Corporation (LRC). LRC's apparent secret: In one body, it's a financial deal maker, design watchdog, preservation advocate, and indefatigable promoter of the neighborhood.

McKnight hoped its $10 million would attract $100 million in Lowertown investment. The latest total: $428 million. Lowertown today has 4,300 jobs and 1,500 housing units, a quarter of them for low and moderate income people. Dynamic "yuppie" couples and retired executives, struggling artists and fixed-income seniors rub shoulders here. They seem to value the diversity.

Lowertown has had commercial ups and downs but now seems on a steady upward course with high occupancy rates both in office and apartment buildings. The cyber village influx is part of the growth, as fledgling firms select historic buildings for their operations.

Why? "They like the funky space, low cost, restaurants, being right next to a park," says Lu—"It's the right mix for folks breaking out of their basements."

"There's a cool, funky thing going on here in Lowertown that meshes well with an Internet company," says Scott Bourne, founder of First-TV, a firm offering real-time Internet-based news coverage, music videos, and documentaries.

Another Lowertown cyberfirm is point2point communications, specializing in private, global television programming for corporations. It's a spinoff of another Lowertown neighbor, Minnesota Public Television.

The Internet address go.fast.net constructs high-speed ISDN (integrated service digital networks) hookups for businesses. HomeStyles is America's largest publisher of home plans (now on CD-ROMs and the Internet). And they're several more like them, all on the lookout for shared opportunities with their new neighbors.

None of this would work, though, if Lowertown didn't offer carefully assembled, preserved amenities, from a farmers' market to historic street lighting to cafes, theaters and galleries and a new children's playground.

After years of effort, Lowertown's Mississippi River connection has been made usable with an attractive riverfront park—now popular for running, walking, fishing, biking. "We want to see more trees planted there, and bring back the birds," says Lu.

Is there opportunity for more such developments around America? The answer has to be yes. Such places as Denver's Larimer Square, the Portland (Ore.) Riverfront, Dallas' West End, and Chattanooga's historic downtown are already on their way.

Urban Land Institute studies indicate high vacancy rates in older buildings in cities across America. Just look for any grouping of old underused warehouses, for example, and you see a potential Lowertown.

Rather than sterile office parks or massive stadiums, Lowertown-type projects may be America's "best practice" model for reviving desolate but historic center cities. It just takes leveraged financing, attention to detail, imagination, patience—and an organization like Weiming Lu's Lowertown Redevelopment Corporation watching the store.

A LEADERSHIP STYLE ASSESSMENT

DIRECTIONS

The following quiz looks at four types of leadership styles often found in the public sector. In each blank, rank the response on a scale of from 1 to 5 (1 = "not like me"; 2 = "not usually me"; 3 = "somewhat like me"; 4 = "usually like me"; and 5 = "very much like me"). At the end of the quiz, add your scores by the questions in each of the four columns. The total gives you an idea of your preferred public leadership style. Explanations of each style follow.

1. _____ I prefer clearly defined ends in making decisions.
2. _____ I have a "sense" for detecting political games.
3. _____ I prefer to solve problems and make decisions that involve working with others.
4. _____ I often look for new possibilities for doing tasks.
5. _____ I am comfortable dealing with multiple and often conflicting goals.
6. _____ I strive for consensus among my followers or organizational stakeholders.
7. _____ I rely on procedures in negotiating my viewpoints with others.
8. _____ I am someone who takes calculated risks to achieve a goal or purpose.
9. _____ I often use compromise and bargaining in making decisions.
10. _____ I like to work toward a goal that gives everyone a shared purpose.
11. _____ I usually succeed when the pressure is greatest.
12. _____ I see my role primarily as an agent of enforcing regulations in my unit or agency.
13. _____ I enjoy working with people from diverse backgrounds and styles.
14. _____ I enjoy competing to attain a valuable prize or goal.
15. _____ I am not frustrated if my plans are changed.
16. _____ I prefer to use "my head" rather than "my heart" when making decisions.
17. _____ I am usually one of the first to try something new.
18. _____ I often use humanistic values in matters involving interpersonal relationships.
19. _____ People see me as technically oriented, predictable, and thorough.
20. _____ Routine and administrative tasks bore me.

Add the totals by each question number in the corresponding column.

Trustee	Adapter	Collaborator	Entrepreneur
1. _____	2. _____	3. _____	4. _____
7. _____	5. _____	6. _____	8. _____
12. _____	9. _____	10. _____	14. _____
16. _____	11. _____	13. _____	17. _____
19. _____	15. _____	18. _____	20. _____
Total _____	Total _____	Total _____	Total _____

Preferred style _____

Secondary style(s) _____

EXPLANATIONS

Trustee: Uses regulations and rules to guide open-ended decisions; prefers clearly defined goals and procedures in working on tasks; tends to approach interpersonal relationships with logical reason rather than with subjectivity.

Adapter: Keenly aware of many political interests in decisions; uses bargaining and compromise to decide how work is to be accomplished; is means-oriented in developing interpersonal relationships; decisions are often based on contingent conditions.

Collaborator: Is comfortable with complex decisions and works toward consensus; concerned with "people" in forming interpersonal relationships; bases decisions on intuitive assessment of what will produce decision benefiting all.

Entrepreneur: "Big picture" thinker who prefers strategic decisions; calculated risk-taker and focuses energies on high-value terminal goals; uses innovation and intuition in creating task and interpersonal relationships.

REFERENCES

Peirce, N. (1997). Cyber villages—New city recovery formula? Washington, D.C.: *Washington Post* Writers Group.

Rainey, H. G. (1997). *Understanding and managing public organizations* (2nd ed.). San Francisco, CA: Jossey-Bass.

Tarrant, D. (1996, March 5-12). The we decade: Rebirth of community. *The Dallas Morning News*. http://www.pic.net/tdmn/wegen.html.

TRANSACTING LEADERSHIP ROLES AND RESPONSIBILITIES

SYNOPSIS

The chapter introduces the concepts of roles and relationships as behaviors leaders and followers negotiate in meeting mutual goals and interests. The chapter discusses how ideas of public leadership roles have developed from perspectives of Scientific Management, human relations, and situational management. Chapter 1 describes the organizational and political contributors to the development of public leadership roles. This chapter also discusses common problems public leaders face in defining and acting their roles and responsibilities, such as role credibility and role stress.

OBJECTIVES

- *To discuss key concepts of roles*
- *To describe common public leadership roles*
- *To describe conditions affecting role development*
- *To define role stress and its varieties*
- *To describe the process of leader credibility development*

KEY TERMS AND CONCEPTS

credibility

inducements as motivators

role

role stress

Scientific Management

scripts in playing leadership roles

transactional leadership

INTRODUCTION

In the Overview, we defined *leadership* as an interactive relationship involving use of power and influence to secure goals and achieve satisfactory rewards. Here, we discuss some important behaviors that leaders and followers use to identify and achieve goals. This chapter defines roles as the development and use of behaviors that people expect of themselves and others in reaching commonly identified ends. We will see that the behaviors follow a standard "script" as people play them in certain social situations. We will observe conditions that enable people to produce the roles and to transact, or negotiate them. In this context, we will look at what influences role development, particularly as people encounter ambiguous or conflicting role situations. Finally, we will describe the importance of credibility in developing role relationships.

TRANSACTIONAL LEADERSHIP

Leaders and followers are involved in a continuous dynamic relationship centered on achieving goals and developing mutually satisfying outcomes. In the process of building this relationship, individuals develop behaviors that follow mutually expected patterns. These behaviors are roles and the relationship that leaders and followers create is based on role transaction. That is, the leader who asks or demands certain tasks of followers is perceived as legitimate because the leader is acting on some recognized and accepted basis of authority. Followers comply to fulfill their interests and needs and to satisfy legitimate obligations.

Transactional roles are commonly used in completing tasks. Typically, a manager offers employees a reward in exchange for services and products. Although theories of exchange are discussed in greater detail in Chapter 3, we note here that transactional leadership is based on perceived equity. That is, an employee must believe that the manager's rewards will sufficiently satisfy a particular need and result in expected outcomes. This also means that a manager must identify which reward will produce the motivation and expected results in the employee.

Much of the transactional relationship is rooted in rational and economic principles of Scientific Management. Frederic Taylor (1911), the father of Scientific Management, believed that employees calculate costs and benefits of work (cited in Shafritz & Ott, 1996). They achieve goals in line with their maximum expectations. Because in Scientific Management managers controlled resources to promote greater employee productivity, managers regulated both employee motivation and actual outcomes in transacting work. The discovery in the famous Hawthorne experiments (in Roethlisberger & Dickson, 1939) that humans had considerably more choices in performing work than just economic survival eroded this. The Hawthorne studies revealed that employees did not work for economic rewards from their managers alone, but also for intrinsic rewards that came from the work they did and the people with whom they associated informally.

Barnard (1938/1996) noted the importance of subjectively determined rewards and levels of performance in *The Economy of Incentives*. Because such employee-driven goals are critical to end products, Barnard stated that managers induce employees to change rational and nonrational motives. This could come about through offering a combination of material and nonmaterial rewards. Particularly important were opportunities to grow on the job, making the workplace physically attractive, developing warm interpersonal relationships, opportunities for more participation in decision making, and fostering communion, or a sense of belonging to a group having similar interests and goals.

Barnard saw the intangible inducements as critical to public leadership. He noted that public organizations have financial and material constraints and consequently cannot reward employees as abundantly as do private firms. Although public agencies lack such incentives as large merit bonuses, stock options, and gainsharing, they can offer employees opportunities to find meaning in their work and enjoy the prestige of service to fellow citizens. By drawing employees' attention to the idealistic qualities of public service, managers could inspire extraordinary performance.

A CASE EXAMPLE

Being motivated by the worthwhile work they do often encourages heroism in public employees. One example is Anita Septimus, a New York City social worker who works with HIV-infected children. After she had begun working with the children in 1985, she experienced a high level of emotional drain. After watching three of her tiny clients die, she turned for advice to Dr. Arye Rubinstein, head of the Pediatric AIDS Center at New York's Albert Einstein College of Medicine. Rubinstein persuaded her to give it three more months, and Septimus did some soul-searching. She remembered a classmate who complained about working in poor areas: "My teacher said, 'Well, my friend, you have not chosen a pretty profession.' Those words were ringing in my head."

The clinic has since grown to become the Family Comprehensive AIDS Center, and Septimus now heads its social work department. She and her staff look after more than 300 families with AIDS-infected children—going to their homes, teaching infection prevention, and helping parents plan for the future. They also give their young clients a semblance of childhood, with trips to the zoo, the circus, and summer camps. "She makes us feel wonderful about ourselves," says Petra Berrios, the mother of a child with AIDS who is HIV-positive herself. That, Septimus says, is her job—helping families make the most of the lives they have. Happily, that time is expanding for some. One AIDS baby wasn't expected to see her first birthday. Now she's 10 years old. Such "long-term" clients give Septimus something in return— what she calls an "indestructible sense of hope." As she puts it, "You don't choose the day you enter the world and you don't choose the day you leave. It's what you do in between that makes all the difference" (*Newsweek*, 1995).

FORMING TRANSACTIONAL ROLES

Transacting leader–follower roles comes about through a dramatic process (Fondas & Stewart, 1995). In dramas, people play roles with actions and scripts that define character and advance plots. The behaviors actors produce audience credibility by being consistent and predictable. In leader– follower relationships, playing roles and following characteristic scripts facilitates transacting work. For instance, a supervisor of a grants review office of a federal agency acts such roles as overseer, rewarder, and consultant and, depending on circumstances, uses language commensurate with the roles. Employees accept these roles because they are consistent with what they expect of a supervisor and accordingly act corresponding roles of compliant, recipient of praise, and student. Transactional roles may come about through playing parts expected of certain organizational positions.

Transactional roles, however, also emerge from characteristics of leaders and followers dealing with particular circumstances; scripts are impromptu. Emergent leader–follower transactions often appear in novel, crisis, or complex problematic situations. If you are driving home one evening and see on the road in front of you victims of an apparent vehicle accident, you play roles associated with helping, such as stopping and checking the conditions of the victims, calling for rescue help, and flagging other motorists for assistance.

WHAT INFLUENCES ROLE DEVELOPMENT?

Although leaders and followers transact roles based on position, authority, influence, and the needs of particular situations, research studies have shown patterns that describe leader–follower role making.

PERSONAL TRAITS AND CHARACTERISTICS

Many studies describe personal leadership qualities as paramount in role making. In an exhaustive review of 163 studies of leadership, Stogdill (1974) identified six leader characteristics associated with leader effectiveness: (1) physical characteristics, such as age and height; (2) social background;

(3) intelligence and ability; (4) personality, such as adaptability, dominance, creativity, and ethical conduct; (5) task-related characteristics, such as drives for achievement and responsibility; and (6) social characteristics, such as ability to enlist cooperation, nurturance, and tact and diplomacy.

FOLLOWER INTERPRETATIONS

Having positive personal characteristics and traits is not enough, however, to ensure effective leadership. Followers must recognize and interpret the characteristics and traits before they accept leader gestures. A great deal of the interpretation rests on the needs, motives, values, and beliefs of followers. Followers undertake roles to meet inner purposes of which they may or may not have full awareness, or be able to define. Leaders gain followers' confidence by the leaders' abilities to articulate what followers may experience as unexpressed feelings or emotions (Kelley, 1998).

SITUATIONAL CONDITIONS

In situations in which followers experience uncertainty, fear, crisis, or novelty, they seek out individuals who can promote direction, structure, and meet certain common needs or purposes. Charismatic leaders often come into prominence during these events (Bass & Avolio, 1994). As the situations pass, however, the need for the leadership role also fades; leaders lose their prominence and legitimacy.

The contemporary element of participation in decision making, ranging from constituent to employee team approaches, has changed the top-down, command-control form of leadership common in public bureaucracies. Banovitz (1994), for instance, observed that city managers' roles are changing from concern with political involvement toward those characterized by technical consultation: City managers are becoming more like "baseball coaches." City managers have added roles as futurists, diplomats in intergovernmental relations, and brokers of interests.

The pervasive use of Total Quality Management (TQM) and the grassroots projects designed to reinvent government have altered the ways in which both leaders and follower constituents interact. Vinzant and Crothers (1996), for instance, point out that the movements are pushing bureaucrats toward higher levels of responsibility; decision making, they note, is being pushed downward to the lowest levels of accountability. This has produced three primary effects: (1) an expanded range of decisions; (2) an increase in the complexity of decisions; and (3) a heightened importance of how decisions are judged in the larger constituent context.

ORGANIZATIONAL STRUCTURES AND PROCESSES

Organizations influence how individuals define and play roles. Bureaucratic organizations, such as governmental institutions, have highly work structures, flows, and characteristics that affect role definition and behavior. Merton (1957/1958 cited in Scott, 1992), for instance, described a phenomenon of goal displacement among bureaucratic workers. Goal displacement occurs as bureaucratic workers implement ambiguous goals. In this process, ends become means; workers become so preoccupied with "how" a goal is met they forget its purposes. One result is that such workers see themselves as forms managers rather than as decisionmakers.

POLITICAL CHARACTER OF PUBLIC ORGANIZATIONS

Dependency on a political decision-making process also affects public leadership roles and practices. Rainey (1997) maintained reliance on legislative appropriations contributed to less incentive to cut costs and reduced decision-making autonomy. The subordinated role propelled leaders into roles as informal influencers, not only to receive support of political appointees but also support from client groups.

Riccucci (1995) studied the political skills used by six career managers in the federal government and how the skills influence role development. She found that in the policy influencing role, the career managers had gained in-depth knowledge of the informal political process. This involved cultivating good working relationships with politically appointed people, but maintaining a distance with any specific appointee. At times, this resulted in tension. But execucrats, as Riccucci terms them, resolved the tension by passing or doing end-runs around obstructive players. They also made direct use of iron triangles or policy issue networks to help them interpret laws and develop and implement programs. Moreover, they relied a great deal on interpersonal skills, honesty, and trustworthiness in confronting unethical behavior and mobilizing public support.

In a survey of over 300 council–manager forms of local government, Gage (1993) found that leaders exercised a participative or consultative style when dealing with controversial public issues. In developing consensus for decisions, the leaders often used outside consultants for advice and involved the media throughout the process. The leaders also had high skill levels in building coalitions among diverse interest groups.

TYPICAL LEADERSHIP ROLES

Several research studies have identified common roles leaders play. Perhaps the most familiar study was conducted by Mintzberg (1997 cited in Grint, 1997), who identified 10 major roles based on structured observations and interviews of five executives over a month. Mintzberg grouped the roles into three major categories: interpersonal, informational, and decisional. In this scheme, however, leadership was only a subset of the interpersonal relationships. Mintzberg cited it as a chief condition in motivating, training, developing, and rewarding staff members.

Other researchers see leadership as more prominent in an array of managerial roles. Yukl's (1994) Integrating Taxonomy Model of Managerial Behaviors shows leadership as the central element in four behavioral categories: (1) making decisions, (2) influencing people, (3) building relationships, and (4) giving and seeking information. In addition, Quinn, Faerman, Thompson, and McGrath (1996) show task structure as an integral part of defining workflow management and interpersonal relationship roles.

STUDIES OF PUBLIC LEADERSHIP ROLES

Several studies of the roles of federal, state, and local government leaders revealed the elements of interpersonal, task, and organizational combining. Yet, the research revealed some ways that public sector leaders' roles differ from those of the private sector leaders. Lau, Newman, and Broedling (1980) examined Mintzberg's 10 managerial roles in relation to federal government managers. In a survey of 370 Department of Navy executives, the researchers found only four of the 10 factors characterized public sector roles: (1) leadership and supervision; (2) information gathering and dissemination; (3) technical problem solving and executive decision making; and (4) allocating resources. Lau and colleagues defined leadership in the public sector as including Mintzberg's guiding and motivating employees; but the definition also included integrating individual and organizational goals.

In a study of local government leaders, Morgan, Bacon, Bunch, Cameron, and Deis (1996) identified four central roles. These included the following:

1. Interpreting and representing work unit's interests. In this role, leaders develop policy responses to the issues of the day. They also meet to discuss the distribution of resources. Moreover, leaders define performance roles and standards of various constituents.

2. Lending and securing assistance. Leaders discovered ways of marketing and delivering follower's collective expertise.

3. Developing interorganizational relationships. Leaders were figureheads or spokespersons for their groups and built relationships with external constituencies through negotiations.

4. Leveraging time. Leaders attend meetings, perform tasks having unclear purposes, and make decisions.

Morgan and colleagues observe some similarities of public leaders to those Mintzberg studied, but maintain public leaders differ in two ways. First, because public agencies' performance and future appropriations are related, public leaders measure "good" service on the common denominator of funds expended to funds saved. Second, public leaders' roles are enacted among a highly pluralistic set of constituencies. This makes coordinating activities across multiple boundaries of authority a primary role. The uniqueness of a public leader's role is to make sense of multiple and often conflicting sources of information in order to motivate others to perform tasks.

ROLE STRESS

Co-participation in governance processes has its costs. Role stress results from a variety of conditions, and is usually felt as a tension between the expected behaviors of a position one holds and actual demands upon it (Rizzo, House, & Lirtzman, 1970). Role stress has three variants: (1) *role conflict,* a feeling of incompatible expectations; (2) *role ambiguity,* resulting from inadequate, unclear, and irrelevant information; and (3) *role overload,* felt in the pressure of incompatibility between work demands and time available to do them, insufficient resources or authority to carry out expected behaviors, and complex regulations hampering individual discretion in decision making.

Often, public leaders' job descriptions consist of "other duties as assigned." These are heuristic, nonstandard, and unwritten job requirements, which fall in the leader's domain and call for immediate attention. Because public leaders serve multiple constituencies, ranging from elected and appointed officials to internal and external constituents, they may feel pressure from numerous conflicting and ambiguous situations.

In a study of municipal clerks, Rusaw (1995) examined role stress in clerks' job responsibilities and reporting relationships. Clerks define their roles by technical competence as well as in accordance with maintaining a positive professional public image. In carrying out this role, clerks saw many of their duties centering around keeping accurate public records and providing liaison with elected officials, taxpayers, public interest groups, and the media. Role stress came from having to give accurate information on ambiguous legislation, fostering interdepartmental cooperation in the context of insufficient resources, "political games," and compromised resource decisions. In their public liaison roles, clerks described the volume and variety of public "drop-in" requests, ad hoc referral questions, media requests, and fraudulent requests for information. Although clerks' formal duties were described in various regulations, the incumbents noted "tradition" as the major factor in defining and enacting role and role relationships.

Felt pressure from playing multiple roles can force developing new ways of thinking and behavioral patterns; it can also lower role performance and job satisfaction and willingness to remain on the job. In a study of a public sector hospital, for instance, Fennel and Alexander (1987) found that workers developed a great sensitivity to cues from actors in their external environment. Newton and Keenan (1987) found that role stress reduced the ability to use technical competencies. Stress from lack of informal authority over external interest groups impaired communications flow in interorganizational networks, creating what Shrum (1990) termed "powerless elites." Finally, the dissonance between professional ethos and bureaucratic norms lowered outputs (Bacharach, Bamberger, & Conley, 1990).

RESPONDING TO ROLE STRESS: BALANCING POWER, INFLUENCE, AND AUTHORITY

Public leaders and followers may address role stress by understanding and balancing use of power, influence, and authority. We shall note in the following chapter that, although the three concepts are interrelated, they require that leaders and followers negotiate their definitions and applications under particular circumstances. We will also note that leader–follower characteristics and traits, in addition to structural features of social interactions, create the setting for improvising role norms and behaviors. To the extent that leaders and followers can agree to share responsibility without negating individuals' expectations and their relationships, they can balance the quantity of role demands.

CREDIBILITY

Balancing public role responsibilities with pressures from numerous clientele followers can produce positive outcomes. One is that the public leader is not only knowledgeable and skilled in a variety of functions but also has the ability to instill confidence. This is credibility: a negotiated process that leaders and followers undertake based on mutual trust and esteem. Credibility results from at least five complex behaviors.

COMPONENTS OF CREDIBILITY

1. Consistency. Consistency appears in harmonious linkages between attitudes and behaviors. It often appears as steadiness, predictability, and a sense of being in control of one's emotional behavior. In times of crisis or ambiguity, followers find security and direction from leaders who appear unfazed and who provide clear instructions. Consistency is also the alignment of beliefs and actions. Consistent actions tell followers that leaders mean what they profess.

2. Visibility. Leaders are people who stand apart from others—in their characteristic behaviors, skill levels, expertise, and interpersonal

relationships. Leaders attain presence through the quality of their participation in multiple internal and external networks. Leaders obtain information and pass along important data to followers. From the networks, they connect themselves, their staff, their superiors, and their peers with each other, other units, and with the external political environment. Because leaders become recognized for their informational skills, they enhance their reputations for goal achievement as well as concern for what followers need to know and act upon.

3. Mutuality. Leaders involve followers in problem solving and decision making, and construct meaning through consensus. They seek to understand the motives, interpersonal behaviors, and interests of others in social relationships. Leaders show empathy as well as support for followers. In the process, leaders use such tactics as counseling, coaching, negotiation, and mediation. Through involvement, leaders foster democracy, increased confidence among followers, promote greater task accuracy, and heighten follower satisfaction with task processes and outcomes.

4. Respect. Leaders show a high level of confidence in the abilities of followers. They also raise followers' aspiration levels so that task accomplishments become challenging and intrinsically rewarding. Moreover, leaders value follower contributions to the quality of decisions. In addition, leaders have definite beliefs and values that their followers understand and accept. These beliefs and values usually pertain to achieving ideals, similar to that discussed by Barnard (1938). Followers come to realize the investment leaders make and value the leaders' determination in the pursuit of ideals.

5. Legitimacy. Leaders gain the right to govern by making their goals and means conform to ethical and moral standards. If followers perceive that what the leader is asking makes sense, is proper, and will produce benefits to the followers as well as to the social order, followers will grant leaders sanction. Because followers set the standards for judging the appropriateness of leader strategies, followers choose leaders who reflect common values, norms, and beliefs. When leaders do not align their personal standards with those of followers, they lose standing. If they force their personal bias on followers, however, they risk being considered tyrannical.

Briefly, gaining credibility is therefore critical to establishing a productive relationship with followers. The relationship is not to exact contributions from followers, but rather to enable followers to voluntarily accept the leader's vision and contribute to the outcomes. The relationship-building process requires leaders to have a thorough knowledge of task requirements, resources, and contexts in which tasks are performed. It also calls on leaders to develop an intuitive understanding of organizational power coalitions, strategies, and tactics for supporting efforts.

SUMMARY

Leaders and followers transact roles based on a calculation of tangible and intangible costs and benefits as well as expected results and rewards. The calculations involve both objective assessments and psychosocial considerations. In influencing followers to act on purposes, leaders offer a range of inducements. In the public sector, appealing to followers' sense of serving the greater needs and interests of the public are quite effective.

Roles are expected behaviors that people perform based on mutual interpretations of needs, goals, and surroundings. Roles may be formally designated from a legitimate authority or emerge from environmental conditions. Qualities that contribute to role definitions and enactment include individual characteristics, follower perceptions and expectations, degree of situational urgency and ambiguity, extent of bureaucratic layering, pervasiveness of politics, and available resources.

Leadership is a main ingredient in developing and maintaining interpersonal work relationships, coordinating information, motivating and developing followers, making decisions, and structuring work. Public sector leadership studies show several different contributions, however. Public leaders spend a great deal of time representing and marketing their organizations to external interests, developing interorganizational ties, and attending problem-solving meetings. Making efficient use of limited resources, coordinating information among pluralistic interests, and responding to inquiries from political authorities and demands for service play particularly strong parts.

Pressure from multiple roles, incompatible constituent expectations and demands, and ambiguous information creates a generalized feeling of stress. Responding to the pressure can involve tapping a reservoir of creativity, but it can also lower job satisfaction and performance. Finding a balance in managing the demands, delegating responsibilities, and supplying sufficient informational, material, and financial resources poses a continuing challenge to public leaders.

Developing follower credibility can help leaders cope with role stress by involving followers in work decisions. Credibility, or trust, allows a leader to influence follower commitment. To achieve credibility, leaders may cultivate five important skills over time. In particular, leaders develop credibility by showing consistency of beliefs and actions. They also form a rich supply of timely and significant information for follower use. By securing prominence in a variety of networks, leaders can effectively pass on information followers need and expect. Leaders can also create empathetic bonds with followers by sharing personal information and showing support and confidence in follower contributions. Lastly, leaders gain credibility by modeling ethical standards in morally ambiguous situations.

In Chapter 2, we will examine in greater depth how leaders and followers develop power and influence in roles. That chapter also focuses on sources of authority that sanction leader activities.

QUESTIONS FOR THOUGHT AND DISCUSSION

1. Why is credibility important to public leaders? How can leaders enhance their credibility among those they serve?

2. In your opinion, what makes a "good" public leader? How do you believe the media influences the public's perception of quality leadership?

3. How does the political character of public organizations influence leaders' roles and behaviors? How can leaders integrate politics and administration in an effective and ethical manner?

4. Think of some things that create role stress in your life. How do you deal with them?

CASE STUDY

WHEN TORNADOES HIT: DEVELOPING SHARED LEADERSHIP ROLES

TIME: APPROXIMATELY 1 HOUR

DIRECTIONS

In the following case exercise, a task force has been assembled to create a plan of action to coordinate emergency services. The task force has been convened by the mayor and consists of three council members, the director of finance and budgeting, the planner, the director of public works, the director of public health safety, the chief of police, the public relations director, a representative from the Federal Emergency Management Agency (FEMA), and a representative from the governor's emergency planning commission. Several community volunteers have asked to join the task force, including the owner of the major retail business, and several community workers.

Assume that it is the day after the storms occurred. After reading the case description, form small groups and respond to the questions following the case.

BACKGROUND

In May 1999, a series of deadly tornadoes destroyed many communities and valuable farmlands from Oklahoma to Nebraska. Over 50 lives were lost. One community, Summers, lost its main business

section and 10 residents of a retirement community in the center of town were killed. A community of about 33,000, Summers is 70 miles south of the capital city. Surrounded by corn, wheat, and dairy farms, Summers' nearest neighbors are Jerome (population 2,100), and Felicity (a town of approximately 25,000) about 20 miles to the west.

In addition to Summers' retail businesses and the retirement community, several tornadoes in succession struck the town's 80-bed hospital. In destroying the town's major business, the tornadoes caused over half the nonfarming residents to be out of work. Fortunately, the tornadoes destroyed only the hospital's laundry and maintenance facilities, and did not kill any patients. However, they did crush the hospital's emergency facilities. Hospital personnel rushed many patients to the nearby high school gymnasium and set up a triage clinic with limited supplies. Initial estimates of the damage put cleanup costs at close to $20 million. Much of the costs are eligible for federal fund reimbursement. But some of the costs, such as for emergency food, clothing, water supplies, and medical equipment require supplemental funding.

Some of the immediate problems the town faces are finding adequate emergency medical care; distributing food and clothing; locating shelters for homeless persons and families; and coordinating state, county, and local protective services, such as fire and police and national guard units.

The committee scouts for information to help in the planning and coordinating of services. Key data include the following:

1. In addition to some farmers' co-ops nearby, there is a large food warehouse in the state capital.

2. The nearest major airport is in the capital city. However, a major interstate is a mile from Summers' northwestern border. A major railroad that ships agricultural products connects the town with other Midwestern cities.

3. In addition to a junior–senior high school, the town has two elementary schools, several large church buildings, a recreational facility, and a senior community center.

4. A medium-sized Air Force base is located about 100 miles away. It has a 30-bed clinic, a general practitioner physician, and a staff of 20 nurses, medical technicians, and assistants. The base also has a contingent of firefighters, electricians, plumbers, and security personnel.

5. Summers has a small daily newspaper. The committee just learned that reporters from state and national media will be arriving later that day and want to have accurate, up-to-date information on the casualties, the extent of damages, and plans for relief.

QUESTIONS AND ACTIVITIES

1. What tasks, in your opinion, must be handled first? Why? Which tasks can be combined with others? Which can be delegated?

2. Select one of the problems and devise a plan of action.

    a. Describe who or what you would use to help bring the ideas into action.

    b. What resources do you need?

3. What obstacles do you expect? How will you deal with the obstacles?

4. Share your plan with other group members. Look for areas that may be combined or functions that will help meet your goals. Put together a coordinated plan.

5. Select a spokesperson to summarize your group's plan and summarize key features.

THE STUDENT LEADERSHIP INVENTORY (SLI): ON BECOMING A BETTER LEADER

William E. Rosenbach, Ph.D.
Marshall Sashkin, Ph.D.
Fred Harburg

DIRECTIONS

The Student Leadership Inventory: On Becoming a Better Leader, was developed by

William E. Rosenbach, Marshall Sashkin, and Fred Harburg of the Eisenhower Leadership Program at Gettysburg College. It assesses the extent of transactional and transformational skills, based on individual and observer assessments. To take the SLI, make several copies of both sides of the score sheets (the back sides contain the 50-item inventory). Give some to your associates: people who know you well and who will give you honest feedback and ask them to complete the forms and complete a copy yourself. When you and your associates have completed the inventory, mail the form in for scoring. The address is:

Dr. William E. Rosenbach
Professor of Management
Eisenhower Leadership Program
Gettysburg College
Gettysburg, PA 17325

Your results will be tabulated and scored, based on large sample norms of all those completing the inventory. Results will be mailed to you. You may then compare your self-assessment to what others have observed. The scores may be discussed with reference to Chapter 11 of the text.

INTRODUCTION

The Student Leadership Inventory (SLI) is designed to help you gain a better understanding of leadership. The SLI does this by focusing on you, as a leader. It provides you feedback on specific behaviors, on certain personal characteristics, and on the effects that you may have on others as a leader. How you see yourself is compared to the average of how the observers you chose see you. You will also be able to compare these results with results for a large diverse sample of other individuals. By studying the feedback provided by the SLI, you can come to understand leadership and, most important of all, you can develop specific strategies to improve your leadership effectiveness.

Leadership is one of the most widely discussed topics, and at the same time one of the most elusive and puzzling. However, it is not really mystical or mysterious, and understanding leadership in theory or practice is not limited to just a few, special

leaders. The potential for effective leadership is widely dispersed in any population, and whatever your potential may be, it can be developed. Leadership in any group or organization is not limited to those in elected or appointed positions. People at all levels can—and must—exercise leadership, in varying degrees.

Leaders are individuals who help create options and opportunities, who help solve problems and identify choices, who build commitment and coalitions, who inspire others and construct a shared vision of the possibilities and promise of a better group, organization, or community. They engage followers in such a way that many followers become leaders in their own right. Effective leaders are comfortable serving in both the follower and leader roles when appropriate.

Learning about leadership means recognizing ineffective as well as effective leadership. It also means understanding the critical linkage between means and ends. Learning about leadership involves understanding the dynamic relationship between leaders and followers. Most importantly, students of leadership can begin to appreciate their own strengths and deficiencies. Feedback from instruments like the SLI will help you learn about yourself as a leader. John Gardner suggests, "It's what you learn after you know it all, that really counts."

Recent leadership theory and research has identified two basic types of leadership: *transactional* and *transformational*. Transactional leaders influence followers by means of a transaction—money, praise, or some other reward (or punishment) in exchange for effort and performance. Transactional leaders recognize the rewards followers want from their work and try to see that they get them in exchange for performance. But good transactional leaders are not simply bosses, they are helpers. They work with followers, first to understand what followers want and then to help make clear what followers must do to get the results the leader wants and the

Mark Reflex® by NCS EM-160883-3:65432   ED06 Printed in U.S.A.

The Leadership Profile

Marshall Sashkin, Ph.D.
and
William E. Rosenbach, Ph.D.

MARKING INSTRUCTIONS

- Use a NO. 2 PENCIL only.
- Darken the circle completely.
- Erase cleanly any marks you wish to change.
- Do not make any stray marks on this form.
- Do not fold or staple.

RIGHT MARK

Each of the following statements describes a certain leadership behavior, characteristic, or effect that a leader might have on a group or organization. Read each statement carefully and decide to what extent it is an accurate description of the person you are describing. For each statement, mark the response that best describes to what extent that statement accurately characterizes the actual leadership behavior of the person being described.

NAME OF PERSON BEING DESCRIBED

Last Name   First Name   MI

RELATIONSHIP TO PERSON BEING DESCRIBED

I am the person being described ○

I am an associate of the person being described ○

For Office Use Only

PARTICIPANT NUMBER   RATER NUMBER

PLEASE CONTINUE ON BACK

THIS PERSON . . .

	To a very great extent.	To a great extent.	To a moderate extent.	To a slight extent.	To little or no extent.
1. makes sure people have the resources they need to do a good job.	VG	G	M	S	L
2. rewards people fairly for their efforts.	VG	G	M	S	L
3. pays close attention to what others say.	VG	G	M	S	L
4. can be relied on.	VG	G	M	S	L
5. respects people's differences.	VG	G	M	S	L
6. creates opportunities for people to succeed.	VG	G	M	S	L
7. acts in ways that have impact.	VG	G	M	S	L
8. enjoys making others obey her or his orders.	VG	G	M	S	L
9. considers how a specific plan of action might be extended to benefit others.	VG	G	M	S	L
10. encourages others to act according to the values and beliefs we share.	VG	G	M	S	L
11. provides information people need to effectively plan and do their work.	VG	G	M	S	L
12. recognizes good performance with rewards people value.	VG	G	M	S	L
13. communicates a clear sense of priorities.	VG	G	M	S	L
14. follows through on commitments.	VG	G	M	S	L
15. shows he or she cares about others.	VG	G	M	S	L
16. designs situations that permit people to achieve their goals.	VG	G	M	S	L
17. can see the results of her or his actions.	VG	G	M	S	L
18. expects others to obey without question.	VG	G	M	S	L
19. concentrates on clear and short-term goals.	VG	G	M	S	L
20. demonstrates that group goals are her or his own.	VG	G	M	S	L
21. helps people get the training they need to perform their jobs effectively.	VG	G	M	S	L
22. expresses appreciation when people perform well.	VG	G	M	S	L
23. grabs people's attention, focusing on the important issue in a discussion.	VG	G	M	S	L
24. keeps promises.	VG	G	M	S	L
25. shows concern for the feelings of others.	VG	G	M	S	L
26. involves others in new ideas and projects.	VG	G	M	S	L
27. makes a difference.	VG	G	M	S	L
28. uses power and influence to benefit others.	VG	G	M	S	L
29. explains long-range plans and goals clearly.	VG	G	M	S	L
30. supports effective coordination by working cooperatively with others.	VG	G	M	S	L
31. supports and encourages people to get the job done well.	VG	G	M	S	L
32. knows the rewards people value.	VG	G	M	S	L
33. listens for feelings as well as ideas.	VG	G	M	S	L
34. acts in ways consistent with her or his words.	VG	G	M	S	L
35. treats others with respect, regardless of position.	VG	G	M	S	L
36. helps others learn from mistakes.	VG	G	M	S	L
37. is confident in her or his own abilities.	VG	G	M	S	L
38. seeks power and influence to attain goals people agree on.	VG	G	M	S	L
39. expresses a vision that engages people.	VG	G	M	S	L
40. encourages people to support their views and positions with concrete evidence.	VG	G	M	S	L
41. makes sure people have clear and challenging goals.	VG	G	M	S	L
42. makes sure that people know what to expect in return for accomplishing goals.	VG	G	M	S	L
43. is able to get complicated ideas across clearly.	VG	G	M	S	L
44. can be trusted.	VG	G	M	S	L
45. makes others feel a real part of the group organization.	VG	G	M	S	L
46. gives people the authority they need to fulfill their responsibilities.	VG	G	M	S	L
47. is in control of his or her life.	VG	G	M	S	L
48. shares power and influence with others.	VG	G	M	S	L
49. has plans that extend over a period of several years or longer.	VG	G	M	S	L
50. values action over maintaining the status quo.	VG	G	M	S	L

rewards the followers desire. Really good transactional leaders go farther, they help followers develop the confidence they need to achieve their goals.

Transformational leadership involves a strong personal identification with the leader; followers join in a shared vision of the future, going beyond self-interest and the pursuit of personal rewards. The transformational leader influences followers to perform beyond expectations. This means first creating an awareness of the importance of achieving valued outcomes. To do this, transformational leaders work to define shared values and beliefs. This is what enables followers to get beyond their own self-interests and commit themselves to team, group, or organizational goals. Transformational leaders then help followers develop strategies for accomplishing goals. They enable followers to develop a mental picture of the vision and transform purpose into action.

DIMENSIONS OF THE STUDENT LEADERSHIP INVENTORY

The SLI gives you a measure of yourself, both as a transactional and a transformational leader. It is important to recognize that these two styles of leadership are two separate and necessary dimensions, not the end points on a single leadership continuum. That is, transactional leadership and transformational leadership do not have an either/or relationship. A person might exhibit just one, the other, both, or neither. A truly effective leader will, however, typically demonstrate a high degree of both transactional and transformational leadership.

The SLI consists of 50 statements. These statements are not in order on the form but are scored in groups of five to give ten scores for ten specific scales. Scales one and two measure transactional leadership. Scales three through six assess transformational leadership behaviors, while scales seven through ten measure the personal characteristics which are necessary for trans-

formational leaders if they are to have a positive impact on their group or organization.

TRANSACTIONAL LEADERSHIP

Scale 1: Capable Management *(Items 1, 11, 21, 31, 41)*

This scale measures how well the leader accomplishes the day-to-day basic administrative or managerial tasks that are necessary for any group or organization to function well in the short term.

Scale 2: Reward Fairness *(Items 2, 12, 22, 32, 42)*

Effective leaders find out what followers want. They promise followers what they want in exchange for good performance, and they deliver on their promises. This scale measures the degree to which leaders make clear and explicit their goals and performance expectations, as well as how well leaders deliver on the rewards they promise for good performance and goal accomplishment.

TRANSFORMATIONAL LEADERSHIP BEHAVIOR

Scale 3: Leadership Communications *(Items 3, 13, 23, 33, 43)*

Overall, this scale assesses the ability to manage and direct the attention of others through especially clear and focused interpersonal communication. Transformational leaders listen and pay especially close attention to those with whom they are communicating. They focus on key issues and help followers' to understand those issues. At the same time they pay attention to and appreciate followers' feelings. They use metaphors and analogies that make abstract ideas clear and vivid. In this way, they are able to get complicated ideas across clearly.

Scale 4: Credible Leadership *(Items 4, 14, 24, 34, 44)*

This scale deals with a leader's perceived integrity. Is the leader reliable, keeping commitments and promises? Are the leader's words consistent with her or his actions? Effective leaders "walk the talk"; that is, they establish trust by taking actions that are consistent both over time and with what they say.

Scale 5: Caring Leadership *(Items 5, 15, 25, 35, 45)*

This scale measures the degree to which a leader demonstrates respect and concern for others. Transformational leaders consistently and constantly express concern for others. They respect other people's feelings, which reinforces others' high self-regard. Transformational leaders value people's differences and let people know it because they see how individuals' unique qualities and abilities can be used to the benefit of the group or organization.

Scale 6: Courageous Leadership *(Items 6, 16, 26, 36, 46)*

Some would say that a leader's courage is measured by a willingness to take risks. Transformational leaders, however, do not take undue risks—they *create opportunities.* While their actions might appear to be risky, they are actually based on careful thought, including an assessment of the ability of followers to perform and succeed. They empower followers by encouraging and allowing them to accept challenges, and they do all that is possible to ensure that followers succeed. What they *don't* do is spend a lot of time and energy worrying about failure. Of course, even effective leaders may at times experience failure. But, when that happens, such leaders use the experience to learn how to do better next time.

TRANSFORMATIONAL LEADERSHIP
CHARACTERISTICS

Scale 7: Confident Leadership *(Items 7, 17, 27, 37, 47)*

Transformational leaders have a basic sense of self-assurance, an underlying belief that they can personally make a difference and have an impact on people, events, and group achievements. Mark Twain said, "If you think you can...or think you can't...you're probably right."

Effective leaders believe they control their own fate. This scale measures the extent to which the leader possesses and displays this sort of self-confidence.

Scale 8: Follower-Centered Leadership *(Items 8, 18, 28, 38, 48)*

Transformational leaders don't seek power and influence because they enjoy exercising power over others. Rather, they realize it is through the positive use of power and infuence that group and organizational goals are achieved. Transformational leaders use power by sharing it with followers. They empower followers to take an active role in achieving group goals. This scale measures the degree to which the leader sees followers as empowered partners.

Scale 9: Visionary Leadership *(Items 9, 19, 29, 39, 49)*

This scale measures a leader's ability to define and express clearly a future for the group or organization. This vision is derived, at least in part, from followers. Groups and organizations that perform well have leaders who have the perspective needed to deal with ambiguity and complexity. Such leaders know what actions are necessary to achieve the vision. They develop plans that extend beyond the present into the long-term future.

Scale 10: Principled Leadership *(Items 10, 20, 30, 40, 50)*

An effective transformational leader helps develop and support certain shared values and beliefs among group members; that is what this scale measures. These values and beliefs reflect the important and fundamental issues faced by people in groups and organizations. The elements of principled leadership include: managing change (especially external pressures for change); achieving goals (including how goals are defined and their importance); how people work together to get the job done; and, the degree to which group members agree that the values and beliefs are important and should guide their actions.

THE STUDENT LEADERSHIP INVENTORY REPORTS

Your SLI results consist of two reports. The first presents your own self-assessment results, the second reports the average results of the observers you chose to describe your leadership style. The second (or latter) report also shows how many observers' reports were returned and included in the scores.

All of the results are shown in standard scores based on the distribution of raw scores among a very large group of people who completed the SLI. "Standard" means that scores range from an absolute low of 0 to an absolute high of 100. The mean or average score is 50, and almost all the scores range from 25 to 75. About two-thirds of all scores fall between 40 and 60, so a score of 60 or above can be considered "high"— an area where you are likely performing well, while a score of 40 or below can be considered "low," an area that probably could be improved.

The first, "Self Assessment," report presents the results of the SLI you completed yourself. The first column of scores are your own scores for each of the ten scales and for the three overall groups. The score for each scale is the average of the five items that comprise each scale. The next three columns are average self-assessment scores and the individual low and high scores for the group that participated with you.

The second, "Observer's Assessment," report shows that the average scores of all the observers who described your leadership style. The first column is the average score of all observers on each of the ten scales and for the three overall groups of scales. The next three columns present the average of observers' scores for all people in your group and the individual low and high scores in the group.

INTERPRETING YOUR RESULTS

Your scores are the result of your responses and those of your associates you asked to give feedback about you on the SLI. By carefully examining your self-assessment results in comparison with those of your associates, you will obtain valuable information about your own leadership and your effects on others, the group, and the organization.

There are almost always some differences between how a person sees him or herself and how others see that person. What's more, we all see things and people from various perspectives; not all observers agree. The observers' ratings may vary because of how long and well they know you. Some observers may be unusually harsh, while others may be unduly lenient in their ratings. And some observers may only know and observe you in a restricted setting, providing limited feedback on your leadership style. Generally, you should not be concerned unless the difference between self and observers' scores is ten points or more. Look especially for patterns of discrepancies among the various scales and groups of scales, patterns of differences in opinion between you and your observers.

If the observers' ratings are consistently higher than your self-ratings, you may be a bit modest concerning your leadership skills and your effect on others; most people are. If on the other hand, your observers' ratings are consistently lower than your own, you see yourself as being a more effective leader than do others. Your self-ratings may reflect an honest, positive belief in yourself, but the fact that observers see you differently may be a critical obstacle to your leadership effectiveness. Such differences are, however, an opportunity for learning and development.

Often, when there is disagreement between one's self and others' ratings, one is tempted to try to determine which is correct. A more constructive course of action is to determine why there is a difference and what can be done about it. For some issues, you may know yourself better than the observers. On other issues the observers' ratings should probably be given more weight. In any case, large differences should be carefully examined, since they can identify problems that impede your effectiveness as a leader.

Use the models (Figure 1.1) that follow to enter your three "Self Assessment" overall scores in the triangle labeled "Self Assessment." Make a mark at the appropriate point on each scale and connect the three points to form a small triangle within the large one. Do the same for the three "Observers" scores using the triangle marked "Observer's Assessment." You can learn more about your strengths and development needs by studying the profile formed by your triangles, as illustrated and explained on the following pages.

HOW TO USE YOUR RESULTS

The information you get from the SLI can be used to analyze and modify your own leadership behavior, to develop further those personal characteristics associated with effective transformational leadership, and to consider how you might go about improving your transactional (managerial) leadership. The three SLI scores, and the specific scales of which they are composed, can help you develop your own leadership potential.

Very few people score exceptionally high on the three overall leadership scores or on most or all of the ten scales. Nonetheless, effective leaders can learn a great deal by acting on the information provided by the SLI. Moreover, it really is a matter of degree, not of "having it" or "not having it." Low scores are guideposts for action, not signs of failure. Use low scores and especially discrepancies between how you see yourself and how others see you as indicators of areas where improvements can be made.

■ FIGURE 1-1

TRANSACTIONAL LEADERSHIP TRIANGLES

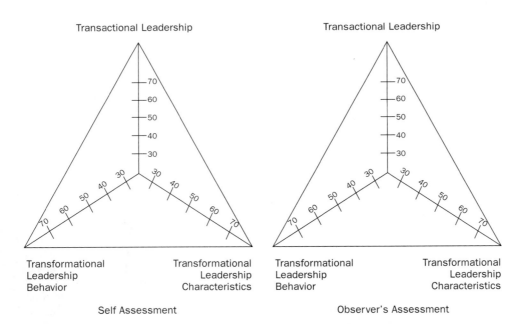

SOURCE: Copyright © M. Sashkin and W. E. Rosenbach, 1995. Reprinted by permission.

Some things are harder to change than others. Most of us find it easier to learn new behaviors than to learn to accept different ways of looking at things, for example, changing our attitudes about such things as power and influence. But, again, this is a matter of degree. You do not have to become a "superior leader" tomorrow, nor must you be at the top of every scale to be effective. Small changes and improvements can make real differences!

The following suggestions may prove helpful, for your personal consideration or for group discussion:

- Select several scales on which your scores were relatively high and represent agreement between yourself and your observers. These scores represent areas of strength or assets, behavior and characteristics that have a positive effect on others. Try to determine how you can integrate these positive perceptions into your self-concept. You should also consider how you might expand the impact of your talents. Identify new projects, situations, or ar-eas of endeavor where your strengths will likely lead to success.

- Consider several scales on which your scores were relatively low and choose one or two that are important to you. Next try to determine specifically what you are doing or not doing in your leadership role that caused these scores. Identifying the causes may be difficult. You must be honest with yourself and may also need to solicit additional feedback from your observers. Finally, determine what specific action you must take to improve your effectiveness in the areas you identified. It may be just a matter of changing your emphasis or focus or it may involve exhibiting different behavior, developing a different characteristic, or taking different strategic actions.

- Do you think that popular public, transformational leaders exhibit the behaviors, characteristics, or strategic actions measured by the SLI? Can you identify specific individuals?

2

LEADERSHIP AUTHORITY, POWER, AND INFLUENCE

SYNOPSIS

This chapter defines authority as the right to lead. It also discusses formal and informal power as derived from legal as well as ascribed authority. In examining various theories and bases of power, this chapter distinguishes power from influence. Emphasizing influence as a product of follower inferences, Chapter 2 describes some techniques leaders use to create positive impressions. Among the techniques are use of political and shared power strategies.

OBJECTIVES

- To define authority, power, and influence
- To describe authority as the source of power and influence
- To define formal and informal bases of power
- To describe influence tactics
- To examine the dilemmas of power and influence in public sector leadership

KEY TERMS AND CONCEPTS

inducement-based power

coercive
reward

influence tactics

blocking
coalition
consultation
ingratiation
inspirational appeals
pressure tactics
upward influence

legitimate bases of power

connection
normative
political
positional

personal power base

expertise
referent

INTRODUCTION

In this chapter, we study the idea of transaction in leadership roles by examining the development and use of authority, power, and influence. First, we will define key terms; review theoretical descriptions of authority, power, and influence; and discuss the development of influence tactics leaders often employ in public settings. Second, we will examine more closely the dilemmas public leaders face in exercising power and influence within the framework of legitimate authority, such as the U.S. Constitution. We shall observe that the limitations on leadership power often produce ambiguous situations, requiring leaders to exercise a great deal of sensitivity and judgment.

AUTHORITY, POWER, AND INFLUENCE

Leaders derive power and the ability to influence from authority. *Authority means the right to do, to create, or to activate movement in others toward a particular aim or purpose.* This right may be spelled out in a legal document or set of socially agreed upon principles. For example, the U.S. Constitution sets forth the duties as well as the limits of the three branches of government. Authority may be legally delegated as well, as when legislators enact laws and administrators carry them out. Moreover, authority can be accepted by group agreement. This frequently occurs as groups develop and adhere to norms or standards for working together.

Power, which is based on authority, is the ability to require or to get followers to act to achieve a goal or purpose. In stating that power is the "ability," the definition implies that power is really a potential; the leader has to activate some latent capacity or force that followers understand as necessary or appropriate to achieve an end under certain circumstances. The ability to "require or to get" means that followers interpret the leader's strategies as authoritative or legitimate. The interpretation can be made on the basis of a formally written document having a legal basis and backed by sanctions for noncompliance. The interpretation can also, however, be made on the basis of informally derived norms or standards of a group that followers acknowledge as having authority. Examples of both formal and informal power occur in public organizations. In the former, a branch chief reviews the budget submissions of a supervisor, modifies particular requests, and makes a decision. In an example of informal power, in the agency where the branch chief works, the norm is for the branch chief to convey to the supervisors priorities of the agency head before the supervisors submit their requests. This way, the supervisors will have a better chance of their requests being accepted.

Whereas power is a *potential* to force or even to persuade someone to perform a particular task or accomplish a certain goal, *influence is how followers view the appropriateness and effectiveness of leader attempts to motivate action.* Influence is based on follower inferences. In deciding to comply with leader requests, followers assess the legitimacy as well as the importance of the requests. For example, in a public school, a principal may order teachers to keep windows closed and locked during class. However, because students may complain they are too warm when the room temperature is 80º, teachers may decide to open the windows. Situational variables, namely the overly warm class and the norm of having students feel comfortable, were prime factors. Moreover, the principal's order lacked sanctions, leaving no penalty for violations.

STUDIES OF POWER

SPECIAL GIFTS

The leader's ability to entice follower performance is based on several conditions. This ability has often been attributed to charisma, or "special gifts." In one of the pioneering studies of leadership, Weber (in Behling & McFillen, 1996) observed leaders having extraordinary abilities to compel follower performance. Weber noted that charismatic gifts often emerged in times of crisis and endowed the leader with savior-like qualities. The special gifts were manifested in six leadership attributes:

1. empathy
2. dramatizing purpose or mission
3. projection of self-assurance
4. enhancing leader image
5. assuring followers of competence
6. providing follower opportunities for success.

Charismatic attributes derive value through others' perceptions and feedback (Shamir, Zakey, Breinin, & Popper, 1998).

The special gifts distinguished leaders from nonleaders and manifested in behaviors, which many early leadership scholars saw as predispositions or inherited traits. Leaders were distinguished by their aggressiveness, above-average height, intelligence, and problem-solving abilities. Leaders also had extraverted personalities and came from higher social strata than nonleaders. Greatly concerned with achievement, leaders showed great drive for accomplishing tasks as well as high regard for follower interests and needs (Stogdill, in Bass, 1974/1990).

PERSONAL POWER BASES AS LEADERSHIP RESOURCES

Gifts and abilities that were absent in followers gave leaders power in the eyes of followers. Personal characteristics became bases of power upon which leaders established trust, loyalty, affection, and identification. Some important bases of personal power include expertise, amiability, and control of rewards and sanctions.

1. Expertise. In Stogdill's (in Bass, 1974/1990) research, leaders who possessed superior intellectual and emotional abilities had the greatest degree of personal power. Because of these features, followers could rely on leaders to solve difficult or complex problems. This personal power often revealed itself as interpersonal acumen, technical skills, and conceptual and analytic talents (Yukl, 1994). When individuals lack specific and highly refined information for solving problems or for making decisions, they defer to those who do possess such information.

2. Referent power. Referent power is based on the fact that followers will do what leaders ask because they admire leader characteristics. Through establishing symbolic ties, friendships, popularity, and esteemed traits, leaders become referents or models for followers. Followers internalize the characteristics in their mannerisms, words, phrases, and even clothing styles.

INDUCEMENT-BASED POWER

As discussed in Chapter 1, roles and relationships arise through the leader's use of symbolic and concrete rewards. French and Raven (cited in Cartwright, 1959, pp. 150–167) in a classic study of inducements revealed leaders used rewards as inducements as a basis of power. Conversely, leaders could withhold the desired rewards or sanctions to get followers to act in a desired direction. French and Raven called this "coercive power."

1. Reward power. To induce followers to act on the basis of an expected reward, leaders need to discover what followers value. The values may be intrinsic rewards, such as recognition, autonomy, discretion in decision making, or personal satisfaction. External rewards also play

an important role in motivating follower performance. To be effective, however, rewards must have value from the follower's vantage point.

2. Coercive power. Leaders also use sanctions to deemphasize undesired follower behavior. Although coercion produces compliance, its overuse can lead to negative outcomes. Followers may become hostile and/or even sabotage projects. Further, withholding rewards may inhibit one person, but fail to deter another. Moreover, leaders who repeatedly coerce followers impair long-term commitment to goals and future productivity.

LEGITIMATE BASES OF POWER

In every interaction, leaders and followers negotiate standards for both expected outcomes and for work relationships. In negotiating the relationships, leaders rely on valid sources of authority, such as legal means, delegation, or position. Followers assess the uses of leader authority by determining if the leader requests are commensurate with explicit or implicit requirements based in authority. To enable followers to make accurate assessments, leaders employ four types of power: (1) normative, (2) positional, (3) connection, and (4) political.

1. Normative power. Clegg (1990, pp. 42–47), citing Etzioni, noted normative power rests upon principles that individuals have internalized as legitimate, such as socially sanctioned rituals, symbols, and artifacts. Normative power enables individuals to achieve idealized ends and to experience community. By engaging in social activities and learning acceptable behaviors, people develop standards for judging value and meaning.

    In large part, cultural norms underlie the base for using normative power, although situational characteristics may allow using different norms if the purpose can be seen as socially beneficial. In many governmental agencies, for instance, employers grant workers "liberal leave" if their locale is experiencing inclement weather. What is "liberal" is set by the manager's expectations and the employees' estimation of fairness and actual commuting conditions.

2. Positional power. Weber (in Behling & McFillen, 1996) noted that charisma, the oldest form of power among human social groups, becomes routinized over time. Before a charismatic founder of an organization dies, he or she often passes the reins to a leader more concerned with survival and growth than with innovation. To redirect an organization to produce effectively and efficiently, second-generation leaders usually create bureaucratic structures. Authority based on position rather than charisma became a recognized form of legitimacy.

3. Connection power. Connection power, based on informal network ties (Burt, 1992), refers to obtaining favors or legitimate requests by virtue

of knowing a person in a position of power. Knowing powerful people and having them grant requests cuts through many bureaucratic barriers. For instance, many managers complain about the slowness of getting needed services because of red tape. However, if such managers know persons who can order computer parts or fill a vacancy quickly and legally, managers may obtain what they want. Those providing shortcuts become informal, but powerful, resources.

4. Political power. Positional power is also related to control of resources, such as finances, staff, technology, and information (Kramer & Neale, 1998). Political power refers to the allocation and distribution made of scarce resources. People in "gatekeeper" roles can regulate who gets what and when. Leaders who can get political gatekeepers to respond to their requests for additional funds, for instance, often use persuasion and other forms of influence. Hult and Walcott (1992, p. 87) pointed out that political power influences how problems are defined and settled. They cited the influence of the "religious right" in the decisions that flowed from the White House to political executives and lawyers, and ultimately to career employees in the Department of Health and Human Services in the early 1980s.

Political power goes beyond the control of resources. It also includes the ability to control decision processes, to form coalitions and alliances, and to institutionalize cultural norms and behaviors (Clegg, 1992). Because governmental bureaucracies have fragmented decision-making structures and processes, power is weakened and diffused. To attain support for administering laws and delivering mandated services, governmental agencies require assistance of key legislators, interest groups, other governmental agencies, and private sector counterparts.

INFLUENCE

Leaders rely on power to add legitimacy to their requests; effective leaders use a variety of tactics that facilitate follower compliance. Influence tactics help change the minds and desires of followers in directions leaders expect and desire. Power, as noted, helps define issues and allocate resources, but influence enables followers to accept the tactics.

Influence tactics often consist of multiple behaviors leaders use for specific purposes. These may be to inform, explain, inspire, motivate, coerce, order, and/or to exchange resources. Some of the more common tactics include the following:

- **Rational persuasion**—explaining important reasons for requests and informing followers of potential benefits
- **Ingratiating**—making followers feel important

- **Upward influence**—gaining credibility by appealing to higher authorities
- **Blocking**—preventing followers from achieving a particular goal
- **Coalitions**—enlisting the collective aid of others to support a particular position
- **Inspirational appeals**—use of symbolic imagery
- **Consultation**—use of expert knowledge and information to assist in problem solving
- **Pressure**—implied or overt threats if actions are not carried out

Leaders having power based on their position may also use their authority to influence follower compliance. Followers may be bound to carry out a leader's request or order, but the leader may wish to emphasize the importance of the demand to affect follower commitment. Leaders may invoke pressure tactics or coercion if followers are reluctant or uncommitted to performing a particular task. Moreover, if the task is unpleasant or requires extra effort from followers, leaders may bolster performance by adding incentive rewards. For example, a supervisor who has been given a "rush" job with a deadline of less than a week realizes that staff will not like having to come to the office on Saturday to work. The leader may pressure workers and threaten them with disciplinary action if they do not comply. But this would worsen the workers' emotional state and probably provoke their resentment. Rather, the supervisor should probably inform the employees of the importance to the organization of completing the job as a whole and might promise them a bonus when the task is completed.

WHAT MAKES INFLUENCE TACTICS "POLITICAL"?

Followers interpret the legitimacy of leader requests based largely on the type of tactics the leader uses. Followers accept tactics that clearly establish and work toward goals benefiting a greater purpose. When the tactics are not as clearly apparent or when self-interests emerge, followers may interpret the tactics as "political." Pfeiffer (in Shafritz & Ott, 1996, p. 362) defined organizational politics as "those activities taken within organizations to acquire, develop, and use power and other resources to obtain one's preferred outcomes in a situation in which there is uncertainty or dissensus about choices."

Porter, Allen, and Anglo (1990) observed that the perception of *political* is based on areas of organizational uncertainty and resource scarcity as well as the need to act because of high personal stake or importance of the issue to an individual. In this light, common undesirable influence tactics include covert transactions, persuasion through specialized knowledge, and manipulation through concealment of actions and intentions. Legitimate political pressure occurs when followers understand the tactics are in line with expected role behaviors, have clearly articulated purposes, and result in fair allocations of resources and rewards.

POLITICAL GAMESMANSHIP, ADMINISTRATION, AND PUBLIC LEADERS

Public administration is inherently political. Separating the goals of policy making from the processes of implementation involves shaping preferences and forming coalitions at every turn. Administrative agencies, asserted Cook (1998), have the strongest direct influence over public policy. Administrators influence indirectly, however, in the ways they define roles and the perspectives they have of their responsibilities. The task of the latter is to find a balance between what is good for the greater social benefit and what is good according to a narrow constituent viewpoint.

LEGITIMACY DILEMMAS IN PUBLIC SERVICE

This balancing is often fraught with dilemmas in the public sector. Leaders derive legitimate authority as delegates of laws and regulations. However, this authority is often unclear, vaguely worded, or incomplete in terms of specifying how administrators carry out laws. This is complicated by the fact that each situation administrators encounter is unique and requires interpretation and judgment. Moreover, because there is no central point of authority in agencies (through a check-and-balance arrangement between branches of government), defining priorities and enacting them involves bargaining, compromise, and trading.

Decisions are difficult to make in such cases. Not only do administrators risk judgmental error, but also particular circumstances coupled with limited resources pose additional problems. Followers may see a leader's decision to expend funds for a certain activity as benefiting one group over another. Others may see such decisions as arbitrary or even made to please higher authorities. Sometimes legal restrictions may pose ethical dilemmas as well. Because the legislature allocates funds based on the preceding year's levels, agency managers try to prevent revenue losses. Accordingly, the requirement that unspent funds be returned to the treasury has propelled many "third quarter" spending sprees among governmental managers.

Wilson (1995) surveyed Senior Executive Service (SES) members in the federal government concerning their perceptions of political power and influence, particularly during the Reagan administration in the early to mid-1980s. This era was characterized by an abundance of political appointees who believed career employees, such as the SES, would sabotage the administration's ideological goals to change the government. The study revealed that the SES perceived the appointees as using autocratic and coercive power in such tactics as abusing performance appraisal ratings, allocating rewards and imposing sanctions, and making punitive reassignments. One of the most prevalent tactics was to invite the SES members to share information under the illusion of democratic participation, but to prevent them from making substantive contributions. In controlling informational as well as financial resources, the political appointees diminished the degree of power of both the SES member and the subunit that he or she administered. The degree of trust of such political supervisors was a key element in the commitment of SES members to remain in the federal government.

Inadequate funding and lack of consistent leadership emerged in the perception of political influence on agency accountability in the Federal Aviation Administration (FAA) (Ott, 1997). In 1996, the FAA lost a large number of technical experts who provided strong leadership in safety. That year was also one that saw a higher-than-average number of fatal air crashes. The exodus came in the swirl of several political interests bearing on the agency, such as a highly judicious National Transportation Safety Board, a critical Congress and news media, Department of Transportation officials, and the White House.

SHARED POWER

Legitimacy dilemmas often involve zero-sum power games in which individuals or coalitions of individuals attempt to exert control over others' resources, beliefs, motives, and actions. This is especially true if organizations have top-down or hierarchical power over resource acquisition, control, and development.

A growing trend in the public sector, which mitigates the win/lose resource fights, is collaboration among government, private organizations, nonprofit groups, and citizens. For example, the pervasive move to privatize many governmental services has resulted in more cross-cutting, entrepreneurial activities (Osborne & Gaebler, 1992). In addition, governments have formed wide-ranging partnerships with community, private and nonprofit organizations, and interest groups to solve such overwhelming societal problems as AIDS, air and water pollution, and homelessness (Rusaw, 1997). Accordingly, power bases for carrying out laws and administrative ordinances are shifting to multilateral agreements among those whom laws affect (King & Stivers, 1998).

In discussing a collaborative policy-making process involving the Environmental Protection Agency (EPA), Weber and Khademian (1997) illustrate this further. The collaboration between the EPA, Congress, oil/alternative fuels industry interests, environmentalists, and state regulators came about, the authors maintain, because of innovative leadership. In such a leadership model, they note, the leader must

> ...be prepared to persuade rather than command,...and be willing to share authority in the selection and design of the means to policy goals. Leaders must convince potential participants that collaboration is desirable, that their stakes in the outcomes will be respected and protected, and that if they cooperate in good faith, others will also (p. 405).

SUMMARY

Leadership plays a vital role in the definition and exercise of power, influence, and authority. Principally, leadership involves the changing of attitudes, beliefs, values, and behaviors in inducing other people to accomplish certain goals. As a reciprocal relationship, moreover, leadership entails influence processes whereby followers accept as legitimate a set range of behaviors.

Power is the potential to achieve objectives by working with and through other people. In transacting roles, leaders and followers use a variety of power bases. Chiefly, these include personal, inducement-based, and legitimate power bases.

Personal power includes having desirable physical characteristics, inherited qualities, and keen intellectual and emotional attributes. Personal power manifests itself in expertise in interpersonal, technical, and analytic areas. It also appears in follower identification with leader beliefs and values through symbols and artifacts.

Inducement-based power lies in the ability of the leader to determine and use wisely appropriate rewards and sanctions to regulate follower compliance.

Legitimate power, based on socially defined norms and expectations, includes the presence of shared beliefs and values, legally recognized authority, and access to valuable resources and decisional points.

Influence involves the activation of follower potential. Leaders employ several tactics, including rational persuasion, inspirational appeals, consultation, ingratiation, and coalition building.

Political influence tactics involve using scarce resources, and self-serving ends. Political influence sets in motion zero-sum games, in which some individuals win at the expense of others. To create situations in which both agencies and constituents obtain desired ends and to produce higher quality decisions, many governmental agencies have instituted relationships based on shared power.

In Chapter 3, we shall observe in greater detail some of the important psychosocial characteristics that motivate the leader–follower relationship. We note especially how public sector leaders can use these characteristics among followers when material and technological resources are scarce and when opportunities for career growth may be limited.

QUESTIONS FOR THOUGHT AND DISCUSSION

1. From your experiences, think of some particularly useful influence strategies leaders have used. What made them effective?

2. In what ways can charismatic gifts be useful to public leaders? What are some circumstances in which using the gifts may potentially be harmful to followers?

3. What are some examples from your own experiences of how leaders get around red tape to accomplish their purposes?

4. What are some necessary conditions for shared power in public leadership? How can they be achieved? Under what conditions is shared power *not* effective for leadership decisions?

THE NUCLEAR WASTE SITE DISCUSSION

DIRECTIONS

Read the following case study silently (5 minutes) and note the interests and needs of the leaders and each constituent group. Also note the base of power each has and some possible influence strategies that will enable leaders and followers to reach consensus. After reading the case, divide into small groups of 9–10 and select parts to role play. Individuals should study the parts and make notes of how they will use power and influence (10 minutes). Observers should examine the role play and note how effectively the players used their power and influence tactics (30 minutes). At the conclusion of the role play, observers share their feedback with the players.

THE NUCLEAR WASTE SITE DEBATE

BACKGROUND

The disposal of low level nuclear waste in America has reached the stage where it is an issue of great sociological, economic, and ecological significance. Congress has passed legislation requiring each state to dispose its own low level nuclear waste. Your state's Hazardous Waste Manage-ment Agency has spent the past two years studying potential sites where disposal would be feasible geologically. Of the sites, the agency has chosen three, but the final decision is complicated by many factors. The state itself is densely populated, and little space exists for nuclear waste disposal. In the three sites that do contain sufficient space, the communities are small and stable, and noted for good schools. There is limited commercial and economic stability in the state, however. Providing a special tax-relief system and other economic incentives will benefit the community selected. Because hazardous waste sites are designed to be safe, no one can foresee an accident near the community chosen. Moreover, while the site can accommodate the needs of the state presently, it is possible that it may in the future take in hazardous waste from neighboring states.

In the following discussion the director of the Hazardous Waste Management Agency and the environmental engineer are meeting with a group of residents of Pillsbury, a community of 25,000, and one of the three sites selected. The purpose is to discuss concerns and arrive at a solution concerning the selection of Pillsbury.

PLAYERS

Pat Nichols: Director of Hazardous Waste Management Agency

Chris Fields: Environmental engineer with the Hazardous Waste Management Agency

Casey LaPorte: Owner of one of the larger retail businesses in the community

Kelly Chan: Restaurant owner

Robin O'Brien: Realtor and parent

Rosario Dominguez: Parent and community volunteer

Stacy Feldman: Teacher

3

Leadership Through Motivating Others

Synopsis

This chapter explores the uses of values, motives, needs, and organizational processes and arrangements that influence follower compliance with leader requests. The text contends that motives are complex forces within individuals that stem from needs, drives, and socialized learning. Historically, differing leadership approaches have specified how to activate motives to achieve leader purposes. Chapter 3 analyzes the approaches and describes applications from Scientific Management, reward-based theories of management, human relations schools of thought, and organizational development models of enriching worker environments and skill development.

Objectives

- To state components of motives
- To describe the scientific approach to motivation, particularly with respect to contemporary public sector applications
- To discuss Expectancy Theory and Equity Theory as reward-based approaches to motivation
- To discuss human relations themes in needs-based theories of motivation and in applications to redesigning workplace structures and processes

Key Terms and Concepts

drives

Equity Theory

Expectancy Theory

gainsharing

Hawthorne experiments

47

Herzberg's Two-Factor Theory

human relations approach to motivation

Job Characteristics' Model
   job enlargement
   job enrichment
   job rotation

Lewin's small group research

Maslow's Needs Hierarchy

McGregor's Theory *X* and Theory *Y* leadership

motivation

needs

Performance-Based Organizations (PBOs)

reengineering jobs

Scientific Management

social learning

Total Quality Management (TQM)

INTRODUCTION

Leadership is a process of defining and carrying out goals using socially sanctioned behavior. Central to this process is identifying those personality traits that will inspire people to reach a given objective. This can prove difficult because what sparks one person into action may fail to motivate another.

Leading public employees requires an understanding of particular values and beliefs that instill the desire to serve. Although public employees continue to value serving the common interest over profit (Perry & Wise, 1990), this altruistic motivation is changing. With the recent trends in "privatizing" public service, government employees have become more attuned to the need to compete for services and private firms have taken on responsibilities for meeting general social needs (Rainey, 1997).

Jurkiewicz, Massey, and Brown (1998) compared 15 central motivators in a survey of public and private employees. They found that having job stability and security was primary among public employees; a chance to learn new things and to develop skills ranked second and third, respectively; and high salary was fourth (see Table 3.1). However, in terms of what public employees actually received, learning new skills and variety of work assignments were at the top of the list. Job stability was fourth, while high salary was next to the bottom (see Table 3.2 p. 50).

In addition to privatization, many public sector jobs are becoming more entrepreneurial and economically competitive (Osborne & Gaebler, 1992). This has led to many changes in the motivation to serve public needs as well as changes in the quality and meaning of work performed. "Customer service," a concept that has borrowed many ideas and practices from the private sector, has become the focal point of providing direct work to the public (Epstein & Olsen, 1996). Public employees are encouraged to identify the particular needs of their "customers" (that is, the individuals and groups they serve) and provide high quality, high satisfaction outcomes and results. The emphasis on discretionary, decentralized, and "user friendly" service

▪ TABLE 3-1

WHAT PUBLIC EMPLOYEES EXPECT FROM THEIR JOBS

A Comparison of Rank Order of Motivational "Wants" by Public and Private Sector Employees

Public Sector Employees		Private Sector Employees	
Rank	Motivational Factor	Rank	Motivational Factor
1	A stable and secure future	1	High salary
2	Chance to learn new things	2	Chance to exercise leadership
3	Chance to use my special abilities	3	Opportunity for advancement
4	High salary	4	A stable and secure future
5	Opportunity for advancement	5	Chance to make a contribution to important decisions
6	Variety in work assignments	6	Chance to use my special abilities
7	Working as part of a team	7	Chance to benefit society
8	Chance to make a contribution to important decisions	8	Working as part of a team
9	Friendly and congenial associates	9	Chance to learn new things
10	Chance to benefit society	10	High prestige and social status
11	Chance to exercise leadership	11	Freedom from pressure to conform both on and off the job
12	Freedom from supervision	12	Variety in work assignments
13	Freedom from pressure to conform both on and off the job	13	Friendly and congenial associates
14	Chance to engage in satisfying leisure activities	14	Chance to engage in satisfying leisure activities
15	High prestige and social status	15	Freedom from supervision

SOURCE: C. E. Jurkiewicz, T. K. Massey, and R. G. Brown (1998, March). Motivation in public and private organizations: A comparitive study. *Public Personnel Management Review, 1*(3), pp. 230–250. Used by permission.

Note: Spearman's rank correlation coefficient = .52 ($p < .10$).

■ **TABLE 3–2**

WHAT PUBLIC EMPLOYEES "GET" FROM THEIR JOBS

A Comparison of "Wants" and "Gets" Rankings of Motivational Factors by Public Sector Employees

Public Sector "Wants"		Public Sector "Gets"	
Rank	Motivational Factor	Rank	Motivational Factor
1	A stable and secure future	1	Chance to learn new things
2	Chance to learn new things	2	Variety in work assignments
3	Chance to use my special abilities	3	Chance to use my special abilities
4	High salary	4	A stable and secure future
5	Opportunity for advancement	5	Working as part of a team
6	Variety in work assignments	6	Chance to benefit society
7	Working as part of a team	7	Friendly and congenial associates
8	Chance to make a contribution to important decisions	8	Chance to make a contribution to important decisions
9	Friendly and congenial associates	9	Chance to exercise leadership
10	Chance to benefit society	10	Freedom from supervision
11	Chance to exercise leadership	11	Opportunity for advancement
12	Freedom from supervision	12	Variety in work assignments
13	Freedom from pressure to conform both on and off the job	13	Freedom from pressure to conform both on and off the job
14	Chance to engage in satisfying leisure activities	14	High salary
15	High prestige and social status	15	High prestige and social status

SOURCE: C. E. Jurkiewicz, T. K. Massey, and R. G. Brown (1998, March). Motivation in public and private organizations: A comparitive study. *Public Personnel Management Review, 1*(3), pp. 230–250. Used by permission.

Note: Spearman's rank correlation coefficient = .65 ($p < .05$).

has given new meaning to the way employees see their work and themselves (Schachter, 1995).

In this chapter, we will examine various views of motivation, from Scientific Management to humanistic and participatory theories. We will also highlight relevant illustrations in the public sector and describe how leaders might apply these theories to working with individuals. The purpose of Chapter 3, then, is to provide a basic understanding of the motives and behaviors important to the leadership process. We will explore techniques for developing these behaviors effectively to reach desirable goals. The phrase "desirable goals," a public relations' term, refers to constitutionally derived laws, policies, or services that encourage societal well-being.

AN INTRODUCTION TO MOTIVES

Before we begin, we need to understand that motives are complex. They result from the unique combination of both inherited traits and learned qualities, such as tolerance or initiative. Motives also develop differently with each person, depending upon his or her personality, experience, and cultural upbringing.

In general, motives consist of drives that produce energy, direction, and tenacity. They often originate biologically to create homeostasis (that is, internal equilibrium). Homeostasis is a response to a stimulus that can be physical, psychological, or an awareness of conditions outside the human organism. Drives are the forces that direct people either toward or away from these conditions. Moreover, while some conditions provoke an instinctual reaction—touching a hot stove, for example—some reactions can be learned. We learn to avoid touching hot stoves as a result of experience. Therefore, responses are based on both external and internal stimuli, and are inborn as well as learned. Drives seek to maintain inner balance by reducing tensions and providing relief.

SCIENTIFIC MANAGEMENT: AN AGENCY VIEW OF MOTIVATION

Perhaps the oldest view of what motivates people is based in economics: People will work for basic needs, such as food, clothing, and shelter. In capitalistic economies, it was believed that workers would produce goods in exchange for tokens that symbolized value, such as bills and coins. In the Industrial Age particularly, value developed as a result of an accumulation of capital in money and machines; labor became an exchanged commodity. In that era, as is evident in Adam Smith's *Wealth of Nations* (1776/1996), capital and labor interlocked on a national scale, producing a combined wealth.

As soon as owners of capital could buy services of labor, they became known as "agents." In "agency" theory today, people are primarily motivated by money as the way to satisfy basic human needs. This view characterized the Scientific Management model of leadership, particularly in the writings of Frederick Taylor (1912/1996). Taylor viewed labor as an essential element of an agent becoming wealthier. By offering workers additional wages, owners could increase output and hence profits. Taylor's principles for effective management included shifting all power of decision to management, and using scientific methods for improving productivity. In this view, managers would select the best-qualified person for a job using measurable criteria and would then provide training. This system of working closely with employees gives owners not only a more capable worker, but also a chance to monitor production to see that exact standards are met (see Figure 3.1 p. 52).

MODERN APPLICATIONS: TOTAL QUALITY MANAGEMENT (TQM)

Many of Scientific Management's ideas of improving organizational functioning through providing worker incentives, setting clear job outcomes and

. FIGURE 3-1

AGENCY VIEW OF MOTIVATION

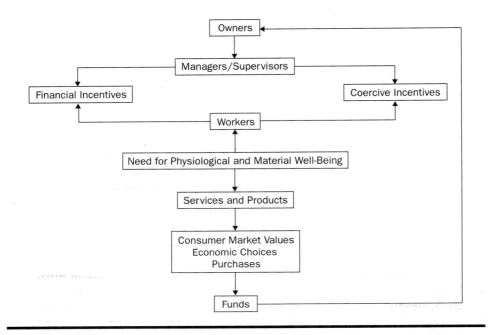

measuring task results, and using management-supplied resources appear in contemporary productivity improvement methods. Perhaps the most familiar is Total Quality Management (TQM). TQM techniques have been used to promote greater motivation by developing clear, explicit, and measurable goals; linking goals with job responsibilities; and providing accurate, timely, and quantifiable feedback to employees. TQM uses the concepts and skills of continuous improvement to promote pride in work, create a climate of productivity improvement through eliminating problems based in organizational structures, involve workers in planning and designing improvement projects, and drive out fear (Juran, 1995).

Since 1988, with the establishment of the Federal Quality Institute (FQI), 70% of federal agencies have adopted some form of TQM (FQI, 1991). Moreover, TQM programs have been launched in several state and local governments. In a review of TQM at the local level, Berman and West (1995) observed that TQM was successful in larger cities having a greater variety and amount of resources. Moreover, TQM was used most often in police, recreation and parks departments, and in human resources management.

Vinzant and Vinzant (1996) reviewed the applications of strategic management and Total Quality Management in government and noted that successful uses adapted methodologies to specific characteristics of public organizations. For strategic management to work, organizations must have a highly influential leader or sponsor who is committed to long-range changes and is willing to accept delays in planning. Successful projects also require a culture that can adapt values of quality organizational performance through employee involvement. Total Quality Management programs that produced expected results navigated numerous obstacles, such as the existence of multiple customers, instability and uncertainty, complex accountability, and the symbolic "products" of public service. Successful TQM programs emphasized concrete goals, measurable performance results, were flexible in terms of meeting the demands of a many-layered clientele structure, and had outcomes that clearly benefited government.

Rago (1996) added that to change both structural arrangements and culture in governmental agencies, leaders of TQM projects need to communicate clearly and constantly throughout all parts of an agency what the vision or purpose of a TQM program is and what it hopes to accomplish. Additionally, leaders need to establish training programs tailored to specific situations users of the program typically encounter.

REENGINEERING

Another common use of Scientific Management principles appears in Business Process Reengineering (BPR). Reengineering involves improving overall work productivity by eliminating wasteful and duplicative tasks and jobs. "Productive" systems are those that reduce waste through eliminating scrap, "downtime," or time spent on task, recurrent problems in performance, duplication, and fragmentation. Systems are reengineered by decreasing waste, combining functions, or eliminating unnecessary steps or task functions. Often, organizations undergoing reengineering use cross-functional teams of managers and employees to identify candidates for systemic change and to develop ways to produce more effective and efficient services and products (Hammer & Champy, 1993).

In a review of case study research from various information resources management documents, Caudle (1994) examined the uses of reengineering in several governmental organizations. Caudle noted several conditions that government managers confronted in using reengineering interventions. First, government work processes and subprocesses had to be defined in relation to a specific customer served. This was difficult because public employees provide service not only to specific customers and clients but also to the larger society, in terms of being accountable for use of public resources. This opened decision-making processes to public scrutiny and invited oversight from several legislative and judiciary bodies. Further, the short tenure of politically appointed managers presented narrow windows of opportunity in which to develop long-term goals and produce tangible results. In addition, vague organizational missions and the inability to develop exact and quantifiable performance measures of service to achieve the mission created problems for identifying and evaluating expected improvements.

Finally, the fragmented human resources systems limited the abilities of managers to hire, train, and reward the individuals conducting reengineering projects. The structural impediments identified made it difficult for managers to coordinate and integrate services and products. Many of the continuous improvement varieties of "reinvention" are incremental interventions.

REWARD-BASED THEORIES OF MOTIVATION

A variant of Scientific Management is the use of rewards and punishments for motivating employees. Although Scientific Management identified economic incentives as critical to increasing work quantity and quality, it is the employees' perception of the value of such incentives that determines what is satisfying. What one employee values, another finds unimportant or even demotivating. To help explain this, we shall look at two important theories of follower perceptions of rewards: Expectancy Theory and Equity Theory. We can also see applications of the theories in Performance-Based Organizations (PBOs) and gainsharing.

EXPECTANCY THEORY

Expectancy Theory holds that individuals will pursue goals depending on how much they value expected results (see Figure 3.2). Expectancy Theory consists of gauging effort according to how likely is the desired outcome. In Figure 3.2, two factors dictate the outcome: how much effort is required and how expectations will affect the desired ends. There is a critical linkage between performance and outcomes. If there is a high probability that performance will result in the expected outcomes, motivation and effort will be high. On the other hand, if probability is low, a person will not expect a high reward and will exert only minimal effort.

If individuals value promotion, for instance, they will perform those tasks they expect will lead to promotion. They may volunteer for a challenging assignment, solve a persistent managerial problem, or attend college courses. For example, Casey volunteers to work overtime to earn extra money as well as to impress the supervisor. In return, Casey expects time-and-a-half plus a highly commendable rating on the next performance evaluation. If Casey receives only compensatory time, or if the supervisor overlooks Casey's extra efforts, Casey will be upset and will probably not volunteer again.

EQUITY THEORY

In Equity Theory, individuals calculate how much effort is required to produce a valuable result. They also assess the ratio of their efforts to their re-

■ **FIGURE 3-2**

A MODEL OF EXPECTANCY THEORY

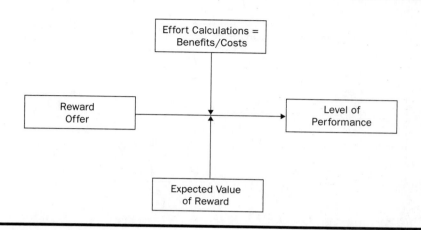

sults, comparing this ratio to that of others. If, in comparison, their performance seems lacking, they will adjust their behavior to achieve a better standing. In Equity Theory, individuals compare their rewards with those who do similar work and adjust levels of motivation. If they discover they are receiving less than others, they will be dissatisfied and their motivation will decrease (see Figure 3.3 p. 56).

For example, Mary, a program analyst in the Department of Defense, has a bachelor's degree, eight years' federal experience, and earns $48,000 per year. She notes, however, that her colleague Barbara, who has the same credentials as herself, but with fewer years at the agency, was recently promoted.

According to Equity Theory, Mary feels that her own contributions to the agency fail to yield the same results as those of Barbara. Since Mary feels that Barbara has received a greater reward for a lesser contribution, she will focus her attention on this difference. Mary will then try to rectify the imbalance of inputs and outputs by doing one or more of the following:

1. *Change outputs.* Mary may try to produce a greater number or higher quality products.

2. *Change inputs.* Mary may simply decide to put more effort into the tasks she already has.

3. *Change self-perception.* Mary may see herself as equally competent as Barbara, but more deserving of rewards because of her greater tenure.

4. *Change perception of the other.* Mary may see Barbara as less competent than herself and treat Barbara as a threat.

. FIGURE 3-3

A MODEL OF EQUITY THEORY

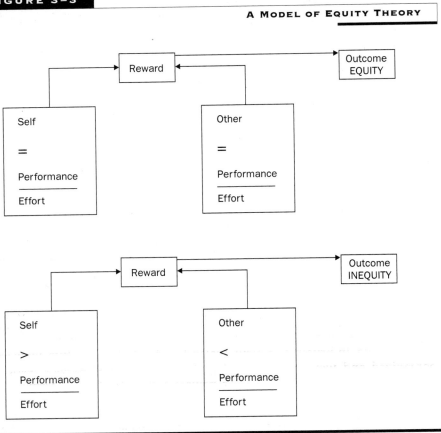

5. *Change referent.* Mary may feel that Barbara's promotion was merely Barbara's blind luck, given her lack of experience. Therefore, Mary may cease being concerned about the incident and redouble her own efforts to earn a promotion "the honest way."

6. *Leave.* Mary may perceive that other women of similar qualifications are glossed over by the agency. She may feel that since only token women are promoted, the effort is futile. Why continue working at a job with no potential of upward mobility?

MERIT PAY

We can see merit pay as an application of Expectancy Theory. If employees believe their payment was assessed fairly and was equal to the effort they exerted, merit pay is motivating (Dow, Markham, & Vest, 1996; Kellough &

Seldon, 1997). However, using merit pay by itself may have the opposite effect. Often, managers do not have discretion over how much merit pay exemplary employees receive. In addition, because many of the jobs in the public sector lack quantifiable criteria, measurement is difficult. Subjective calculations of expected benefits to actual results may differ between employees and managers. Finally, merit pay systems have widespread rater bias and greatly limit individual performance improvement (Campbell, Campbell, & Chia, 1998).

A study of public/private sector pay comparability illustrates the use of Equity Theory (Lewis & Durst, 1995). Federal salaries lagged behind private sector salaries by 3% in 1978 to 25% in 1990. To close the gap, particularly in high-cost-of-living metropolitan areas, Congress enacted the Federal Employee Pay Comparability Act (FEPCA). Lewis and Durst found some support for higher government employee turnover in areas where private sector pay was higher.

PERFORMANCE-BASED ORGANIZATIONS

The National Performance Review recommended Performance-Based Organizations (PBOs) as a means of stimulating employee motivation (Roberts, 1997). Performance-Based Organizations are based on governmental organizations in Britain, New Zealand, and Canada that reduce legal and regulatory constraints on agency performance and offer new incentives to improve outputs. In Britain and New Zealand particularly, executive agencies reorganized and were given annual performance targets. Agency leaders were recruited from both public and private sectors for limited terms and paid according to how well their organizations met goals. A "Next Steps" review of the British agencies showed significant improvements in both performance and employee satisfaction. Yet, such results may not be achievable in the United States for several reasons. Centralized administrative oversight, as in Great Britain, interfered with decentralized goal setting. Further, the inability of agencies to use resources other than government-operated central services and the legislative control of agency funding hamper agency discretion and entrepreneurial activities. Moreover, paying government officials high bonuses for top performance is likely to draw criticism from taxpayers who have been consistently unwilling to raise taxes to fund innovative governmental programs. In brief, unless agency leaders can have authority and resources to chart innovative courses, Performance-Based Organizations will not likely succeed.

GAINSHARING

Perceptions of equity in distribution of rewards also occurs in gainsharing. Gainsharing—the dividing up of profits or surpluses—has been used more often in private than in public sector organizations. In governmental organizations that have introduced "privatization" or competition for performing public services, cost savings (rather than profits) may be redistributed as bonuses.

Although this concept of gainsharing has improved financial job satisfaction, one case in Zebulon, North Carolina, suggested lack of discretion in goal setting may limit gainsharing's effectiveness (Patton & Daley, 1998). In Zebulon, elected council members and department heads set strategic goals and established performance measurements and standards for employee performance. The new goals and measurements resulted in budget savings. However, a survey of the town's employees revealed that workers were dissatisfied with the gainsharing process because they felt they had no input in setting the goals and performance standards.

HUMAN RELATIONS' VIEWS

Scientific Management emphasized the use of objectively derived performance standards and the subordinate role of noneconomic motives in improving productivity. Since the Hawthorne (Rothlisberger & Dickson, 1939) experiments of 1930s, however, individual needs, psychological drives, and the prominence of cultural learning in motivation have recast the economic basis of productivity. In these experiments Mayo and Rothlisberger manipulated the lighting levels in an Illinois Western Electric plant to observe the effects on workers, they found, as predicted, that output grew when they increased the intensity of lighting. To their surprise, however, production also grew when they *decreased* the light level. After further investigation, the scientists found that the productivity increased not because of the variations in lighting, but because they had given special attention to the workers. This discovery ignited the human relations' view of management. In this view, a worker's nonrational needs—such as working for recognition—became just as valid as the needs of those working to sustain a vital existence.

TWO VIEWS OF MOTIVATION: THEORY *X* AND THEORY *Y*

The Hawthorne Plant discoveries led to increased attention to the role of emotional needs as motivators. It also raised issues of reward systems, management styles, and work structures imposed by organizations. In brief, two branches of human relations were born: human needs as motivation and organizational contribution to motivation. Douglas McGregor (1960) perhaps best describes these two branches of human relations in his Theory *X* and Theory *Y* opposition. McGregor placed motivational theorists into two camps: (1) those who favor a scientific view, where managers control workers' behavior with a system of rewards and punishments; and (2) those who champion a humanistic basis, where workers determine their own goals and the means of achieving them.

In his Theory X and Theory Y discussions, McGregor illustrated fundamental differences in the views. Theory X proponents, for example, believe
people have an inherent dislike for work. They are lazy, self-centered, and
resist change. Managers, therefore, have the right to motivate them through
rewards or sanctions: carrots and sticks, respectively. Theory Y advocates,
however, see workers' higher needs as the basis for motivation. This philosophy maintains that workers want to fulfill their potential, but organizations hinder them by failing to provide self-development opportunities and
incentives. Accordingly, people may *appear* passive and resistant, but, in
fact, are not.

As the human relations' view of behavior began to explore the relationship between psychological and material motivation, several theories of
needs-based motivation emerged. Notably, these included: Maslow's Hierarchy of Needs and Herzberg's Two-Factor Theory.

MASLOW'S NEEDS HIERARCHY

Early in the 1940s, Abraham Maslow (1954) published his seminal work on
a hierarchy of human needs. Maslow's five-tiered model revealed that while
needs do encompass a basic survival mechanism, they also include needs
for affection and for belonging to a valued group. His model incorporated
needs that help develop self-respect, autonomy, and achievement. Maslow
also highlighted the need for status, recognition, and the capability of realizing potential. Figure 3.4 (p. 60) depicts Maslow's Needs Hierarchy.

Maslow divided this hierarchy into three main groups: (1) lower, such as
physical and safety needs; (2) middle range, such as social and esteem
needs; and (3) higher needs, such as self-actualization. Maslow maintained
that external motivators such as wages, benefits, and tenure satisfy lower
needs. But workers satisfy higher needs internally, by working with others,
learning, and finding fulfillment in the work. Once lower needs are satisfied, Maslow contended, individuals pursue higher needs. Conversely,
when lower needs emerge, people give them priority. Hence, Maslow believed that when individuals receive sufficient wages and benefits, they become concerned with finding social identity in an organization. They then
seek fulfillment in their work. If, however, organizations reduce wages,
workers revert to emphasizing job security.

HERZBERG'S TWO-FACTOR THEORY

Herzberg (1966) believed that Maslow's organizations that used extrinsic incentives, such as pay, benefits, pleasant working conditions, and ample
parking spaces, did not produce desires to perform more effectively (Burke,
1994). The only true motivators were intrinsic rewards individuals earned
from performing a particular job or task, such as feelings of accomplishment, recognition for expertise, self-actualization, and doing something

■ FIGURE 3-4

A MODEL OF MASLOW'S NEEDS HIERARCHY

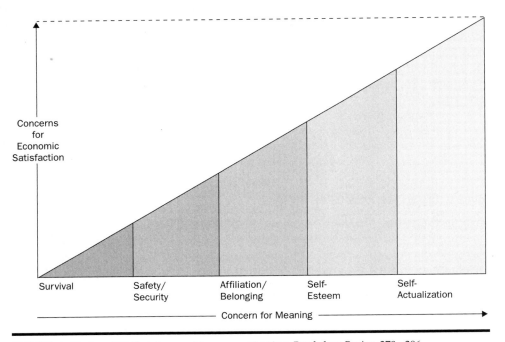

SOURCE: A. Maslow (1943). A theory of human motivation. *Psychology Review,* 370–396.

"worthwhile." Herzberg saw organizational attempts to motivate, such as through increases in wages and benefits, as merely "hygienic"; at best, they prevented workers from reverting to primitive, physiological maintenance-based behaviors. As indicated in Figure 3.5, Herzberg saw job performance motivation resulting from features of the work itself that allowed for involvement, self-direction, and producing opportunities for personal growth and development. Extrinsic rewards, such as pay, benefits, yearly bonuses, and even promotions only masquerade as motivators. Ultimately, they produce greater drives to gain more extrinsic rewards and are only hygenic attempts to motivate.

SOCIOTECHNICAL CONTRIBUTORS TO MOTIVATION

Organizations highly contributed to what drove individuals to perform. Organizational components include the structure of work, the satisfaction derived from certain aspects of work, the scope of responsibility, and the opportunity for independent decision making. An organization is also concerned with the degree of specialization and the types of rewards (mate-

■ **FIGURE 3–5**

HERZBERG'S TWO-FACTOR APPROACH TO MOTIVATION

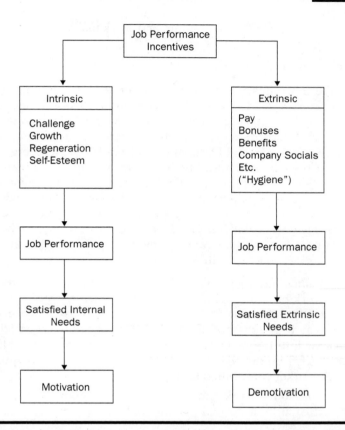

SOURCE: F. Herzberg (1966). *Work and the nature of man.* Chicago: World Publishing Company.

rial and nonmaterial) attached to a job's completion. Therefore, the focus of the sociotechnical theorists lies in the relationship between the types of work performed, the degree of satisfaction in the work, and the structure of work flow, rewards, and motivation. Job motivation encompassed not only the technical aspects of how work was organized and rewarded, but also the social needs that humans presented.

LEWIN: SMALL GROUP GOAL SETTING

Kurt Lewin (1947), a psychologist interested in how organizational structures and processes affected role development, was a leading figure in human relations in organizational development (French, Bell, & Zawacki,

1994). Lewin's studies of small group behavior in a Virginia pajama plant in the 1940s showed how workers developed their own systems of rewards, work output quotas, leadership dynamics, and criteria for satisfaction. Lewin's research emphasized the need to create opportunities for participation in decision making, goal setting, and work management.

JOB CHARACTERISTICS' MODEL

One of the most illustrative sociotechnical theories of job motivation is the Job Characteristics' Model (JCM). McGregor's Theory X and Theory Y—which maintained that lack of incentive stifles human potential—endorsed changing job structures so workers might derive more satisfaction from the work itself. Hackman and Oldham (1980), as well as Herzberg, adopted the theme that the characteristics of jobs greatly influence motivation and productivity. Work that provides satisfaction has certain characteristics. As shown in Figure 3.6, they include skill variety, task identity, and task significance. These jobs also have a strong element of autonomy; they enable workers to assume responsibility for feedback and the outcomes of their work.

To foster an intrinsic motivation in the workplace, Hackman and Oldham (1980) suggested four ways in which it could be redesigned.

1. *Job rotation.* Job rotation enables workers to develop a broader idea of the work by transferring to other departments, both horizontally and vertically. Job rotation provides a range of experiences that allow workers to see the premise upon which the work is based. They gain insight into the main objectives of the work, and are able to see the product from the client's point of view. They can also appreciate how each worker contributed to that product.

2. *Work modules.* Work modules are task periods of approximately 2 hours each. In a normal, 40-hour week, a workday would consist of

■ FIGURE 3-6

WHAT MAKES JOBS MEANINGFUL:
THE JOB CHARACTERISTICS MODEL (JCM)

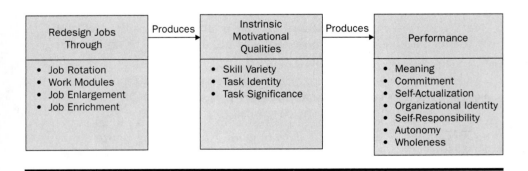

four modules for 5 days. Modules increase the variety of tasks that workers perform and provide more opportunities to determine the nature of the work itself. Workers select modules they would prefer in order to relieve monotonous, boring, and/or highly segmented tasks.

3. *Job enlargement.* Enlarging jobs, or doing whole jobs rather than parts, increases the horizontal scope to encompass a variety of tasks. Frequently, job enlargement combines several overspecialized tasks with limited promotion potential.

4. *Job enrichment.* Job enrichment expands the vertical scope of work by increasing control over designing and carrying out whole projects. Through enriched jobs, employees may work with increased autonomy. They develop greater responsibility for outcomes, and learn how the job is meeting desired goals.

SUMMARY

Motivation is a complex process that enlists a range of drives and desires in achieving goals that leaders deem important. Leaders help to produce desired outcomes by tapping these drives to meet economic and security needs. Drives consist of an individual's needs for affiliation with a larger community and fulfilling his or her own potential. How leaders tap these drives, however, has been seen differently throughout history. Chapter 3 has described three key philosophies:

1. **Agency** or **Scientific Management** viewed individuals as parts of an organization's architecture. In this view, owners provided incentives to workers through the mediation of managers and supervisors. Motivation was primarily a matter of economic rewards and punishments handed down by management to increase productivity.

2. **Human relations** centered on finding a balance between economic and noneconomic incentives. The success of the organization depended on how well the social and self-actualizing needs of the workers were met. Motivation consisted of empowering workers to define, develop, and implement goals on their own discretion. The promise of a desirable outcome provided further motivation.

3. **Sociotechnical theories** described organizations that provided increasing opportunity for individual worker fulfillment. These programs encouraged social relationships as well as a restructuring of the workload. Over the past 40 years, sociotechnical views have emphasized a revision of how work is apportioned and how management is structured. Other sociotechnical ideas included work teams to improve product quality and participatory management. Motivation was a consequence of this workplace restructuring that allowed employees to find an intrinsic meaning in it.

Underlying all three of these approaches is the philosophy that needs, or subconscious drives, operate within to reduce tensions individuals experience in performing tasks. Needs stem from a perceived gap in one's work situation. Dissatisfaction may result from states of mind in which a worker feels the job, which represents his or her means of survival, is threatened. Insecurities also arise when an individual feels excluded or unfairly treated in social groups. This can also occur when an employee perceives the work as irrelevant to a larger public mission or to the worker's own personal growth.

Moreover, needs may arise when people assess their efforts and rewards and compare them to those of others. If the person perceives inequality, then needs—as well as a drive to rectify the imbalance—emerge. In this situation, workers may try to alter the effort they must exert to achieve their desired outcome and payoff. To be motivated people need to identify the connections among their work, the fulfillment of greater social purposes, and the feeling of acceptance among peers.

Motivation challenges a leader's resourcefulness. It requires understanding not only the general needs that motivate individuals, but also finding particular combinations of needs and incentives that encourage individual fulfillment. As we shall see in Chapter 4, the concept of motivation involves multiple interdependent factors that affect followers. We will see that these factors exist within the follower, within the situation, and even within the leader.

QUESTIONS FOR THOUGHT AND DISCUSSION

1. From your experience, does motivation differ between public and private sector employees? Explain why or why not.

2. From the discussion of pay and benefits in the public sector, how do you see economics influencing motivation for public employment today? How can leaders deal with some detrimental aspects of merit pay or "pay for performance"?

3. What are some barriers to motivation you see in the work public employees perform? What might leaders do to remove the obstacles?

4. In your opinion, how can leaders create a Theory Y organization from one that is Theory X?

CASE STUDY

TURNING ON THE TAX DEPARTMENT
MOTIVATION STRATEGIES IN A STATE AGENCY

TIME: APPROXIMATELY 1 HOUR

DIRECTIONS

In the following case study, identify as many motivational theories and applica-

tions from the chapter as you can. Then, working in small groups, discuss how Gene Gavin, Commissioner of the Department of Revenue Services, applied the theories to the demoralized situation. In your opinion, would a similar strategy be effective in similar instances where public service work is being changed by competitive forces? Share your group's responses with the larger class.

When Gene Gavin became Commissioner of Connecticut's Department of Revenue Services (DRS) in 1993, he faced a demanding task. Taxpayers demanded better quality of services, yet refused to increase funds for them. Rumors of downsizing drifted through the agency continually. People also called the DRS with questions pertaining to the state tax code—a document so complex and arcane even the experts had trouble giving answers. Discouraged, overworked, and confused, department employees had become quite demotivated.

Gavin saw in the employees a great deal of potential. And he saw them as allies. He often spoke of them as "my" people. He recognized their fear of job loss and the meaning work had for his employees. He knew many of them personally before he was appointed commissioner. As a certified public accountant and attorney, Gavin had contact with five of the nine divisions of DRS and praised their professionalism, fairness, and courtesy. He was well aware of the distrust that had been kindled by the frequent changes at the top and the lack of tax knowledge exhibited by many of his predecessors.

To connect his goals of cost effectiveness and efficiency with his staff, Gavin identified common irritants in the tax law administration. He realized that neither the public nor even the employees liked the cumbersome, vaguely written tomes; both desired simplicity and ease in administration. He remarked in a 1995 personal interview,

> The 26 tax credits and the statutes that were written were so complicated that sometimes it took me, as a practitioner, more time to understand the statutes and write a memo to my clients that I had to bill them more for my time. Something was wrong with that.

Accordingly, Gavin made the simplification of tax language (in terms that laypersons could understand) a priority. He found the Small- and Medium-Sized Users Business Committee (SMSUBC), which the state general assembly had created that year, willing to help out. Comprised of business people from small- and medium-sized organizations, trade professionals, and tax professionals, the SMSUBC worked with employee volunteers to publish three handbooks the first year of Gavin's appointment: "A Guide to Connecticut Sales and Use Taxes for Building Contractors" (February 16, 1995); "A Guide to Connecticut Corporation Business Tax Credits" (February 16, 1995); and "Sales and Use Tax Guide for Manufacturers, Fabricators, and Processors" (November 3, 1995).

Since Gavin became commissioner, the workforce has fallen by 7%. But Gavin insisted that no person be laid off. Instead, he did not fill jobs when employees left or retired, he transferred people to divisions with vacancies, and retrained people whose jobs had become obsolete. He said:

> I know how important a job is to people, and I don't want to cut a job. One of the things that might happen in the process is that there might be new opportunities, new retraining for people who are here. I made the commitment to them. I will give them the right training, if that's something that impacts them. I see this as an opportunity to learn something new about the agency. This will make you more valuable and keep you interested.

Gavin saw that the agency lacked a focus, a vision. In the wake of frequent management changes, people had no idea of what the agency was expected to do or what their particular roles were. Gavin recognized that because of this ambiguity, the nine division directors had built up "walls" around themselves and had managed each division as a business unto itself. People inside the agency did not talk with each other and relationships with outside clients were sometimes tense.

To create a common identity among the employees, Gavin asked employees to draw up their own mission statement. It gave them a chance to determine what they wanted in the agency and write it in concrete terms. After employees wrote the final version, Gavin had it printed on the backs of business cards. He pointed out that this reminded employees of their purpose and gave them a reason for serving taxpayer needs and interests. Business and professional clients as well as employees have told Gavin how that has improved their relationships. "The positive feedback," Gavin noted, "was applauded. Psychologically, that's very important. When they started getting the feedback, the sense of hard work they had put into the publications was worthwhile."

In addition to seeing and communicating possibilities for change and stimulating others to share the vision, Gavin uses many team metaphors. The Public Service Excellence Program (PSE), a variant of Total Quality Management, uses cross-functional teams of managers and employees to develop and carry out incremental changes in operations. Gavin referred to the incremental changes as "base hits," and added that "When you have 860 people hitting a single, you have a lot of home runs by the end of the program." Sometimes, an innovation that nets large cost savings is a "grand slam."

Empowering division directors and employees to identify, carry out, and evaluate changes emerged as a result of education. Gavin coined words such as *torchbearers* and *disciples* to signify their shared interpretation and commitment to change in their own organizational units. To create an optimistic outlook for redeploying employees in the workforce reduction, Gavin proclaimed that he would "insource" work. He would develop a cadre of specially trained employees to take over the data-entry functions outside vendors

used to perform during the busiest tax-collection season. Through changing the frameworks of meanings of delegation and contracting work outside the agency, Gavin used words to educate employees for greater ownership of work processes and outcomes.

Gavin's approach to working with and through people is intensely personal. He often speaks of DRS in human terms, for instance, saying to employees, "The agency is listening to your ideas." He also showed that he shared their "pride in production," and used internal motivators as levers for change. In addition, he appealed for help by referring to them as equals in power: "If you help me be successful," he told them in small group meetings, "I will help you."

Gavin used the personal approach even in all-employee messages. He relied on his broadcast mail to tell employees about their colleagues who had accomplished major results through the PSE small wins applications projects. He also announced via the broadcast line his pride in what all the employees had contributed when the Connecticut Quality Council awarded DRS its 1996 Gold Connecticut Innovation Prize. In introducing a strategic planning process and inviting volunteers to participate, Gavin held 10 face-to-face meetings with all 860 employees. And each Friday, at the informal "Breakfast with the Commish," he listened to whatever employees wanted to tell him.

Gavin's personal, direct, and participatory approach to leading organizational change inspired others to bring about changes. In developing team-based "small wins" of the PSE, employees had to question why they had been doing work as they had always done it. In developing an understanding of problems and issues, employees opened up for critical inspection many of their unquestioned assumptions that framed the organization's culture. In addition, because they had training in problem solving, the commitment of their directors and the commissioner, and delegated authority to make changes within two to four weeks in how they did work, employees developed their own ideas for future changes. In fact, in their employee newsletter, employees recognize colleagues who have begun incremental changes on their own.

The favorable responses have a snowball effect, Gavin commented. Employees began to experience rapid success with new ideas they had introduced; in fact, one private sector official said that employees accomplished in 6 months a particular reform that would have taken anywhere from 2–3 years. External customers have been so pleased with the changes that they have built internal bases of support for DRS. One contractor newsletter, for example, praised "Gavin's Posse" of employees who prosecute home improvement contractors' refusing to pay taxes. The contractor newsletter asked members to contact the DRS "Discovery Unit" if they knew of tax violations.

Gavin commented, "We're getting a lot of business and industry people and taxpayers saying 'We want to talk to DRS because they seem to be getting things done quickly and fairly.'" The federal government has also taken note. The U.S. Congressional Ways and Means Committee, hearing of the DRS' successes, last year cited Connecticut as one of three states as models of innovation. The committee has asked DRS to share its revenue-finding tactics with the Internal Revenue Service.

The commitment to the commissioner's goals of cost effectiveness and efficiency, moreover, influenced legislative appropriations. When the legislature became aware of how the 860 DRS employees recovered over $900,000 in lost revenue, they granted Gavin's request for funds to replace the 1977 vintage computer system.

APPROACHES TO LEADERSHIP:
Normative, Situational, and Contingency

SYNOPSIS

Chapter 4 introduces conditions, such as individual characteristics, culture, types of preferred power and influence strategies, and conditions within environments that make using any particular style of leadership faulty. To examine how situational leadership has evolved and how it is used today, this chapter highlights several prominent theories, including Fiedler, Hersey and Blanchard, Vroom and Yetton, House, and Kerr and Jermier. By knowing individual preferences and readiness for independent decision making, degree of environmental ambiguity, and availability of leadership substitutes, leaders can attain the results they desire through different followers.

OBJECTIVES

- *To describe conditions in leaders, followers, and situations that require use of different interactional strategies*
- *To describe the key ideas in five major theories of contingency, normative, and situational approaches to leadership:*
  Fiedler's Contingency Theory
  Hersey and Blanchard's Situational Leadership Theory
  Vroom and Yetton's Normative Decision-Making Model
  House's Path–Goal Theory
  Kerr and Jermier's Leadership Substitutes

KEY TERMS AND CONCEPTS

follower maturity (readiness)

instrumental (task-oriented) leadership style

leadership substitutes
  neutralizers

Least Preferred Coworker (LPC)

Normative Decision-Making Model

Path–Goal Model leadership types
achievement-oriented
directive
participative
supportive

Situational Leadership types
autocratic
participating
delegating

Supportive (relational) Leadership style

INTRODUCTION

Leadership is a complex process involving both leaders and followers as they work toward a desired goal effectively. As we shall see, leadership effectiveness is based on several characteristics. In this chapter, we examine some leading theories describing effectiveness and give examples of each theory from the perspective of public administration. The theories discussed include: (1) Fiedler's Contingency Theory; (2) Hersey and Blanchard's Situational Leadership Theory; (3) the Vroom–Yetton Model; (4) House's Path–Goal Theory; and (5) Kerr and Jermier's Leadership Substitutes. By understanding the theories, public leaders can adjust their leadership style to match the needs and interests of followers as well as to conditions in the transactional environment.

CONTINGENCY THEORY

Contingency Theory implies that there is no "one best way" to lead others. There are at least seven variables that influence the leader–follower relationship:

1. Individual characteristics. The talents of leaders and followers complement each other. Individuals contribute unique qualities such as creativity and intelligence to reach a common goal.
2. Previous events. Individuals bring particular backgrounds to each situation. Their beliefs are a blend of culture, family, and education. As leaders and followers interact, these personal histories inform their behavior.

3. Objective versus perceived task requirements. Because individuals have unique histories, they perceive reality differently. Leaders help find a common ground by offering objective definitions of how followers can achieve a goal.

4. Subjective and objective accounting. There are subjective and objective interests in every interaction between leaders and followers. Both parties must therefore agree to terms of a contract, and act on those terms once a balance has been achieved.

5. Bases of power. Both leaders and followers have valuable abilities that can be used as bargaining chips in negotiation. They can greatly influence others with expert advice, authority, and/or the ability to inspire.

6. Influence strategies. Leaders and followers require tools to convince others to work toward a goal. This influence depends on tactics such as rational persuasion, ingratiation, and forming coalitions.

7. Heuristics. An encounter between a leader and follower occurs in a unique setting, where varying conditions of time and place can either encourage or hinder an exchange.

Because of changing conditions, the things that happen in one context cannot happen again. Figure 4.1 (p. 72) shows how these qualities come into play. The degree of shared perception influences to what degree leaders and followers can agree on what exists. The congruence of perceptions, in turn, allows leaders and followers to choose roles and scripts to play. Feedback helps individuals adjust choices and behaviors.

FIEDLER'S CONTINGENCY THEORY

From his studies on leadership traits, Fiedler (Clement, 1993) observed that various conditions affected the outcomes of leader–follower transactions. Fiedler noted two types of leaders who were effective in different circumstances. Task-oriented leaders were effective in situations that demanded clarity of purpose and structure. Such leaders often performed well during crises or periods of corporate instability. On the other hand, leaders who focused on interpersonal problems were able to help followers find acceptance within their group. These leaders also gave direct feedback to group members on their performance.

To understand how these types of leaders defined their roles according to their situation, Fiedler developed and tested a scale of coworker characteristics (Chemers, 1997). The scale contained 16 paired adjectives, such as *pleasant–unpleasant,* and *friendly–unfriendly,* that described coworker preferences. Fiedler determined that leaders who described their least-preferred coworker negatively valued task completion. Leaders describing their least-preferred coworker positively, however, put relationships before tasks.

■ FIGURE 4-1

MODEL OF LEADER–FOLLOWER SITUATIONAL RELATIONSHIP

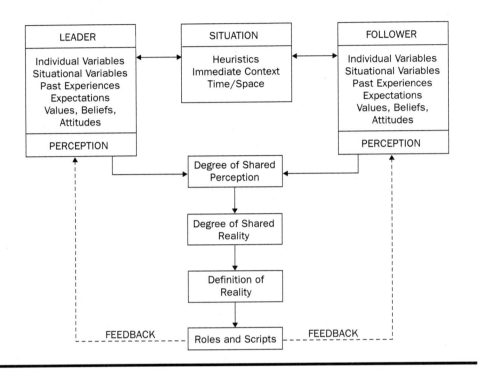

From this Least-Preferred Coworker Scale (LPC), Fiedler defined task-oriented leaders as having low LPC, and relationship-oriented leaders as having high LPC.

In addition, Fiedler determined kinds of situations in which both leader types functioned best. He identified three main situations, or "contingencies," that determine which style is more effective:

1. **Leader–member relationships**—the amount of respect and trust between leaders and followers.

2. **Task structure**—the amount of clarity and simplicity in each task.

3. **Position power**—the amount of a leader's authority according to his or her place in the organization's hierarchy.

Fiedler also developed a scale in which individuals ranked their perceived influence in particular situations. The sum of ranks, arranged into eight cells, indicated the strength of a leader's influence. For instance, a leader is influential when the situation affords good relationships, specific task assignments, and high leader authority. When these conditions suffer, so does a leader's influence.

Fiedler's research indicated that task-oriented leaders (low LPC) are effective under extreme circumstances—both favorable and unfavorable situations. Relationship-oriented leaders (high LPC) are best suited for situations where leader–member trust, task structure, and leader authority are moderate. When an organization is restructuring, personal conflicts arise because workers feel uncertain and helpless. Since this is an unfavorable situation, the most suitable leader would be one who could mediate conflicts and assign specific goals.

Fiedler maintained that the most significant factor in each situation is the relationship between leader and follower. Trust and commitment, he said, are essential to a leader's success. Fiedler believed that this relationship was based on a leader's innate rather than taught qualities. Thus an open and supportive leader was more capable than one who had a negative attitude toward group members. Fiedler also found that task structure was only moderately important to follower commitment. Of least importance was the leader's positional power. We can see Fiedler's Contingency Theory illustrated in the following scenario.

The heads of each department meet to discuss the budget, often a strained situation. Each manager typically vies for increased funds and attempts to exert control over the allocation of money. Moreover, the tasks are often ambiguous because legislative bodies often fail to set firm targets. Further, each department head has a limited power of decision, as the ultimate choice rests with the legislature. The situation would likely fall into the eighth cell in Fiedler's scheme; that is, highly unfavorable. Thus a task-oriented leader is a most suitable choice. Such a leader might be expected to identify spending priorities, find common ground among the managers, and develop a bargaining strategy with legislative officials.

A situation that demands a relationship-oriented leader can be seen in the example.

A supervisor with strong positional power helps resolve a conflict in an office where workers compete for limited resources. Lou complains that Pat has monopolized the copier, creating a backlog in his work that will keep him from meeting an important deadline. Pat argues that he'd been instructed to use the machine to copy reports for an emergency briefing.

As emotions escalate, their supervisor Terry, enters. Terry encourages Lou and Pat to share their opinions on who should have use of the copier. Terry listens actively to them and gives feedback. After the two have calmed down, Terry identifies both their needs and uses them in planning for similar problems in the future. Terry gets further suggestions from Lou and Pat so they can meet their deadlines. Through negotiation, Lou and Pat agree to use a copier in another department when necessary. Since Lou and Pat have expressed their concerns—and since they see that Terry has listened to them and is willing to help—they are ready to resume work.

HERSEY AND BLANCHARD'S SITUATIONAL MODEL

Fiedler's Contingency Theory focused on how a leader's qualities affect task outcomes. Fiedler's theory did not, however, sufficiently address the traits of the followers. In particular, the theory omitted the motivation, skill, and experience that followers lend to each situation. Paul Hersey and Ken Blanchard (Hersey & Blanchard, 1969; Blanchard & Nelson, 1997) developed a model that identified these characteristics. In the model, eventually called Situational Leadership Theory (SLT), a follower's motivation increases with competence (see Figure 4.2).

As followers gain confidence through a leader's guidance, they become more competent; the more competent followers become, the less guidance they need. SLT enables leaders to assess their followers' competence and motivation. It also allows them to apply leadership styles accordingly. Thus leaders become effective when they match their own approach to their followers' development.

Similar to Fiedler's high and low LPC leaders, Hersey and Blanchard recognized two main types of leadership styles. Hersey and Blanchard described an "autocratic" style similar to Fiedler's low LPC. Their "delegating" style corresponds to Fiedler's high LPC. Hersey and Blanchard, however, recognized a range of styles between autocratic and delegating, depending on follower variables. The authors describe four styles: S1, or autocratic; S2, or telling; S3, or participating; and S4, or delegating.

These leader styles correspond to the ability and motivation of followers, depicted as "readiness." S1 leadership is helpful to followers in R1, S2 for R2, and so on. Task-oriented leaders (S1 and S2) are effective when defining project goals, and when follower skills are low but improving. Relationship-centered approaches (S3 and S4) are needed when working with followers who have advanced skills and close work relationships.

Follower characteristics (R cells), are defined in two types of maturity. Job maturity refers to the amount of experience, skill-based knowledge, and ability followers have. Psychological maturity relates to the ability to act independently and with self-confidence. Central to improving followers' maturity is a leader's ability to craft the leadership style to the maturity level of followers. Unlike Fiedler, Hersey and Blanchard believed leader style was not fixed but could be altered through training.

To illustrate the Situational Leadership Theory, we look at an example of a recent graduate of a public administration program.

Chris takes a job as planner I in a city government organization. In cell R1, Chris is eager to learn, and gains much information by reading regulations, asking the supervisor questions, and talking to veteran employees. Chris's supervisor explains how he can use public administration principles in practical decisions. After 2 years, Chris feels comfortable with his job. From time to time, however, he needs help with some problems, and seeks advice from his supervisor, who suggests solutions—a strategy, perhaps, for working with a difficult client. Chris, now in R2,

■ **FIGURE 4–2**

MANAGER LEADERSHIP STYLES

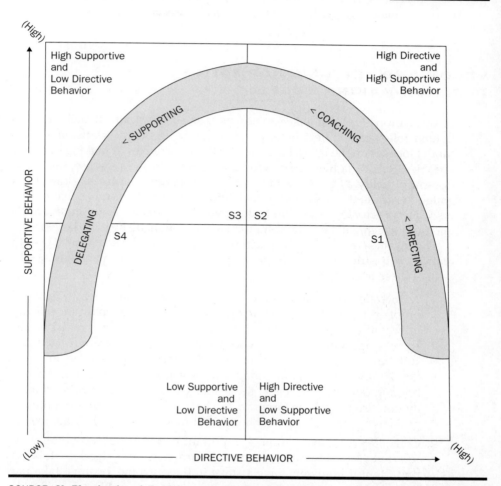

SOURCE: K. Blanchard and B. Nelson (April 1997). Recognition and record. *Executive Excellence, 14*(4), 15.

needs the supervisor to broaden his repertoire of responses. Chris builds confidence and technical knowledge, and thus gains a promotion.

As planner II, Chris's expertise is desirable to the junior staff. Chris's supervisor asks for innovative solutions. After 20 years, Chris has reached full performance potential. Considered trustworthy and competent, Chris shoulders large responsibilities and serves as liaison to the city council. As Chris contemplates retirement, however, the city government undergoes reorganization and the position of Chief Planner is abolished. Chris takes a less senior job in highway planning, reverting from R4 to R1.

Although Chris had performed well before, it will take years before he can reach that level in the new position. Chris's motivation may diminish with this change. Nevertheless, as Chris increases proficiency, the new supervisor may begin to solicit Chris's opinions and give frequent rewards in the form of recognition and praise.

VROOM AND YETTON'S NORMATIVE DECISION-MAKING MODEL

Fiedler emphasized leader characteristics, and Hersey and Blanchard highlighted follower abilities. Vroom and Yetton's Normative Decision-Making Model focuses on the importance of situational variables in making decisions (DeVries, Roe, & Taillieu, 1998; Vroom & Yetton, 1973). In a sense, the model does not qualify as a theory, but rather a technique that leaders can use to gauge the amount of follower participation. The model assumes that followers who participate in decision making will have greater commitment to the decision, which will be more solid than a decision made by a leader alone.

The Vroom–Yetton Model specifies three levels of participation: (1) autocratic, (2) consultative, and (3) group process. Definitions and examples for each of these terms follow.

1. Autocratic. In the autocratic level of participation, a leader solves a problem without follower involvement. The leader may use relevant information from followers, but makes the final decision alone. This style is appropriate when working under strict deadlines. It is also suitable when a decision requires a single perspective or when confidential information is intended for a restricted audience. If a leader is briefing department heads, the leader gathers and summarizes information from various programs. The leader may indicate potential problems to the department heads, but merely solicits their advice.

2. Consultative. Consultation is important because followers often have relevant and useful information to inform a leader's decision. It is also important if followers have a stake in the outcome, or must take part in its implementation. Setting overall goals and making decisions requires input from all those affected. In planning budgetary projections, for instance, a leader may ask followers to set their programming priorities or needed resources. The leader should then meet with followers to discuss the plans and seek consensus on which requirements are most important.

3. Group process. The leader may enlist help from followers in defining the problem, developing a solution, and examining possible consequences to the clientele. The group method is important when the leader is confronting controversial situations, or when the commitment of followers is crucial to the goal. This method is also helpful when followers know highly influential people and can call on them for assistance or technical expertise.

An example of the group process can be seen in a scenario where a department's operating budget must be cut by 7 percent.

The leader calls a meeting to generate ideas to cut costs and/or increase revenues. The group might suggest the department should appeal to businesses and nonprofit organizations for money, rather than cutting popular programs or eliminating jobs. The group argues that cutting programs or staff would harm relationships with these constituents, but soliciting donations would build goodwill and involve the community in solving a common problem or interest.

Vroom and Yetton identify five levels of decision-making involvement, including two autocratic, two consultative, and one group-based. As shown in Figure 4.3, these are as follows:

▪ FIGURE 4–3

VROOM AND YETTON DECISION PROCESS FLOWCHART

A. Does the problem possess a quality requirement?
B. Do I have sufficient information to make a high-quality decision?
C. Is the problem structured?
D. Is acceptance of the decision by subordinates important for effective implementation?
E. If I were to make the decision by myself, am I reasonably certain that it would be accepted by my subordinates?
F. Do subordinates share the organizational goals to be attained in solving this problem?
G. Is conflict among subordinates likely in preferred solutions?

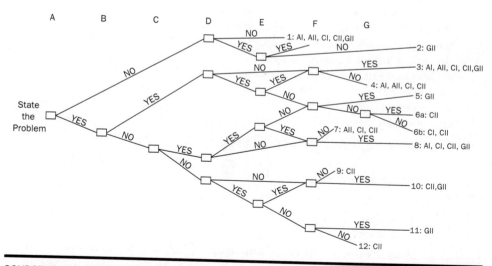

1. **Autocratic**

   A1. The leader solves the problem or makes the decision alone using available information.

   A2. The leader obtains information from followers and uses it to make the decision alone. However, the leader may or may not tell the followers the problem.

2. **Consultative**

   C1. The leader shares the problem with relevant individuals. Based on data collected, the leader makes the decision. The outcome may or may not reflect the followers' suggestions.

   C2. The leader shares a problem with followers as a group.The leader asks them for ideas, advice, and relevant information. The leader may or may not use the group's suggestions.

3. **Group Process**

   GII. The leader shares the problem or concern with followers as a group. The leader and group construct and assess possible alternatives. The decision is based on consensus.

In the Normative Decision-Making Model, Vroom and Yetton identify eight contingencies that influence which leadership style is appropriate. They incorporate these variables into a series of questions a leader may use. Questions are arranged into branches that take shape depending on how the leader answers each question. The first three variables help the leader assess the project—the importance of how a leader would use this decision tree in implementing flex-time in a government agency. Flex-time is a system of varying work shifts. In this system, employees agree to work a standard number of hours, usually 8.5. However, some workers would start work at 7:00 A.M. and finish by 3:30 P.M., whereas others would begin at 9:00 A.M. and end by 5:30 P.M. Thus, there are always workers present during the core hours of the day (9 to 5), when the agency conducts public business. In deciding the flex-time issue, a leader might *ask the following questions. Eight is the maximum number of yes/no questions in the Vroom/Yetton decision tree. In the following example, the leader has had to answer only 6 of the 8 to satisfy the conditions. The "move" refers to whether the leader needs to ask himself or herself another question, based on the response.*

1. **Q:** Is the decision important to the quality of the product?

   A: Yes, it bears on employee satisfaction and productivity. (Move to commitment requirement)

2. **Q:** Is subordinate commitment necessary?

   A: Yes, since they will be using the system. (Move to 3, leader information)

3. **Q:** Does the leader have sufficient information to make the decision?

   A: Yes, based on extensive research in similar organizations. (Move to 5, group commitment)

4. **Q:** If the leader makes the decision alone, will subordinates commit to it?

   A: No, they will likely resent having been excluded. (Move to 6, goal agreement)

5. **Q:** Will employee and organizational goals coincide if flex-time is implemented?

   A: Yes, if employees are satisfied and productive, the organization's capability increases. (Move to 8, subordinate information)

6. **Q:** Do employees have enough information to make a good decision?

   A: Yes, employees should have a sense of peak business times and how variables like child-care needs or traffic congestion could affect their schedules.

According to the Vroom–Yetton Model, this leader would use the GII or group-centered style to decide the flex-time issue.

By using this system to guide their problem solving, leaders can generate a "feasible set" of alternatives. This means that although their style of decision may work, there are many options available to devise an effective solution. Thus, in the above example, the leader may use group-centered approach to test the feasibility of flex-time. Through this group process, however, the members may believe that the question of flexible work schedules will not address other, more serious problems in their work environment. Perhaps the work itself is tedious or coworker relationships are strained. These factors can influence how satisfied and productive the workers feel. Based on the group's input, therefore, the leader can weigh these other elements, and may look at other options. Perhaps measures such as job enlargement or paying workers weekly instead of biweekly would better solve the productivity problem.

In addition to using the model to adjust their decision-making style, leaders also need to consider other factors. These include time constraints, availability of resources, and which improvements both leaders and followers would value.

PATH—GOAL THEORY

Follower commitment and the quality of a decision are important factors in the Vroom–Yetton Model. The model does not, however, address the impulses that would yield commitment, or how leaders can ensure rewards for employees. The Path–Goal Theory compensates for this by helping leaders create clearer paths for the employees to reach a goal. In so doing, the Path–Goal Theory enables the follower to build satisfaction by working toward a challenging, yet reachable aim. The developer of the theory, Robert House (1971, p. 324), said that the

...motivational function of the leader consists of increasing personal payoffs to subordinates for work-goal attainment and making the path to these payoffs easier to travel by clarifying it, reducing roadblocks and pitfalls, and increasing the opportunities for personal satisfaction en route.

Path–Goal Theory bases its assumptions on Expectancy Theory described earlier in this text. Expectancy Theory, briefly, holds that followers calculate the value of a particular accomplishment. They weigh the benefits, such as monetary or positional gain, against the effort needed. Together, these theories describe the pivotal role a leader plays in helping followers to succeed. A leader might help define tasks, for example, thus reducing worker anxiety. A leader might provide coaching or give praise for increased effort. In all, leaders must use both task-oriented and relationship-oriented styles to enable employees to reach objectives.

Path–Goal Theory addresses variables such as what employees expect for rewards, and how they perceive their job in general. House observed that the workers' abilities and personalities influence how these perceptions are formed (Chemers, 1997). Other factors in workers' reward expectation include how workloads are assigned and how the reward system itself is structured.

For instance, in a governmental organization, managers may not have the ability to award many financial incentives, and those incentives available may have a limit of perhaps $1,000. Often, the incentives are awarded to only a chosen few. Receiving such a reward thus bears more value in recognition than monetary gain because of the high visibility it creates. To allow employees a greater chance to receive such an award, managers could provide opportunities to serve on high-level task forces or take on a challenging field assignment. Some employees, however, may not respond to these opportunities. Some may not like the ambiguity of a task force, but prefer solitary assignments that have clear parameters. Leaders can thus enhance follower commitment and performance by considering the limitations of an organization's reward policy and the particular motivations of the workers.

The way in which workers' personalities dictate their response to incentives prompted House to set up four types of leadership within the Path–Goal Theory: directive, supportive, participatory, and achievement-oriented. Figure 4.4 depicts the model.

1. Directive leadership. The leader tells followers what they are expected to do and specifies the task. Examples include a highly specific job description to clarify responsibilities, setting and monitoring work, and assigning deadlines.
2. Supportive leadership. A supportive leader is one who expresses concern for the needs of followers, solicits their suggestions, and shows courtesy toward followers.
3. Participatory leadership. Leaders spur followers to participate in making decisions on giving and carrying out assignments.

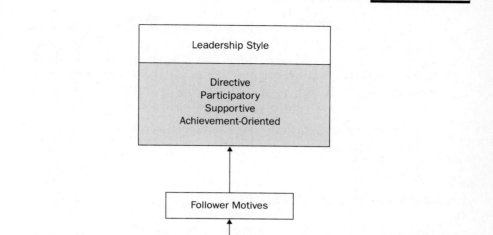

- FIGURE 4-4

A MODEL OF PATH–GOAL MOTIVATION THEORY

4. Achievement-oriented leadership. Leaders using this approach set high goals for their followers while giving them the means to reach the goals. These leaders demand the best performance from followers and prepare them for even greater challenges in the future.

In Path–Goal Theory, three conditions moderate which styles leaders select: (1) the nature of the task itself—a tedious or unclear task, for example; (2) the structure of authority in the organization; and (3) the quality of relationships among group members and between a leader and follower. As an example, take the case of the mayoral budget reform in St. Louis, Missouri (Rubin & Stein, 1990).

St. Louis municipal budgeting was the duty of the Board of Estimate and Apportionment, including the mayor. The group's rigid structure cramped all visionary budget reforms for over a century. The ceaseless checks and balances the board en-acted, for instance, inhibited activism and limited property taxes.

A problem emerged in the 1980s when citizens demanded a greater role in gov-ernment, thus pressuring the stubborn system. As one strategy to provide flexibil-ity, the mayor centralized departmental authority, thereby limiting the discretion of each department head. In addition, the mayor replaced the existing department heads with persons of his own choosing. This action weakened the roadblock erected by well-established political interests. The mayor also sought to make the system more accountable by starting a new planning process. He further changed the budget calendar so that much of the power fell on his shoulders.

Overall, this case illustrates the need for directive leadership in response to a critical situation.

LEADERSHIP SUBSTITUTES

House's Path–Goal Theory sparked the possibility that job conditions alone can motivate followers. Some conditions can take the place of directive lead-ership. Such a condition would be a routine task, or one that provides an immediate indication of performance. A job that defines a clear and un-changing direction renders directive leadership superfluous.

Kerr and Jermier (1978; Gordon, 1994) developed a Leadership Substi-tutes' Model to identify conditions that either nullify or duplicate manage-rial leadership. The authors used the term "neutralizers" to describe condi-tions that made a leader's role redundant.

Kerr and Jermier classified substitutes and neutralizers according to lead-ership types: supportive (relationship-based) or instrumental (task-based) leaders. As depicted in Table 4.1, Kerr and Jermier list types of workers, tasks, and organizations that either provide or inhibit leadership.

Under subordinate characteristics, for example, highly educated workers substitute their own expertise for leadership. Such expertise not only pro-vides them with the ability to assess their own performance, but it also fos-ters a desire to assume additional duties. On the other hand, employees who do not seek personal growth resist both supportive and instrumental leadership; they remain as unmotivated by a challenge as they are by mate-rial incentives.

Work having clearly defined tasks and intrinsic rewards can substitute for both types of leadership. Strong within-group relationships can also pro-vide direction. Networks of public administrators, for instance, can substi-tute for directive leadership. O'Toole (1997) describes how such a network requires standards based on negotiation rather than specific authority; a net-work's power rests with many people rather than a single leader. A network often provides support through allies who give emotional support to co-members.

SUMMARY

▪ **TABLE 4-1**

LEADERSHIP SUBSTITUTES AND NEUTRALIZERS

Follower Qualities	Organizational Structures	Task Features	Effects on Leadership Style
Professional	Cohesive work group	Intrinsically satisfying	Substitutes for supportive leadership
Indifferent to organizational rewards	Leader has low position Leader isolated physically	Rules limit discretion	Neutralizes supportive leadership
Experienced	Cohesive work group	Structured routine unambiguous	Substitutes for instrumental (task-oriented) leadership
Indifference to organizational rewards	Leader has low position power	Rules are basis of decisions	Neutralizes instrumental (task-oriented) leadership

SOURCE: Based on S. Kerr and J. M. Jermier (1978). Substitutes for leadership: Their meaning and measurement. *Organizational Behavior and Human Performance, 22,* 375–403.

SUMMARY

In this chapter, we examined five models for understanding the leader–follower exchange. Fiedler's (1967) Contingency Theory emphasizes how a leader's qualities influence the willingness of followers to act. Based on a scale of "Least Preferred Coworker" (LPC), Fiedler identifies two leadership orientations: task (low LPC) and relationship (high LPC). Fielder maintains that three factors determine the favorability of the situation. Most important to Fiedler is the role of interpersonal relationships. Of secondary importance is the clarity of task structure. Least important is positional power. Task-oriented leaders excel in the extremes, in both favorable and unfavorable situations. When situations are of medium favorability, a relationship-oriented leader is most appropriate.

Hersey and Blanchard's (1969) Situational Leadership Theory (SLT) indicates that the traits of followers, such as skill level and motivation, dictate the appropriate leadership style. Hersey and Blanchard maintain that leaders need to match four leadership styles to the state of follower readiness. These styles range from autocratic or "telling" to democratic or "delegating." New tasks and low commitment (R1), for instance, require an autocratic leadership style. However, as followers become more proficient and confident (R2) leaders assume a persuasive or "selling" style. Highly skilled followers with high levels of confidence (R4) should participate in group decisions.

Vroom and Yetton's (1973) Normative Decision-Making Model outlines five levels of how involved followers can become in decision making. These levels range from autocratic, where the leader makes the decision alone; to consultative, where the leader solicits opinions; to a group process, in which the leader consults with a group and the decision is based on consensus. Leaders can apply a suitable decision-making style by asking themselves up to eight questions on whether followers need to be involved, and how the decision will affect follower commitment.

House's (1974) Path–Goal Theory holds that followers will be more willing to devote themselves to an assignment if a leader gives them both clear goals and support if they complete the assignment. Leaders often play dual roles. On the one hand, they must be task-oriented in clarifying goals and their importance to both company and employees. On the other hand, they also assume a relationship-oriented role in helping followers achieve desired ends. As with Fiedler's Contingency Theory, the Path–Goal Theory maintains that the approach a leader uses hinges on situational variables, the leader's authority of position, and the quality of personal relationships.

Kerr and Jermier's (1978) Leader Substitutes' Model indicates that situational variables may either supplant a leader's function or merely weaken leader influence. Conditions that render a leader superfluous occur when workers are highly skilled, the tasks are intrinsically rewarding, and work group members support each other. However, a leader's influence suffers when company policies are too rigid, leaving the leader little control over decisions and employee rewards.

In the leader–follower exchange, leaders must develop a keen understanding of their own qualities as well as qualities possessed by others. A leader must also be sensitive to the various situations that affect how tasks and approaches are defined. Five main situational models have pointed to the relationships, task structures, and power available to the leader. Because leadership rests ultimately with the persons involved, the quality of personal relationships is crucial. Leaders can modify their approach depending on the degree of structure required in a task and their level of authority. Two main leadership styles are open to a leader: relationship-oriented and task-oriented approaches. Situational theories not only enable leaders to achieve good results, but they also help develop trust-based relationships, which extend well beyond any single project.

In Chapter 5, we will examine the role of building trust in the relationship between follower and leader.

QUESTIONS FOR THOUGHT AND DISCUSSION

1. Think about an important leadership decision in which you participated recently.
   a. What were the goals you wished to achieve?
   b. How clearly defined were they?

    c. Did they differ from the goals of others who had a stake in the decision?

    d. How were differences of opinion dealt with?

2. Based on your own experiences, how do differences in individual motives and expectations affect levels of commitment? How can a leader influence the motivation of a team, for instance, when each member has different aspirations?

3. Recall a recent time when you were unsure of what needed to be done on a particular project.

    a. What did the project involve?

    b. What were some circumstances surrounding the task or project?

    c. What were some thoughts and feelings you had?

    d. What did the leader do to clarify the task? to relieve feelings of confusion?

    e. Were these leader efforts successful in your view?

CASE STUDY AND ROLE PLAY

CITY OF SPRINGFIELD: PRACTICING SITUATIONAL LEADERSHIP SKILLS

TIME: APPROXIMATELY 1 HOUR

DIRECTIONS

In the following exercise, you will practice Situational Leadership skills in leading employees in the City of Springfield to work together as a team and solve the city's central problems.

To prepare, read the City of Springfield Background Sheet and examine the characteristics, needs, and levels of readiness of each player. Decide how you would apply Situational Leadership strategies in dealing with the problems each person presents. Jot down the type of SITUATIONAL LEADERSHIP STRATEGY you believe appropriate for the person with whom you are interacting. Also describe the POSSIBLE SOLUTIONS you believe will help that person solve their problems. (The Instructor's Manual will contain the correct solution.)

After you have completed your analyses, divide into three-person groups (triads). One person plays the Town Manager, one person plays one of the other charac-

ters and should state the person he or she will be playing; the third person is the group process recorder and observes responses and feeds them back to the dyad at the end of round one (10 minutes).

In round two, the triad members trade roles: A different person plays the Town Manager, a second plays a different employee, and a third person takes on the job of group process recorder (10 minutes).

In round three, the process is repeated, with the Town Manager role rotated, another character selected, and the third person observing the interactions (10 minutes).

At the end of the exercise, each triad member records his or her reactions on the feedback sheet and shares them with the others in terms of strategy effectiveness and satisfaction (10 minutes). Following the sharing, the facilitator asks for reactions to adjusting leadership styles, depending on the needs of the situation, follower competencies and needs, and the leader's own characteristics and competencies.

BACKGROUND

The City of Springfield is a suburb of a large southern city. Its population of about 40,000 has almost doubled in the past 10 years. The size of the city's government has not. Springfield employs a city manager. The mayor and council members are local businesspeople who take their roles seriously and who are concerned about finances. They have promised their constituents that taxes will not be raised.

The new city manager, who recently earned a Master's of Public Administration degree, came to Springfield about 9 months ago and inherited a staff in which all department heads and secretaries, with the exception of three part-time employees, had worked for the city for many years. Prior to the new city manager's tenure, the department heads had been accustomed to operating their units independently; they are all tough-minded individuals who believe that they, as directors, know the facts and should make the decisions in their own areas. Support staff members pitch in and do what needs to be done as crises occur or as the public demands. Employee morale in city government is poor. The city has no plan for managing its phenomenal growth, and the existing positions of employees are obsolete.

The new city manager firmly believes in a team approach to leadership and has instituted biweekly staff meetings in the hope of encouraging communication. The department heads attend reluctantly, feeling that meetings are a waste of time and teamwork a fad devised by some management professor in an ivory tower. The meetings usually deteriorate quickly and end with arguments about the fact that the department heads have been making independent decisions without consulting the city manager. The city manager has good relationships with most of the other city employees, except the secretary to the city manager, who is the mayor's cousin.

CITY MANAGER'S SECRETARY

All of the secretarial staff members are housed in offices adjacent to the city manager's. The secretary to the city manager gossips a lot and complains of being bored and ill informed about city business. The city manager asks for clerical help from the secretary to the municipal clerk when sensitive matters are involved and confidentiality must be maintained.

The secretary feels bewildered by the fact that the city manager gives her less to do than had been the case with the previous city manager. The secretary has been with the city for 12 years and feels capable of handling more work. The secretary feels bored. Lately, the secretary has relieved her boredom by going to the coffee machine area to chat with some of the other secretaries.

MUNICIPAL CLERK

The municipal clerk, formerly a member of the secretarial staff and now the supervisor of this staff, feels overwhelmed by the new supervisory duties and hesitant to make requests of subordinates. When an errand needs to be run, the city manager tends to go directly to a member of the secretarial staff without first informing the municipal clerk.

The municipal clerk wishes the city manager would observe the chain of command and stop giving work and errand assignments to the clerk's subordinates without first checking. The municipal clerk has been with the city for over 7 years and has the reputation of knowing more about the city's operation than does the city manager. The municipal clerk, however, has not supervised before and feels overwhelmed by the new duties. Knowing how and when to delegate, for instance, is problematic.

RECEPTIONIST

The receptionist, a 3-year-employee, is also responsible for collecting city fees, complains about being interrupted more than 500 times a week, and about not being appreciated. Other clerical staff members resent the receptionist's complaints. Although the work volume is plentiful, the receptionist believes the skill levels required to perform the work are below her expertise. The receptionist is the only member of the secretarial staff who has a professional certificate in secretarial science. The receptionist feels it is ridiculous, for instance, to be responsible for collecting city fees, such as those charged for use of recreational facilities. The receptionist, in addition, has had a lot of money problems because her spouse left recently. Also, the receptionist does not have good interpersonal relationships with the accounting clerk. However, the accounting clerk is secretive and quiet and never seems to want to sympathize with the receptionist's problems.

ACCOUNTING CLERK

The accounting clerk, also a member of the secretarial staff, has withdrawn from the group and stays busy at a computer terminal. The accounting clerk would like to be left alone to do the job. Because of many problems at home, the clerk does not want to be bothered by hearing about the receptionist's problems. The clerk is also annoyed by the gossiping secretary. The accounting clerk works hard, but would like to quit. Paying children's school tuition is perhaps the main reason for staying on.

DEPARTMENT HEADS

Police Chief—The police chief, who supervises one secretary and eight police officers, has been with the city for 10 years. The chief has the reputation of being the toughest law-enforcement official in the area. The long record of successful law enforcement has proven that the chief has accomplished the primary goal of ridding the city of crime. The chief

believes the city manager wastes time by requiring staff meetings, which only end up in petty squabbles.

Public Works Director—The public works director is responsible for a crew of 72 people plus a meter reader and a secretary. The size of the public works staff has not increased in the past 10 years, and no new equipment for the staff has been purchased in that time. Meanwhile, citizen demands for services have increased. The public works director, feeling overwrought by staff, budgetary, and equipment resource depletions, faces resolving several internal employee grievances as well as many citizen complaints because of inefficient, late, and sloppy services.

Director of Parks and Recreation—The director of parks and recreation, with the city 6 years, wants to build a new community recreation center. In the meantime, members of the city secretarial staff do the director's correspondence and collect fees for the use of recreational facilities because the director's assistant works only part-time and must help with program planning and teaching. The director feels the department has been ignored in the past, but believes the city manager is farsighted and willing to support funds for expanding the recreation center.

SITUATIONAL LEADERSHIP STRATEGIES TO USE

1. City Manager's Secretary
2. Municipal Clerk
3. Receptionist
4. Accounting Clerk
5. Police Chief
6. Public Works Director
7. Director of Parks and Recreation

FEEDBACK RESPONSES

OBSERVER NOTES

What particular words and behaviors enhanced follower compliance? satisfaction? What detracted from them?

DEBRIEFING

1. What Situational Leadership Strategies did you use with which role player? Why?

2. Did the strategy change during the course of the interaction? If so, how?

3. As the city manager, how satisfied were you with the leadership strategy you selected?

4. How satisfied do you think the other player was with the city manager's leadership strategy?

5. What helped achieve your goal? What hindered it?
   a. As City Manager?
   b. As employee?

6. What are some important things you learned about Situational Leadership in this exercise?

BUILDING TRUST

SYNOPSIS

Effective leader–follower relationships are built on mutual trust. To transact roles and responsibilities and achieve ends, leaders must create conditions that followers accept as valid and useful, and followers need to commit their resources fully. Chapter 5 discusses some conditions that facilitate trust building, such as aligning intentions with actions, personal integrity, self-control, degree of perceived similarity of interests and goals, ability to disclose one's personal thoughts and feelings and use information to improve other and self-understanding, and organizational politics and climate. By developing sensitivity to self in relation to others, leaders can facilitate trust and enhance collaboration among followers.

OBJECTIVES

- To define trust as a reciprocal relationship involving mutual obligations and exchanges of resources
- To identify trust as a product of attitudes, behaviors, values, situations, and organizational contexts
- To state the importance of building trust among followers
- To describe 11 variables in building trust
- To develop trust in interpersonal relationships through practicing feedback and self-disclosure
- To discuss ways of increasing trust among public sector constituents

KEY TERMS AND CONCEPTS

interdependence

Johari Window

Leader–Member Exchange Theory

locus of control

normative trust

organizational climate

organizational culture

reciprocity

self-disclosure

INTRODUCTION

Building trust in governmental institutions and the people who work in them is a persistent challenge for public leaders. The notoriously slow processes of paperwork and lack of centralized accountability have been just a few of the frustrations that have dogged governmental employees as well as citizens. Scandals involving personal ethics and illegal behavior in public service have further weakened public confidence. Apathy, cynicism, and even violence have been just a few responses. Calls for "reinventing" basic administrative processes continue.

How can public leaders restore a sense of trust among internal and external constituents? Developing trust entails creating a balance of several elements, such as individual characteristics, relationships between and among diverse followers, goals, aspirations, and constitutional values and laws. Shaping these elements to achieve larger aims while at the same time promoting good faith is critical to leadership competency.

Trust enables followers to comply with a leader's orders and to put their best foot forward. In particular, this chapter focuses on: (1) defining trust as a mutually beneficial exchange between workers; (2) the importance of trust in leader–member relationships; (3) factors contributing to trust; (4) fostering trust through feedback; and (5) building trust through participation. We examine studies and theories that will illuminate our understanding of building trust. We will also use these concepts in practical exercises.

WHAT IS TRUST?

We define *trust* here as attitude or behavior that yields a reciprocal relationship with others. As noted earlier, experiences mold an individual's behavior and perspective. Accordingly, trust is rooted in earlier life events. Persons approach new situations with varying levels of trust, from high to low; and base this level on the assumption that others will not exploit their goodwill (Parks & Hulbert, 1995).

We also note that trust is a *relationship of reciprocity*. Cooperation can exist without reciprocity, as giving time or money to another often obliges the recipient to return the favor (Hollander, 1997). Likewise, the original giver is beholden to return that favor, and so on. However, this is merely a tit-for-tat approach. It binds a person to a standard of giving and getting, rather than to voluntarily giving without the expectation of payback.

Note, too, that this definition includes not only trust for other people but also trust for institutions. As we shall see, trust among people encourages trust within organizations. This is especially true in the supervisor–worker relationship since it dictates how workers feel about the company as a whole. Further, just as people affect their work environments, environments affect people. Employees in an organization plagued by suspicion will react with an equal amount of distrust.

The way personal trust is interwoven with trust for a company is complex. Sitkin and Roth (1993) identify four main components of trust as: (1) an attitude, (2) a behavior, (3) a situational feature, and (4) an institutional context. Trust lies not only in each person, but also in that person's perception of the setting.

THE IMPORTANCE OF BUILDING TRUST

Developing relationships of trust is crucial to leaders for several reasons. Trust of leaders has been linked to greater satisfaction in followers and to their willingness to cooperate (Buessing & Broome, 1999). Having a trusting relationship has also enabled leaders to manage effectively and increase productivity (Butler, Cantrell, & Flick, 1999; Coyne, 1998). In addition, trusted leaders can help transform the human resource policies of an organization (French & Bell, 1999).

VARIABLES IN BUILDING TRUST

Building trust is a delicate process for leaders. It requires insight into relationships and their tangible and intangible aspects. From research studies, we can identify factors that influence trust between leader and follower. These include: (1) alignment of intention and action, (2) personality traits, (3) locus of control, (4) degree of perceived similarity, (5) expected role behaviors, (6) self-disclosure and feedback, (7) situational ambiguity, (8) interdependence, (9) politics within organizations, (10) how organizations coordinate employees, and (11) climate in an organization.

ALIGNMENT OF INTENTION AND ACTION

People often gauge their level of trust on the sincerity of others' intentions. Individuals are considered trustworthy based on how faithfully they execute their intentions. Often, however, persons conceal their intentions if society dictates such behavior. For example, a used car salesman convinces a buyer that a 10-year-old car runs flawlessly because it was owned by an elderly lady who used it only to drive to church. The salesman does not mention that since the woman never changed the oil, costly repairs will soon be needed. Does this mean the salesman is lying? Perhaps his failure to mention the car's condition is because the woman neglected to mention it to him. In this case, he would be considered trustworthy because he acted on sincere—though misguided—intentions.

PERSONALITY TRAITS

Over time, individuals develop certain thinking patterns that inform their behavior. In a study of health care managers, Schindler and Thomas (1993) find that five personality traits influence employee trust. In order of importance, these include: (1) integrity, or exhibiting honesty; (2) competence, or the level of technical and interpersonal skill; (3) consistency, or reliability; (4) loyalty, or a benevolent desire to protect others; and (5) openness, or freely sharing ideas and information.

LOCUS OF CONTROL

People have many reasons to be distrustful. Many grow hardened from experiences with coworkers or family members, and carry over this distrust into each new situation. These persons eventually feel powerless and subject to the will of others. Since they believe that others have power over them, they are said to believe in an *external locus of control*. Conversely, people with an *internal locus of control* believe their own efforts affect circumstances. They therefore have high levels of trust and exhibit empathy, enthusiasm, and frankness (Mishra, 1996).

Johnson, Luthans, and Hennessey (1984) investigated how productivity and authority are effected by a leader's locus of control. They found that leaders with an internal locus of control—confident, energetic, trustful— were seen as more effective and trustworthy than leaders who felt control rested with others. The more trustful, confident leaders also inspired higher performance and team spirit in their followers.

DEGREE OF PERCEIVED SIMILARITY

Trust depends, too, on how similar others seem to a person. People tend to trust those who have similar economic, social, or racial backgrounds. Steel (1991), for example, finds that individuals tend to reveal more about themselves to family members than to outsiders. Women, he finds, tend to be more trustful than men, and thus reveal more about themselves.

EXPECTED ROLE BEHAVIORS

For trust to have meaning, others must perceive and define it. As we noted in an earlier chapter, individuals play roles in social interactions. Roles involve understanding, interpreting, and producing required verbal and non-verbal behaviors commensurate with expectations of particular situations. People who visit doctors expect doctors to show competence in their diagnoses, recommendations for treatment, and helpful, if not compassionate, concern. When doctors show by both their verbal as well as nonverbal behaviors that they do meet patients' expectations, patients trust them.

The relationship between expected and actual behaviors reflects the cognitive and the affective character of trust. McAllister (1995) studied these twin characteristics and noted that factors influencing cognition include a reliable role performance, cultural and ethnic similarity, higher level of profesional credentials, socially-acceptable, "citizenship" behaviors, frequent interactions, and high-levels of affection. Affective-based trust, McAllister noted, is the extent to which another person shows sensitivity and caring for individual needs.

SELF-DISCLOSURE AND FEEDBACK

Trust is founded on openly sharing personal information and on receiving valuable responses from others. Steel (1991) finds that trust is essential for revealing one's feelings or ideas to others. Moreover, Corcoran (1988) points out that when counselors assured clients of confidentiality, they were more willing to discuss their problems. Sabatelli, Buck, and Dreyer (1983) established a connection between feeling confident (an internal locus of control) and feeling comfortable in opening up to a group.

Goliembiewski (1995, p. 58) calls feedback "information concerning the efficacy of some data processor's adaptations to the environment." He states that feedback provides a clear way to foster personal development. Feedback enhances interpersonal skill, promotes autonomy, and brings subconscious thinking into the open. How readily feedback is accepted relies on the recipient's level of trust.

Deutsch (1994) points out that others must perceive trust for it to have meaning. As noted earlier, people behave according to the expectations of others. Individuals monitor the verbal and nonverbal cues of each situation, and act accordingly. For example, persons who visit doctors expect the doctors to demonstrate confidence in their diagnosis and to be helpful, even compassionate. When doctors behave according to these expectations, they gain the trust of their patients.

Deutsch's connection between expected and actual behavior reveals much about the character of trust. Trust is based on rationality and emotion.

McAllister (1995) notes that these two traits factor into one's decision to trust someone. Other factors include how faithfully an expected role is played, similarity of cultural background, professional credentials, how often one sees the person, and the level of affection displayed.

SITUATIONAL AMBIGUITY

People often define reality according to social norms. Their conception of reality is altered by meanings they assign based on their surroundings. Because the perception of the world is subjective, people look to an objective definition of *trust*. Individuals therefore trust others based partly on their own ideas and partly on the ideas of society.

Some situations, however, are not as straightforward. Some have what Zand (1997) terms "objective uncertainty"; that is, incomplete information, unclear rules, and elements of fear can confuse people. Leaders attempt to clarify ambiguities and establish order in such circumstances. When distrustful people misinterpret these actions as hostile, they exhibit what Zand calls "social uncertainty." This general distrust further impedes a leader's attempt to control a situation.

INTERDEPENDENCE

The exchange of resources such as time, goods, and expertise is often asymmetrical. That is, people are indebted to others who grant them favors. Vulnerability results in those receiving goods because they must trust the givers to do them no harm. Those who lend their resources to others tend to amass power and influence. This is especially true in organizations where top officials and supervisors provide the means for sustaining employee livelihood. Yet, because of the expectation that no harm will come to the recipients, managers have a moral obligation to use their power judiciously.

In the Leader–Member Exchange Theory (LMX), leaders establish strong ties with followers whom they feel are more loyal and competent. In return for this extra attention, followers show gratitude. Wayne and Green (1993), for instance, find that hospital employees who have established relationships with their managers are more likely to reinforce the influence of their managers.

POLITICS WITHIN ORGANIZATIONS

If trust relies on an interdependent relationship between manager and worker, it also depends on the amount of resources available. Scrambling for scarce resources often involves politics; that is, manipulating others for personal gain. For example, Brann and Foddy (1987) examined how competition for a resource reflected on trust. The authors find that when resources grow depleted, trustful people consume less than the distrustful. If, under these conditions, distrustful people consume more resources, they are highly likely to hinder others to ensure more for themselves.

Kumar and Ghadially (1989) note that cynical people use the following tactics: limiting information access, strategic employee replacement, alliance formation, and threats. The psychology of these opportunists, they maintain, entails the assessment of how much (or how little) they have compared to others. These political games emerge from real or perceived losses of power.

COORDINATION

The interdependence of individuals is particularly evident, as noted, in organizational contexts. Although normative behavior specifies socially accepted behaviors in resource exchanges in the workplace, they cannot guarantee equitable treatment. Because of the possibility of exploitation, organizations set up written policies, rules, and contracts to take the place of normative trust. These formal methods of promoting trust have legalistic procedures and carry sanctions. But as formal substitutes for trust, the documents fail to foster voluntary commitment (Creed & Miles, 1996). Wagner (1995) points out that group cooperation, in contrast to formal policies, emerges from a collectivist approach. That is, when group members are interested in meeting their own goals by means of corporate goals, overall cooperation results. Wagner finds that conditions such as small group size and few shared responsibilities encourage cooperation.

ORGANIZATIONAL CLIMATE

Various factors contribute to a climate of trust within organizations. The term "climate" describes employees' perception of how organizations treat them. People often describe climates as warm, hostile, or trusting. One thing that contributes to the climate is how individuals satisfy their societal or corporate roles. For example, if an organization implies that employees should be treated as family, people will characterize that climate as warm and friendly. How managers assess and enforce these norms of behavior greatly influences the climate (Whitener, Brodt, Korsgaard, & Werner, 1998). This managerial presence likewise affects the amount of trust employees develop (Victor & Cullen, 1988).

Carnevale and Wechsler (1992) studied this trust–climate relationship in the public sector. They conclude that the climate imposed by supervisors is the most important factor in nurturing employees' trust. Supervisors have the most frequent face-to-face contact with employees and significantly influence their motivation to serve the public.

IMPLICATIONS FOR BUILDING TRUST

We have seen how leaders play a significant part in how trust is built. Leaders can promote trust in three ways: (1) giving feedback, (2) encouraging openness, and (3) increasing follower participation. Let's now turn to how leaders can develop trust-building skills.

GIVING FEEDBACK AND SELF-DISCLOSURE

One of the most widely used methods for developing personal skills is the Johari Window. Developed by Joseph Luft (1984) and Harrison V. Ingham in 1950s, the Johari Window incorporates an understanding of conscious behaviors and subconscious motives. As depicted in Figure 5.1, the Johari Window contains four quadrants that describe degrees of self-awareness and awareness of others, including the extent to which this knowledge is revealed.

Quadrant 1 is the open quadrant. It refers to behavior and motives known to oneself and to others.

Quadrant 2 is the blind quadrant. It refers to behavior and motives known to others, but not to oneself. In Quadrant 2, behavior is driven

. FIGURE 5-1

THE JOHARI WINDOW MODEL

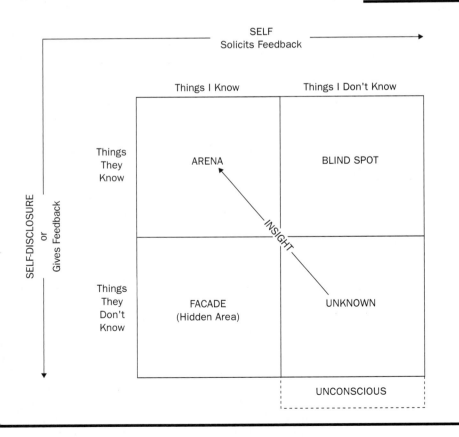

by the subconscious. Others observe this, but may not always comment.

Quadrant 3 is the hidden area. It refers to behavior motives known to oneself, but not to others. In Quadrant 3, people choose what to reveal to others. Luft (1984) notes that self-disclosure is important when: (1) it is part of an ongoing relationship, (2) it is mutual, (3) it is appropriately timed, (4) it concerns all involved, (5) it moves in small increments, (6) others can confirm it, (7) its affect on others is taken under consideration, (8) it creates a reasonable risk, and (9) it is sped up in a crisis.

Quadrant 4 is the unknown area. It refers to behaviors and motives known neither to oneself nor others. These behaviors may become apparent in times of crises. They may also indicate latent abilities that a person could develop.

Luft maintains that a person can strengthen the Quadrant 1 identity by using feedback and by carefully revealing personal information. In so doing, the individual pushes back the boundaries between Quadrant 2 and Quadrant 3 and shrinks the area of Quadrant 4. This process also enables the person to tap any latent talents in Quadrant 4.

We can understand the Johari Window's use in interpersonal communications more by observing how people expand or shrink the two dimensions of communications, exposure and feedback. In Figure 5.2 (p. 98), we see persons who fit Type A communications' styles. Type A communicators tell little about themselves and want to know little about others. The shaded area, representing their "public selves," is small. We consider them as cold, withdrawn, and aloof. Type B persons give too much feedback to others, but reveal little about themselves. In requesting information, but not telling what is going on inside themselves, Type B personalities are often suspect. Type C individuals are those who reveal too much about themselves and do not find out much about others. They may come across like "bulls in a china shop," and others soon ignore what appears to be pomposity. The "public self" area of Type D persons shows a balanced proportion of feedback and disclosure. Type D personalities have learned to share themselves by seeking feedback from others. Consequently, we learn to trust them in interpersonal communications relationships.

At the end of this chapter, we offer a group exercise using the Johari Window. This will promote an awareness of your own blind spots and hidden qualities.

INCREASING TRUST IN GOVERNMENT

The capacity to build individual relationships of trust is also related to organizational linkages. Lawson (1994) studied the influence of public leader personality characteristics in relation to achieving organizational objectives, in-

. FIGURE 5-2

INTERPERSONAL STYLES AS FUNCTIONS OF EXPOSURE:
USE AND FEEDBACK SOLICITATION

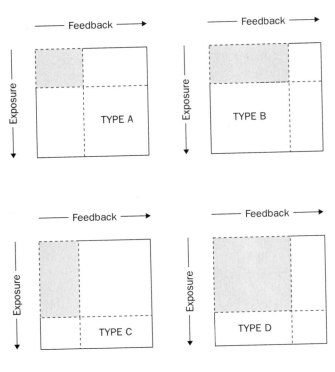

INTERPERSONAL STYLES

spiring subordinate commitment, and organizational productivity. He finds that leaders lacking subordinate trust fail to instill follower commitment to top performance. Typically, this lack of trust shows up in the leaders' aggressive, selfish behaviors. This engenders low commitment to task and, consequently, deflates performance. External constituents see the consistently poor results and develop a negative characterization of the organization.

Denhardt (1994) studied effective relationships of trust that public leaders in four Western countries had established. He notes five recurring themes, based on the leaders' commitment to democratic values, service to constituents, involvement in programs, use of available resources to make extraordinary opportunities for mutual growth and development, and empowerment in making and carrying out decisions.

Trust depends on establishing openness and collaboration among followers. This leads to a feeling of community. Terry (1995) lists several ways leaders can develop such communities from diverse constituents within and outside government. Primary is fashioning a favorable public image. This results from inviting feedback on agency products and services and, at the same time, sharing those that exemplified quality. Leaders use techniques of organizational learning, which uses timely and accurate customer feedback to promote continuous quality improvement (Kofman & Senge, 1994).

Terry (1995) also maintains that developing openness in informal communications networks strengthens agency image. Such networks form and thrive on exchanges of information, expertise, responsiveness, and mutual involvement in events, such as conferences and speeches. Ties through mutual participation over time lead to trust.

Agency credibility also emerges through adherence to regime laws and values, professional ethics, and industry-defined standards of quality for products and services. By demonstrating that the leader and the agency acknowledge and uphold higher-order rules, leaders can demonstrate their concern for personal integrity and institutional accountability. Further, by publishing agency performance information, leaders enhance the perception of agency honesty. They also promote the idea that an agency's services and products are reputable (Herzlinger, 1996; Teasley, 1999).

SUMMARY

Instilling trust in followers is crucial for leadership. Trust enables workers to succeed through commitment. Commitment, in turn, produces higher employee confidence and satisfaction. This enhances a level of productivity that carries through to future projects. Trust is like credit in a leader's bank account: The leader can draw on it anytime, but it is particularly valuable in times of crisis.

Chapter 5 described 11 variables that affect building trust:

1. how closely leaders' intentions match their actions;
2. leaders' traits which followers emulate;
3. an internal locus of control, or confidence that individual efforts shape events;
4. the degree of perceived similarity among group members;
5. sharing one's ideas and giving authentic feedback;
6. assuming and interpreting expected roles;
7. adapting to ambiguous situations;
8. not exploiting those who depend on help from others;
9. understanding how company politics affect trust;
10. using formal policies to augment the unspoken rules of trust; and
11. creating standards that foster an open and respectful work climate.

In this chapter, we have introduced skills that are essential in building a trustful relationship with followers. As we shall see in the following chapters, this relationship is the foundation for establishing effective leadership. We will see how leaders use trust to strengthen communication, build productive teams, and solve problems creatively.

QUESTIONS FOR THOUGHT AND DISCUSSION

1. What conditions have you experienced that enhance trust in leaders? reduce trust?

2. How can public sector leaders promote trust among citizens? In particular, how do citizens lose trust in government? What are some specific instances?

3. How can organization trust facilitate perceptions of organizational commitment? organizational justice?

INTERACTIVE EXERCISE

COAL TO DIAMONDS: LEARNING THE GOOD FROM THE BAD
AN APPLICATION OF THE JOHARI WINDOW

TIME: APPROXIMATELY 1.5 HOURS

DIRECTIONS

We think of coal as a dirty, unpleasant substance. We also think of intense pressure as undesirable. Yet, you may remember comic-book stories in which Superman used intense pressure to squeeze a lump of coal and turn it into a diamond. So, too, we can transform unpleasant experiences into gems of wisdom for others and ourselves.

Below are three questions. Write down your responses to the first two, and select one you wish to convey to others in a *small group* (10 minutes). The *large group* will divide into groups of four people. There will be three rounds of 30 minutes each, with each person playing the role of *storyteller* and *listener*. All participants act as spotters twice. One spotter will observe the storyteller and the other, the listener. In the last round, participants will brainstorm ways the unpleasant experience in each story might be used positively.

ROUND 1 *(30 MINUTES)*

After 5 minutes, the *facilitator* will call time. The storyteller, the listener, and the *spotters* will write answers to the questions on the observation sheets (5 minutes). Each person will then share his or her responses. The spotters will provide their observations to the storyteller and listener (10 minutes). The listener and the storyteller will exchange feedback (10 minutes).

ROUND 2 *(30 MINUTES)*

The storyteller and the listener become spotters and the other two group members take turns as storyteller and listener. At the end of 5 minutes, time will be called and participants will write their observations (5 minutes) and share them, as in Round 1 (20 minutes).

SOURCE: From M.K. Prokop and D. A. Kline (1995). Coal to Diamonds: Learning the Good from the Bad. In J.W. Pfeiffer (Ed.), *The 1995 Annual, Volume 2: Consulting* (pp. 9–12). San Diego, CA: Pfeiffer and Co. Used with permission.

ROUND 3 (30 MINUTES)

The two members who did not have an opportunity to share their stories and play the role of listener will act their parts (10 minutes). After each person has written comments (5 minutes), they provide feedback (20 minutes).

ROUND 4 (15 MINUTES)

After the second group has completed their discussion, the group can brainstorm how the two unpleasant experiences (the coal) can be transformed into a learning experience (a diamond).

QUESTIONS

1. What was an experience you've had in your life or work when you learned something from someone else's mistake? Make a few notes in the space below, then share the experience with the person designated as the listener.

   _____

   _____

   _____

   _____

2. What was an experience in your life or work when you were unhappy with the results? Perhaps you made a decision that turned awry, or any mistake that you would hope no one else would make. Make a few notes in the space that follows.

   _____

   _____

   _____

   _____

3. Brainstorm with the other members of your subgroup about what good has or could come from these experiences. Draw some conclusions and discuss these in the small group.

OBSERVER SHEET

OBSERVATIONS OF THE STORYTELLER

Self-disclosure occurs when individuals reveal something about their **inner states,** such as feelings, attitudes, and values concerning an event.

1. Approximately how many self-disclosure statements did you observe?

   _____

   _____

   _____

   _____

2. Give some examples of self-disclosure conveyed to clarify or illustrate meanings.

   _____

   _____

   _____

3. In your opinion, are there ways the storyteller might improve using self-disclosure? If so, what are they?

   _____

   _____

   _____

OBSERVATIONS OF THE LISTENER

Feedback includes verbal and nonverbal responses, helpful comments, suggestions, and questions. It should be objective, or relevant to what is being said. It should be helpful, rather than critical, and shared honestly.

1. Approximately how many times did the listener give verbal feedback to the storyteller? nonverbal?

   _____

   _____

2. Did the listener stay focused on what the storyteller was saying?

   _____

   _____

3. What were some important examples of feedback the listener shared with the storyteller?

_____

_____

_____

_____

_____

_____

SELF-OBSERVATIONS

STORYTELLER

1. In thinking back to the experience you chose to reveal, how well do you think you revealed your feelings?

_____

_____

_____

_____

2. Do you feel the listener gave you valid and helpful feedback?

_____

_____

_____

_____

3. What did you learn about trust from this exercise?

_____

_____

_____

_____

LISTENER

1. What was it like to listen to the storyteller?

_____

_____

_____

_____

2. How did you feel about giving feedback to the storyteller?

_____

_____

_____

3. How did the storyteller respond to the feedback? What did this mean to you?

_____

_____

_____

_____

CREATING MEANING
Approaches to Leadership Communication

6

SYNOPSIS

Based on the work of Krone, Jablin, and Putnam (1987), this chapter describes four central approaches to analyzing communications relationships: mechanistic, psychological, symbolic interactionist, and systemic. Chapter 6 discusses the formation and use of symbols in creating meaning as well as some common perceptual errors that occur in interpreting verbal and nonverbal language. This chapter depicts key leader roles in producing organizational culture and managing interpersonal communications networks. Describing impediments that occur frequently in hierarchical organizational structures, this chapter points out distortions in conveying and decoding messages.

OBJECTIVES

- To discuss four approaches to leadership communications
- To define communications as a relational process of transacting symbolic meaning
- To describe ways leaders shape meaning in interpersonal and organizational communications contexts
- To discuss common communications distortions
- To describe uses of formal and informal communications networks

KEY TERMS AND CONCEPTS

Communication networks

Communication ties

Communications channels
   Formal
   Informal

Communications contexts

    Physical
    Psychological
    Cultural

Deep structure political games

Information overload

Models of communication
    Mechanistic
    Psychological
    Symbolic
    Systemic

Network roles
    Gatekeeper
    Liaison
    Bridge
    Opinion leader
    Cosmopolite

Perceptual meaning making

Power games/political games

Open Systems' Model of communication
    Input
    Transformational processes
    Outputs
    Subsystems

Referent

Symbolic communications
    Metaphors
    Rituals and rites

INTRODUCTION

Throughout this text, we have emphasized how leaders use their relationships with followers for particular purposes. The quality of these relationships, however, depends a great deal on the frequency, clarity, and openness of communication. Communication therefore becomes an important but difficult art to master. Further, it is more than just a volley of words; it is a complex exchange that includes body language and hidden meanings.

To understand how a leader encourages communication in a group, we turn to Krone, Jablin, and Putnam (1987), who define four approaches to leadership communication: (1) mechanistic—how communication can be broken into components, (2) psychological—how a person's reason and emotion affect communication, (3) symbolic—how patterns of behavior indicate meaning, and (4) systemic—how the behavior of surrounding people affects communication.

In this chapter, we examine some of these approaches. First, we focus on errors in communication; that is, how individual or cultural differences can lead to misunderstanding. Second, we examine the symbolic qualities of language, pointing out the leader's role in defining an organization's identity. Finally, we discuss how leader–follower communication thrives or suffers in the context of an organization.

A MECHANISTIC MODEL OF INTERPERSONAL COMMUNICATION

In order for communication to occur, eight elements are needed. As shown in Figure 6.1, these include: (1) a sender; (2) intended meaning conveyed through a context and a code of symbols; (3) a receiver; (4) the receiver's interpretation of symbols; (5) the meaning the receiver ascribes to the interpretation of the symbols; (6) feedback on receiver's interpretation; (7) interpre-

. FIGURE 6–1

A MODEL OF MEANING MAKING

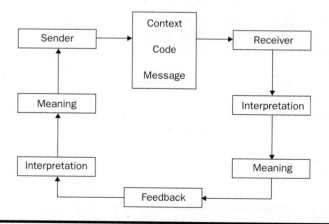

tation of the receiver's feedback by the sender; and (8) meaning the sender ascribes, based on feedback received.

In this model, a sender intends to convey a thought to a receiver. The sender encodes this intended meaning into a set of symbols such as words, sounds, or gestures. These symbols are in turn transmitted by various means, perhaps oral or written. The receiver decodes the symbols and interprets their meaning using contextual cues. This interpretation relies on how logically or randomly the symbols are linked, and on the physical conditions that affect understanding, perhaps a headache or cold. Having interpreted the message, the receiver gives a similarly encoded response.

This basic framework of communication shows how each person is altered by the exchange. They both walk away with something that informs their behavior, such as a new insight or method to reach a goal. Mutual feedback, by producing such results, makes communication a dynamic process.

On the surface, this model seems simple. Yet, between the use of encoded symbols and their interpretation, many conditions arise that affect the quality of communication. First, let's look at how interpretation can be affected.

THE PSYCHOLOGY OF CREATING MEANING

People communicate with symbols that represent thoughts, concrete objects, or even other symbols. Each symbol refers to something—that is, a *referent*. Surrounding the referent are concentric layers of meaning. Like an onion, a referent has external meanings all understand, as well as deeper metaphorical meanings (von Cranach, Doise, & Mugny, 1992).

We will use the word *hit* to illustrate this. As a verb, *hit* means to strike something: "Mary hit the ball." It can also be used as a metaphorical noun: "The song was a hit," meaning, "The song was popular." The speaker can also color this statement with a sarcastic tone of voice, mocking the song instead of extolling it. *Hit* can refer to different actions: "The batter made a hit" differs drastically from "The gangster made a hit." Any word can therefore have varied meanings depending on its context.

Since a single word can refer to different things depending on the surrounding words, the more specific the context, the more specific the meaning. The use of *hit* with *man*, for instance, is used specifically to refer to gangsters. In a similar way, certain groups distinguish themselves from other groups by means of slang and technical jargon.

CHARACTER OF CONTEXTS

Context, as noted, affects how people derive meaning. We may note, however, that contexts themselves can vary. We may classify these variations into three broad categories: (1) *physical contexts,* or the immediate surroundings of an exchange; (2) *psychological contexts,* including intellectual, emotional and physiological states; and (3) *cultural contexts,* or socially defined speech patterns and values.

> *Physical context.* The physical setting of a conversation can affect how well people communicate. For instance, a noisy setting would make it difficult to hear others. Likewise, if circumstances change rapidly—as when people are working under deadline—certain nuances of conversation may be lost in the shuffle, resulting in misunderstanding. Errors can also happen if the message is carried through faulty channels—if, for example, the two people are separated by distance, encouraging an incorrectly sent e-mail or memo.

> *Psychological context.* Perhaps the most significant factor in communication is the mental state of the participants. This state can include the following variables: perceptual limitations, style of processing information, emotional states, and physical readiness.

> Let's look at an illustration of the effect psychology has on communication. Our organs of perception (eyes, ears, nose, tongue, skin) absorb an enormous quantity of information; we are aware of much of it immediately, whereas some information is registered only by the subconscious. We store this information, much like a computer, according to categories. Over time, a person connects similar memories to form unique patterns, which in turn form the foundation of broader meanings. As these meanings grow, the specific information that built them is sacrificed. Concepts become abstract, and their meaning becomes difficult to relate.

> Take, for example, the word *book.* Our experiences tell us that a book is a stack of pages bound together, containing words and sometimes pictures. As children, we learned this by listening to someone reading to us. They may have shown us pictures and asked us questions. We associated *reading* with *book,* and formed a definition of *book* as something that would convey information. We soon learned that there were different kinds of books, such as fiction and nonfiction. These differences were made distinct in school, where English literature was distinguished from chemistry. Growing older, some may have formed negative feelings for everything associated with the word *book.* Any book, no matter how potentially valuable, could evoke a stressful memory—perhaps the memory of failing a test, or an overbearing teacher.

> *Cultural context.* Culture, which imposes patterns of behavior accepted by the group, affects how each person interprets information. Language itself evolved from the need to unite groups that were threatened by their environment or by other groups. Culture is expressed not only through language, but also through customs and religious beliefs.

ERRORS IN PERCEPTUAL MEANING MAKING

Each process or context may also contain elements that lead to mistakes in creating or interpreting interpersonal meaning (MacKay, 1992). For example, we may "leap to conclusions" without checking out the "facts." Certain behaviors, in similar fashion, arise automatically. For instance, if we pull out into an intersection immediately after a traffic light has turned green, we may not account for "a red-light runner" right in front of us. Other errors arise from visual and auditory limitations, such as not seeing or hearing an approaching train at a railroad crossing. We may also fail to understand the jargon of professional and/or technical groups as well as the contexts in which they occur. For instance, we may assume that if a lawyer has reviewed a particular document and has made a decision, the decision is "correct." Additionally, thinking that is not open to new information or information received from different sources may produce stereotypes and block understanding. When we shop for clothing, for instance, we may buy only from a certain manufacturer, assuming that the name will guarantee high quality. When we realize the garment was made in Guatemala rather than Paris, we feel uneasy about buying it.

CREATING MEANING THROUGH CORPORATE CULTURE

Leaders use several forms of symbolic communications in creating corporate culture. Culture includes the values, beliefs, and assumptions that characterize a particular group of people and help them adapt and survive to changing environmental conditions. Leaders build and maintain culture verbally and nonverbally. Common types of symbolic communications are stories or narratives and metaphors (Czarniawska, 1997). Cultural symbols appear in how organizations design tasks and interpersonal relationships; also in how people dress and arrange their work spaces. Public organizations that value order and authority will give these priorities prominence in regulations, standard operating procedures, rigid hierarchical chains of command, and people who wear "uniforms."

RITUALS AND RITES

Leaders create activities that enable organizations to adapt and survive. Leaders and followers develop rites and rituals to help them carry out both repetitive, everyday behaviors as well as significant events (Trice & Beyer, 1993). Many greetings are ritualized behaviors, such as what one says and does when a visitor comes to an office. Filling out standard forms has its own rituals as well. Trice and Beyer identify six that organizations have in common: (1) *rites of passage*—ways to identify significant milestones in careers, (2) *rites of degradation*—ways to demote people, (3) *rites of enhance-*

ment—ways to publicly recognize individuals and their accomplishments, (4) *rites of renewal*—ways to highlight positive outcomes, (5) *rites of conflict reduction*—ways to obtain control in disputes, and (6) *rites of integration*—ways to encourage and revive bonds.

AN EXAMPLE OF CREATING PUBLIC CORPORATE CULTURE: LILIENTHAL AND THE TVA

David E. Lilienthal, one of the early leaders of the Tennessee Valley Authority (TVA) used symbolism to create a "grass-roots" organization. The TVA, established in 1933 as part of Franklin D. Roosevelt's New Deal, integrated various industries, local governments, and volunteers into a unified goal. Neuse (1983, p. 491) observed that the TVA developed and sustained a vision of "utilizing public powers to develop natural resources, foster economic development, and enhance the quality of human life—all within the context of a...partnership." The TVA also blazed trails in its attention to workers' rights, the hiring of African Americans, establishing nondiscriminatory wage scales, and labor relations.

As one of TVA's three board members, Lilienthal shared the view that participatory government would prevent bureaucratic strangulation. To Lilienthal, the TVA needed to establish a "clean slate" in how it planned and carried out its mission. In a new vision of democratic governance, Lilienthal linked democracy, wholeness, and morality (cited in Shafritz & Hyde, 1987, p. 155):

> Here is the life principle of democratic planning—an awakening in the whole people of a sense of this common moral purpose. Not one goal, but a direction. Not one plan, once and for all, but the conscious selection by the people of successive plans.

SYSTEMIC APPROACHES TO COMMUNICATIONS: COMMUNICATING MEANING IN ORGANIZATIONS

Thus far we have examined how individuals affect communication in a company. However, organizational structure also influences how people communicate. Bureaucratic structures limit the flow of information. Further, people in organizations where power is centralized compete for access to information. This competition makes it difficult to gain accurate information. In the following pages, we will examine the limitations of bureaucratic agencies. But first it is important to understand organizations as open systems.

OPEN SYSTEMS' VIEW OF ORGANIZATIONS

We speak of organizational communication as occurring in "systems," or structured channels and patterns within organizations. Because of the

. FIGURE 6-2

AN OPEN SYSTEMS' MODEL OF ORGANIZATION

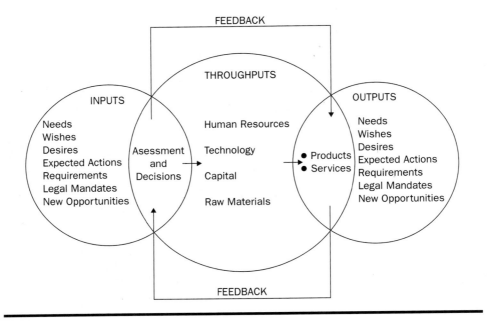

connections between the systems, organizations rarely act as discrete entities. They are influenced by the people and events surrounding them. Accordingly, organizations open themselves to the external environment to assimilate materials or skilled workers. Figure 6.2 shows an Open Systems' Model of an organization.

In an open system, organizations have a dynamic, give-and-take interaction with their environments (Scott, 1992). Open systems have three main features: (1) *inputs*, (2) *transformation processes*, and (3) *outputs*. Surrounding the organization is a *boundary*, or a meeting point for outside clientele. In Figure 6.2, transformation processes produce goods and services, which are transmitted from the organization to its constituents. Organizations adjust the goods and services quantity and quality depending on conditions in the external environment. Regulation of the boundary shifts takes place as *feedback*, as indicated by the arrows. The *transformation processes* consist of *subsystems* that work together to create goods and services. The subsystems, in turn, are united by *facilitative processes*, or ways that raw materials (inputs) are changed into goods or services (outputs).

We can see an open system in the example of a municipal recreation department. The external environment consists of taxpayers who fund the department, city council members, and state regulators. As inputs, the department hires staff members from pools of qualified individuals, uses sports equipment, and obtains operating funds. Inside the organization, various subsystems may design programs for a specific group, such as senior citizens or children's arts and crafts. To make programs work for these outside groups, the staff communicates with each other and applies their specialized knowledge to solve problems. They also demonstrate to taxpayers that they are using their funds effectively. Surveys of clients are conducted to gauge the success of the programs. These surveys, which take place in specially set up offices, represent the boundary of the organization. Here, information is absorbed and used by the organization.

COMMUNICATIONS IN AN OPEN SYSTEMS' ORGANIZATION

Depending on the broadness of the organizational mission and the varieties of outputs an open systems' organization produces, subsystems and facilitative processes vary in complexity. Large, top-down bureaucracies that have broad public purposes have highly formalized subsystems and specialized facilitative processes. This means that communications' flows travel through a myriad of structures to reach all internal and external clientele. Often, communications occur through *formal channels*, such as directives from chains of command and written memos. Bureaucracies may also use *informal channels*, such as "grapevines" that carry the latest information about office politics.

COMMON DISTORTIONS OF FORMAL CHANNEL COMMUNICATION

In formal organizational arrangements, communication generally flows from top to bottom. Leaders may make task requests on the basis of written and legal documents, such as organizational charts or job descriptions. Because formal communications' flow is typically one-directional, however, there is little opportunity to ask for and receive direct feedback to questions. Individuals at each level of the organization may interpret the formal communications according to differing perspectives, values, and purposes. Moreover, because local conditions may not be addressed in formal communications, those receiving messages "from on high" may develop suspicion of intent and perhaps mistrust.

It is also difficult to communicate information upwardly in steep, hierarchical units. One of the chief barriers is the fear that any negative or discordant information from a lower level will cast an unfavorable image on the bearer. If the organization's culture is based on the assumption of punishing individuals or units that reveal views that differ from the "party line," errors of any magnitude will not likely be reported. If inquiries are made, individuals may try to frame mistakes in a positive light. Presidents, for instance, may be "misinformed" or "out of the loop" when scandals erupt.

RESPONSES TO INFORMATION DISTORTIONS

The communications' distortions that occur in hierarchies may contribute to several types of responses centered around power and control of resources. As available resources become more scarce as they reach operating levels, employees often play competitive games—among themselves, with supervisors, and with other units. The notorious federal government budget battles that erupt yearly reflect the types and degrees of hostility over who gets what that employees also experience.

POWER GAMES

Because power exists at the top of a bureaucracy, the lower echelons have little personal discretion to exercise. Employees are not allowed to disobey or question orders. This leads to a variety of automatic responses, such as acting in stereotypical ways, or ignoring information that contradicts personal opinion.

The use of power that leads to employee silence is one form of game power holders play. These games involve estimating risks, rewards, and possible moves and countermoves. Although players may realize they are in a power game, they often make up the rules as they go. Their success depends on calculation and adaptability.

In organizations where resources are scarce and are the objects of negotiation, trade-offs, and often tough bargaining, political games flourish. Winning or gaining resources becomes a major objective. Players will devise strategies to attain resources, often at the expense of other players.

Frost (1987) identifies four major categories of political games, played on different levels as follows:

1. *Individual Games.* Individuals try to gain control of resources in an organization. Those who have a mentor stand a better chance for moving up in a company than those who do not (Kram, 1983). Thus mentoring is a form of career gamesmanship. Mentors who are protective of their power tend to assert their authority heavily on those reporting to them. Moreover, individuals who fear losing the small amount of territory they manage may assert their authority strongly over those reporting to them (Kanter, 1977).

2. *Games Within Organizations.* Perhaps the most notorious games within organizations are played out using reorganization. These reorganizations grant departments power over their rivals by eliminating staff or reconfiguring resources.

3. *Games Between Organizations.* Groups or teams may compete for resources by playing collaborative or win–lose games. Prime examples are debates over yearly budget allocations.

4. *Deep-Structure Games.* Deep-structure games try to change the basic approaches employees use in their work. A good example is the train-

ing of new employees. Recruits undergo a process of standardization where they adjust their views of motivation and advancement to those of the organization.

TANGLED WEBS

Public organizations take in and convey information through a complex web of sources. Information may come from governmental agencies, business groups, the media, as well as from a myriad of individual clients and employees. Finding the proper channel to obtain precise, current information is often frustrating. Agencies are fortunate if reliable gatekeepers can help them navigate this maze to reach a goal.

INFORMATION OVERLOAD

Demand for information from several different sources strains the organization and often causes the system to overload. Bureaucracies therefore build into the system circuit breakers to help guard against overburdening it. These mechanisms can take the form of standard operating procedures or centralized public relations' offices. Many organizations now respond to inquiries over the Internet with form letters. These narrow channels of communication are useful for ordinary problems. But when a crisis strikes, the sudden need for fast and accurate responses can stress and/or cripple the system.

HIERARCHICAL HURDLES

The upper echelons of a bureaucracy control decisions of resource acquisition, distribution, and expenses. Because legislators grant a limited amount of money to agencies each year, top managers guard how much each part of their group receives. Invariably, scarcity sets off competitive games between mid-level managers and supervisors.

REGULATORY TRIPWIRES

Although organizations attempt to prevent information overload, they may falter because of their overreliance on policies that can be contradictory and binding. In emergencies, when accuracy and clarity are required to solve problems, too many strict regulations can hinder prompt action.

DEFERENCE TO POSITION

Because power is centralized at the top of bureaucratic structures, managers and employees at lower eschelons have little discretion in obeying orders. Employees may not openly question the premises of the top officials nor subvert carrying out the commands. This may lead to a variety of automatic responses, acting in stereotypical role sets, or screening out discordant information so that messages are consistent with what the receiver expects to hear.

Adams (cited in Stillman, 1992) recounts how, as an analyst for the CIA, he tried several times to tell officials about serious discrepancies in the reported numbers of enemy troops in Vietnam. Each time Adams would send a report or even meet with officials, they ignored his message.

FORMAL AND INFORMAL COMMUNICATION

In formal group structures, communication generally flows from top to bottom. Individuals in management roles use language appropriate for getting tasks done. Leaders base their requests on official documents, such as charts or job descriptions. Because formal communication typically moves in one direction, workers find it difficult to communicate with each other, with higher-ups, and especially with outsiders. Workers therefore often open their own lines of communication. These informally created channels may take the form of gossip, rumors, and/or casual chatting. Informal networks of communication supplement formal networks.

NETWORK ROLES

Because of inherent limitations of formal communications in complex organizations, individuals form informal channels and play certain roles in facilitating meaning. These may include formal structures that supplement a central purpose or create flexibility in addressing a particular topic or problem. Governmental agencies frequently use task forces and special committees, for example, to handle specialized or controversial issues. Informal channels, however, may also emerge without long-term purposes or structures. These usually consist of networks that people create for particular purposes. Brass and Burkhardt (1992) identify several types of common networks, including those for workflow interactions, power and influence, and friendships.

In communicating informally, people may adopt one of the following five roles (Farace, Monge, & Russell, 1977): (1) *gatekeeper*, (2) *liaison*, (3) *bridge*, (4) *opinion leader*, and/or (5) *cosmopolite*. Each person is connected by outward and inward lines of communication, called "ties." Let's examine these roles, shown in Figure 6.3, in more detail.

1. *Gatekeeper.* The gatekeeper regulates communication among members of the network. Gatekeepers often control schedules, as when the Speaker of the House prioritizes the introduction of bills. Executive secretaries also function as gatekeepers. Gatekeepers exert a great deal of behind-the-scenes, informal power.

2. *Liaison.* A liaison carries information between two or more parts of the network, but is not a member of any specific division. Often, a head-

- **FIGURE 6–3**

NETWORK ROLES IN A FEDERAL AGENCY

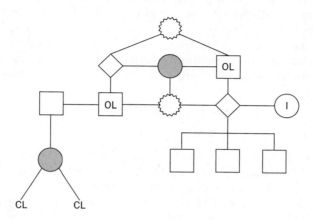

Cosmopolite—has high degree of environmental communication	Gatekeeper—controls message flow
OL — Opinion Leader—influences attitudes and behaviors informally	Liason—connects cliques, but is not part of them
CL — Clique—limited contact of members with internal units	Isolates—individuals who receive and transmit limited information to external units

quarters staff will use a liaison to communicate with officials at a field office. Liaisons are responsible for relaying information in an accurate, timely, and concise manner.

3. *Bridge.* Unlike liaisons, bridges have membership in particular network divisions. Bridges link different sections of the network, and help spread key information across departmental boundaries quickly.

4. *Opinion Leader.* Opinion leaders usually have a great deal of power. They are persons who are respected for their advice as well as their ability to persuade others. In groups, others look up to them as consultants.

5. *Cosmopolite.* Cosmopolites work with groups outside the network. In government, they usually understand the needs of special interest groups, business groups, and legislators. The information they secure helps the organization adapt to outside conditions.

NETWORK DISTORTIONS

Although networks may facilitate informal communications in organizations, they have their own forms of message distortion. Networks can produce illusions of agreement that can stifle decision making. Janis (1989) calls this "groupthink" and notes it was a chief contributor to the policy-making failures in the Bay of Pigs invasion under the Kennedy administration and in the decision to launch *Challenger*. Harvey (1996) calls the unwillingness to voice disagreement the "tyranny of agreement" in his popular book, *The Abilene Paradox*.

PARTICIPATION DILEMMAS

Inviting stakeholder participation in policy making is essential to developing policies that stakeholders can accept. Yet, participation also opens up possibilities for dissent and discordant information—both of which can disrupt problem-solving and decision-making processes. Often, employees who experience trust become empowered to form and express their own opinions. Dissent is then a logical by-product and, by extension, a healthy sign of conscientiousness. The challenge for leaders is to encourage followers to dissent and protect their rights to do so, even though the information the dissenters bring up may refute standard norms and assumptions (Kassing, 1998).

SUMMARY

In Chapter 6, we looked at four different approaches to leader–follower communications. In communicating, leaders share a vision of follower and organizational direction, gather support and commitment, prepare to achieve goals or purposes, and provide links to internal and external clientele. How leaders and followers create and transmit meaning has been categorized in terms of: (1) mechanistic, sender–receiver relationships; (2) psychological constructs of perception and affective conditions; (3) symbolic interpretation of words and phrases, artifacts, and rites and rituals; and (4) organizational structures involving formal and informal communications.

Examining the four approaches to leader–follower communications has revealed several ways communications may become blocked. Difficulties arise from the physical and psychological contexts of leader–follower communications. Examples of physical obstructions include noise, distance, and shortcomings in transmission and receptive apparatus. Psychological barriers include such phenomena as frames of reference, differences in culture, confusing inference with fact, emotive characteristics of certain words and phrases, and stereotypical thinking.

Organizational structures, moreover, create impediments to communication. In the public sector in particular, the presence of numerous, competing interest groups, centralized power, scarcity of resources, and an overabundance of legal rules contribute to communications' distortions. As responses to organizational communications' barriers, members create informal groups and play one of several roles. Moreover, people may play several types of "games" to secure control and expand influence.

Inclusion of stakeholders in policy making is important for building trust as well as exchanging important information. Especially in teamwork, diversity of viewpoints can limit the appearance of "groupthink." Encouraging followers to express their disagreements, however, may pose leadership dilemmas. In Chapter 8, we will explore these in greater detail and discuss particular ways leaders can manage conflict, diversity, involvement, and ethical conduct.

QUESTIONS FOR THOUGHT AND DISCUSSION

1. Leaders need to monitor their thinking processes for bias, and particularly, stereotypical reactions. How, in your opinion, can leaders examine these processes? What roles do followers and constituents play in looking at and correcting possible biases?

2. The drafting of bills can be seen as a type of forging common meaning through symbolic exchange. Compare the changes in meaning of a particular bill's intent to how it is interpreted among administrators. How can public leaders ensure that meaning of a law, ordinance, or statute, is shared among those affected?

3. Think of a public organization with which you are familiar. How have past (and current) leaders interpreted mission and operational goals? In what ways have the leaders' values and beliefs been translated into cultural rituals and rites? Who are the heroes and heroines? the villains? How have narratives inspired followers?

4. Examine an informal network in a public agency. Why was it formed? Who are the constituents? What roles do they play in passing on information? Who are the leaders? Do they allow members to dissent? How does the group handle differences of opinion?

CASE STUDY

56 MINUTES BEFORE PEARL HARBOR

By Hugh Russell Fraser

DIRECTIONS

In the following case study, you will see many of the interpersonal and organizational communications' concepts at play. After you have read the case, answer and discuss the questions with others in a small group. Select a spokesperson to share a summary of your responses with the larger group.

My task was to investigate the 56 minutes of warning we had of the Jap air attack on Pearl Harbor, December 7, 1941. What I learned amazed me. I reported every detail to the Assistant Chief Signal Officer—specifically, Maj. Gen. James A. Code.

Now, nearly 17 years later, I can tell that story. The facts, incredible as they are, became a part of my history in the U.S. Signal Corps in World War II. To most Americans who know merely that we had some radar warning of the sneak attack on the "Day of Infamy," the history of those 56 minutes will come as a shock.

Radar could, and did, detect the approach of the Jap air fleet. But not, of course, as it should have been detected, and not as it would have been detected if authorized radar equipment had been installed. Actually, the island of Oahu was to have been ringed with permanent radar warning installations. It was not. As early as November of the year before, the Corps of Engineers was directed to install six permanent radar warning sets to be operating around the clock beginning July 1, 1941.

These sets were not installed by July 1. They were not installed by December 1, nor by December 7. Four mobile radar warning units, mounted in trucks, were provided in their place. Regarded generally by the men assigned to them as toys to experiment with, they were in operation only from 4:00 A.M. to 7:00 A.M. Why were those hours chosen? Probably it was because these were the three hours of the 24 when the enemy—any enemy—was most likely to attack. If this was the theory, then it came very close to being 100% right.

The open mobile radar set, manned by privates Joseph Lockard and George Elliott, was the one that detected the approach of the Jap air armada. Singularly enough, it was supposed to be shut down promptly at 7 o'clock on the morning of December 7, but, by one of those fortunate accidents of history, the truck coming at that time to take the two men back to base camp and to breakfast was late. So Lockard and Elliott decided to leave the set on until it arrived.

Thus, after 7:00 A.M., the open unit was the only radar unit on the island operating. The other mobile sets, also mounted in trucks, had shut down promptly. One was located at Punaluu on Kahana Bay, 30 miles to the southeast, another on the extreme west side of the island near Makua, and the fourth near Waipahu on the southwest coast, 11 miles west of Pearl Harbor itself.

The Opana unit, which made history, was located about 22 miles due north of Pearl Harbor and about 28 miles northwest of the city of Honolulu. In other words, it was north of the mountains on the island of Oahu, which itself is about 43 miles long and 30 miles wide.

As the seconds after 7 o'clock ticked off, Lockard, who kept his eye idly on the machine, noted noting unusual until, suddenly, at 7:02 A.M., there appeared what he later described as a "huge blip of light—bigger than anything I had ever seen before on the set—moving slowly from the extreme left side of the scope to the right. It was, you might call it, a pillar of light. It startled me, for the flight of one plane is represented by a mere dot, several planes a collection of white dots, but here was something different. The whole left side of the scope suddenly took on light!

"My natural reaction," he continued, "was to infer the radar unit as out of order. So I asked the mechanic, Elliott, to check it. He did so in a couple of minutes and reported it was working all right. By then it was 7:04 A.M. Something unusual, I knew, was before my eyes. Elliott thought so, too, although neither of us could imagine what it might be.

"Quickly we plotted it. The calculations were easily made, and it appeared to be definitely a large flight of planes approaching from due north, three points east, and about 137 miles away.

SOURCE: From *American Mercury*, (August 1957), pp. 80–85.

"We looked at each other, and Elliott was the first to reach for the phone. At first he couldn't get anybody at the Army Information Center at Fort Shafter. The line was dead. Then he tried another line. It was open, and soon Private Joseph McDonald at the switchboard answered. Tersely, Elliott told him what we were seeing on the scope. McDonald's answer was: 'Well, what do you expect me to do about it? There's nobody around here but me.' Elliott told him to find somebody and then hung up.

"What happened, I learned later, was that there was an officer reading a book in the next room. McDonald had supposed he had gone. He was Lt. Kermit Tyler.[1] McDonald told him what Elliott had reported. Lieutenant Tyler looked up from his book, thought a while as if to take it all in, then said: 'It's all right, never mind.'

"Joe McDonald then called back, and I answered the phone. He told me what Tyler had said. I thereupon insisted on talking to the officer myself. I was a little excited and puzzled and didn't want to let the matter end with McDonald. Joe then asked the lieutenant if he would be good enough to talk to me. The officer then came on the phone and said, 'What is it?'

"I made my reply as brief as possible. 'The scope,' I said, 'indicates a large flight of planes approaching Oahu from the north, three points east, about 137 miles away at the last reckoning.'

"There was a pause for a few seconds. Then Tyler said, 'That is probably our B-17s coming in from San Francisco.' I know there was such a flight coming in, but I knew also those planes would hardly be approaching us from due north.

"At once I made this point clear, and he replied, 'Well, there is nothing to worry about. That is all.' The last words he said with some emphasis, and I judged he didn't want to hear anything further about it, so I said: 'All right, sir,' and hung up.

"Meanwhile, somewhat startled by the whole business, although not alarmed, as now the matter was out of my hands, I continued to watch the set. The pillar of light, or 'blip,' as I call it, continued to move steadily from left to right, and the truck still had not arrived. At 7:25 A.M., we made a quick computation, and the flight of planes, whatever it consisted of, was 62 miles out. By 7:39 A.M., just as we heard the truck arriving outside, I made my last computation, and the flight was 22 miles away!

"It was at 7:30 A.M. that we closed down the radar unit and climbed into the truck for a long ride back to base. I was still turning over in my mind what we had seen on the scope as the truck bounced over the badly rutted road. I said nothing to the driver about it, nor did Elliott—not because we were alarmed but because I knew that what didn't make sense to us would hardly make sense to him.

"After we had been driving about 20 minutes, the driver called our attention to a heavy black pall of smoke that lay on the Pearl Harbor horizon to the south. 'Looks like all smoke,' he commented. Soon we were hearing what sounded like explosions and even anti-aircraft fire. It was all very puzzling, and somebody suggested it was a practice raid on Pearl Harbor.

"However, on we went over the rugged road. Actually, it was only 20 miles back to base camp, but because of the road it took almost 40 minutes. As we drove into view of the

[1] A report of the Army Pearl Harbor Board, which was published in the *Army and Navy Journal*, September 15, 1945, reads in part: "The Navy was supposed to have detailed officers in the Information Center to be trained as liaison officers, but had not yet gotten around to it. In the Information Center that morning was a Lieutenant Kermit A. Tyler, a pursuit officer of the Air Corps, whose tour of duty thereat was 8 o'clock. It was Tyler's second tour of duty at the Center, and he was there for training and observation, but there were no others on duty after 7 o'clock except the enlisted telephone operator. He was the sole officer there between 7 and 8 o'clock that morning; the rest of the personnel that had made the Center operative had departed." (Reprinted by permission.)

camp and the truck slowed down, we saw a lot of soldiers running toward us, shouting questions the words of which I couldn't quite at first make out. Finally, it was plain they were asking, 'What happened?' 'Did you report it?' and the like. I never saw a camp so collectively excited.

"As we started to get out of the truck, a major came elbowing his way through the group of men surrounding us and said sharply to us: 'Shut up! Don't say a word! I'll talk to you!'

"With that he took us off to his office and questioned us for 15 minutes. It was not until then I realized the Japs were at that very moment attacking Pearl Harbor, and that what we had seen on the screen was the Jap air fleet approaching.

"Now, as I look back, the position of the flight, the vast number of planes, made sense. I learned later the enemy aircraft carriers had sailed far to the north so that when the planes took to the air they would be coming in from an unexpected direction."

Lockard at one point told me that except for the brief questioning by the major on the island of Oahu on the morning of December 7, 1941, I was the first to interrogate him in detail to those 56 minutes—namely from 7:04 A.M., when Elliott reported the set was not out of order, to the time the first bomb fell on Pearl Harbor.

The tracing of the history of those 56 minutes, however, led me into a further investigation of why the permanent radar sets had not been installed on the island of Oahu by July 1. Here I ran into a curious and amazing story, which I tried in vain to have the Congressional Investigating Committee explore.

My investigation disclosed that the colonel in the Corps of Engineers, who was charged with the duty of having those permanent radar sets installed and operated around the clock by July 1, 1941, had spent most of his time in the summer of 1941 drinking. His entire record demonstrates incredible negligence of duty. Not only did he fall down on his job, but the toll in lives and ships that we had to pay for his failure was heartbreaking.

I tried to bring my evidence before the committee. To that end I prepared a long memorandum, setting forth the facts as I saw them. I requested that this colonel be summoned and be cross-examined under oath.

To my surprise, the Democratic members of the committee, whom I knew personally and regarded highly, handled my request—made in my capacity as a citizen—as if it were a hot potato. They not only refused to *set* on it in any way or request that he be summoned, but they told me in essence "to forget it"!

Amazed that members of my own party would take this view, I turned to the Republicans. I knew only one personally. He was Representative Bud Gearhart of California. Mr. Gearhart read my memorandum carefully and promised to do his best to get the colonel summoned. Later he reported back he had failed, but he had tried his best.

"Why won't they go into this question of radar units?" I asked. "Surely you know their importance!"

"Yes," he said, "of course. My opinion is that somebody failed and failed terribly, but I ran up against a stone wall. The chairman flatly refused me, and when I asked one of my Democratic friends what was the real reason for what I thought, and still think was an obvious runaround, he said, 'Look, Bud, you can do what you please and maybe you can get somewhere, but don't forget. I'm a Democrat and a loyal one, and I take my orders from my commander in chief, and my commander in chief happens to be the president of the United States!'"

QUESTIONS FOR DISCUSSION

1. What were some major perceptual errors in the account? How did they affect the credibility of the report?

2. What particular errors affected the credibility of Lockhart and Elliot? In your opinion, why did no one apparently take their warnings seriously?

3. What role did politics play in the communications? In your opinion, what might a public employee who finds himself or herself in a political "hot potato" do?

4. What are some strategies you might use as a leader who encounters seemingly "incredible" information from one of your followers?

CASE STUDY

THE PREVIOUS ADMINISTRATION'S LIQUOR LICENSE SCANDAL

TIME: APPROXIMATELY 45 MINUTES

DIRECTIONS

Read the following scenario and jot down your thoughts and feelings. Write your answers to the questions that follow. Then, working in small groups, share your responses. Select a spokesperson to summarize the responses and report them to the larger group at the end of the time allotted.

SCENARIO

You are the new director of a State Department of Consumer Protection. One of your agency's responsibilities is to enforce state liquor laws. A leading newspaper in the state recently ran an editorial chiding the agency for not enforcing a law that fined bars featuring exotic dancers. The lax enforcement stemmed from a tacit agreement of the previous administrator and bar owners. The logic, the editorial reported, was that the owners said they would not allow prostitution, gambling, and drunkenness if the agents overlooked the nude dancers.

QUESTIONS

As a public servant, you realize that the information has damaged trust and impaired constituent relationships.

1. How would you set up a strategy to close the breach?

2. Which constituents would you target?

3. How might you establish a new relationship with them?

lead 7 & 10

Section 7

Classics

Leading Diverse Followers

7

Synopsis

This chapter contends that there are multiple forms of "diversity" that affect the character of leader–follower relationships. These include not only race, gender, and age, but also socioeconomic background, culture, thinking styles, and viewpoints. The strategies for leading diverse followers stem from attributions, ideologies, past experiences, lack of direct and continuing contact, authoritarianism and ethnocentrism, and degree of physical attractiveness. Strategies that fail to integrate follower differences may be based in prejudice and manifest themselves in stereotypical leadership behaviors, which produce low trust, poor individual motivation, reinforcement of existing stereotypes, and creation of sharply defined role behaviors. Leaders can develop more inclusiveness in thoughts and interactions, however, by understanding the importance of critical thinking, self-reflection, discussion, and participation. To foster collaborative work, leaders can also understand and practice sharing power.

Objectives

- To define diversity as multifaceted differences among followers that influence leadership relationships
- To describe cultural attributes that influence institutional practices with regard to diversity
- To discuss five concepts that affect prejudice
- To describe effects of prejudice on work relationships
- To discuss ways leaders can reduce prejudice and promote inclusiveness in follower relationships

Key Terms and Concepts

"adaptive work"

Attribution Theory

authoritarianism

bias

cognitive fluidity

critical thinking

discrimination

diversity (among individuals and groups)

ethnocentrism

"feminine" characteristics of leadership

group process

ideology

inclusion

in-groups

"just world" beliefs

"masculine" characteristics of leadership

normative reeducation leadership strategy

out-groups

power sharing

prejudice

self-fulfilling prophecy

status boundaries

theories-in-use

transformational leaders

INTRODUCTION

Leading persons who have diverse backgrounds and personalities is perhaps the most critical skill for public managers to master. When we speak of
diversity, we include not only people from different races or cultures, but
also people who have different thinking patterns and beliefs. In the public

sector, diversity is even more complex because it includes citizens, all three branches of government, business, and nonprofit organizations. To understand diversity, one must understand the interests of each person involved in public service. How can leaders achieve this goal when the scope of diversity is so vast?

In this chapter, we provide tools to enable leaders to satisfy their public duties while keeping their followers' diversity in mind. The first step is to gain insight into the richness of diversity itself, and to see how diversity can strengthen administrative ability. We also look at activities that inhibit use of diverse characteristics. Third, we discuss how leaders can incorporate diversity by assuming an open, inclusive attitude.

A DEFINITION OF *DIVERSITY*

In defining *diversity*, we note that each person is a unique blend of experience and culture. Although each person has particular qualities, we tend to categorize persons with similar traits. The difficulty with this approach is that we ignore individual characteristics and treat the category as fact.

Millikin and Martins (1996) observe that studies have defined *diversity* with reference to observable traits such as gender or age. Other studies, they note, have defined it according to less visible attributes such as education or tenure. Millikin and Martins note that these studies draw a correlation between observable and underlying attributes.

Although individuals of similar race or gender may often think and act alike, these similarities mask real differences. For example, organizations typically reward the so-called masculine characteristics of leadership, such as aggression and decisiveness (Hofstede, 1991). Some organizations foster this "masculine model" because many high-level officials, who embed their views in company policy, feel these traits are essential to productivity. Yet, even when practiced, this model of leadership does not ensure high productivity. The most effective models are those that combine "masculine" and "feminine" traits according to circumstances. Inflexible adherence to the "masculine" model yields low productivity because it devaluates each worker's abilities, thus lowering motivation.

COMPONENTS OF *DIVERSITY*

The concept of *diversity* enables one to see the differences that make people, events, and ideas unique. In this sense, diversity stands in contrast to the idea of prejudging. Whereas diversity recognizes individuals, prejudice views people with similar backgrounds as identical, thus eclipsing individuality. To understand which conditions promote prejudice, we shall

PREJUDICE: A VICIOUS CYCLE OF CONTRIBUTORS

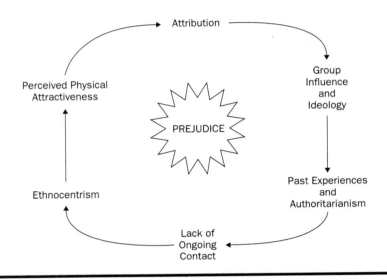

examine the following concepts: (1) Attribution Theory, (2) group influence and ideology, (3) past experiences and authoritarianism, (4) lack of exposure to dissimilar cultures, (5) ethnocentrism, and (6) perceived physical attractiveness (see Figure 7.1).

ATTRIBUTION THEORY

Attribution Theory explains much of prejudice's origin. This theory holds that when individuals have insufficient information on a phenomenon, they will identify with similarities and ignore differences (Heider, 1994). Moreover, the mind links similarities and places them into "bins" for quick access in the future (Kruglanski & Webster, 1995). Such processes are ways of simplifying complex phenomena.

GROUP INFLUENCE AND IDEOLOGY

Prejudice is related to one's level of adherence to the values and attitudes of other group members. Because a strong adherence to a group yields feelings of loyalty and belonging, members see themselves as part of "in-groups," whereas persons having different views belong to "out-groups." This mentality often breeds isolation and tension (Archer, 1988). Stephan and Beame (1978), in testing their notion that in-group members show bias, find that ethnocentrism has a favorable influence on group members when outsiders fail in a task. If outsiders perform well, however, dissimilar values diminish a negative reaction.

A coherent set of beliefs and values comprises an in-group's ideology or mental framework for defining *social reality*. Howard and Pike (1986) find that ideology strongly affects how group members perceive the race and social class of outsiders.

PAST EXPERIENCES AND AUTHORITARIANISM

Zanna (1994) points out that past experiences with out-groups shape negative attitudes, especially among those who have authoritarian worldviews. Authoritarianism is an unquestioned faith people show for institutions that claim to have the "truth." When ambiguous circumstances arise, these people expect authorities to restore order and predictability. Baden (1994) notes that adherence to an authoritarian view strongly affects racial prejudice.

LACK OF EXPOSURE TO DISSIMILAR CULTURES

Cultures that vary widely in worldviews, practices, and attitudes may develop biases toward others. Individuals having limited contact with others from dissimilar cultures may produce strictly defined boundaries between the cultural groups. People may associate with outsiders on a limited basis, or perhaps not at all. Over time, this isolation generates stereotypes that can last for long periods. One example of this is the U.S. government's confinement of ethnic and racial groups to specified compounds: Native Americans being forced onto reservations with westward expansion, and the confinement of Japanese Americans into camps during World War II.

ETHNOCENTRISM

Hofstede (1982) defines these attitudes as *ethnocentrism:* an exaggerated tendency to see one's own group as superior to other groups. One group prejudges another, reacting to them in an automatic, biased way. Triandis (1995) describes *ethnocentrism* as seeing events as "good" if they are similar to things that occur in one's own culture. Stephan, Ageyev, Coates-Schrider, and Stephan (1994) find that ethnocentrism is correlated with a reliance on authoritarian leadership and low self-esteem.

PERCEIVED PHYSICAL ATTRACTIVENESS

A tendency to focus on common or favorable attributes may also produce prejudice. One need only look to television advertisements or magazines that exploit thinness in women, muscularity in men, or flawless skin and teeth. Advertisers try to boost sales by linking attractiveness and their product.

This perceived link between beauty and quality goes beyond the physical. It also extends to what is called "belief in a just world." Dion and Dion

(1997, pp. 775–776) state that a "just world" is where "people get what they deserve and also deserve what they get." They also state that this view rewards attractive people, labeling them "winners," thus encouraging an association between attractiveness and success.

HOW PREJUDICE AFFECTS WORK RELATIONSHIPS

Prejudice affects how people relate to their work and to each other. Taylor Cox (1993) points out that overall productivity suffers when a company fails to recognize diversity, and when workers are insensitive to it. Managers may also contribute to a general mood of segregation and prejudice. At the group level, this climate produces an overemphasis on cultural differences, favoritism, and between-group conflict. These attitudes appear in the very fabric of company policy as well. The result is often low job satisfaction, bias in managing personnel, and low productivity. Some particular outcomes of prejudice are discussed below.

Low Interpersonal Trust

Prejudice can erect barriers to trust. If people feel that others dislike them because of certain ascribed (or hereditary) characteristics, such as skin color or gender, they will not feel accepted. The same can happen for persons with differences in education or social class. This kind of distrust is marked by a mutual hostility that impairs communication and thus the ability to form productive teams (Gibb, 1978).

Individual Motivation

Prejudice dampens motivation. Managers, for instance, may believe that women or African Americans cannot perform complicated tasks. These managers may scrutinize performance, look for errors, or provide limited or even negative feedback. Employees may respond with sabotage, poor performance, or low motivation. Prejudice will affect future work relationships as well (Nachmias, 1985).

Self-Fulfilling Prophecy

When people allow stereotypes to inform their thinking, they expect others to behave according to those preconceived ideas (Cox, 1993). When others behave according to expectation, stereotypes are reinforced. Over time, even the stereotyped person comes to see this behavior as normal and acts accordingly. For example, female managers may be expected to behave emotionally in a crisis. If a woman accepts this as normal, she may fill that role. In so doing, however, she strengthens and perpetuates the stereotype.

DRAWING ROLE AND STATUS BOUNDARIES

There are several ways that prejudice can hinder communication within a company. First, prejudice fosters erroneous thinking because it bases assumptions on limited or biased information. Second, prejudice leads to the formation of factions who have infrequent contact with each other. Third, prejudice leads to typecasting. Over time, biased thinking may infect company policy and appear as discrimination. Unchecked discrimination results in the assignment of "dead-end jobs" based on gender or race (Massey & Denton, 1993). Figure 7.2 illustrates how prejudice affects the careers of the members of an organization.

LEADERSHIP ROLES IN REDUCING BIAS

As already discussed, prejudice appears in a variety of acquired attitudes and actions. *Because prejudice is learned, one of the most effective weapons against it is education.* Leaders assume an active role in combating prejudice by

▪ FIGURE 7–2

HOW PREJUDICE AFFECTS ORGANIZATION MEMBERSHIP AND CAREERS

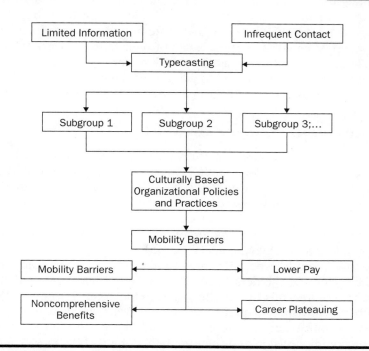

SOURCE: Based on T. Cox (1993). *Cultural diversity in organizations: Theory, research and practice.* San Francisco: Berrett-Kohler.

identifying its effects on workers and organizations and by telling others how prejudice affects task and relationship processes. Leaders also perpetuate, by their own behavior, standards that teach tolerance for individual differences.

Etzioni (1961) calls this leadership process "normative–reeducative"; that is, leaders can bring about change by developing new norms of behavior among followers. Leaders accomplish this by openly sharing visions and purposes with followers. Through reeducating their followers, leaders inspire a commitment to change.

Heifetz (1994, p. 22) describes this sort of reeducation as "adaptive work." By this, he refers to the type of learning that shrinks the gap between the values people hold and the actions they take. Leaders base their influence on building trust and aligning common beliefs with their followers.

Argyris and Schon (1978) point out that leaders may change their followers' biased views by unraveling their "theories-in-use." *Leaders critically confront those attitudes that their followers have adopted.* They must do this in a way that illustrates the harm that bias inflicts on interpersonal relationships. Following confrontation, leaders offer to openly discuss the issues raised (Argyris, 1993). This fosters critical dialogue and helps to establish a common framework of meaning (Gergen & Gergen, 1991).

To get their followers to comply, leaders use both critical and reflective thinking strategies. Tichy and Devanna (1986) address leaders who exploit both the intellect and emotions to produce long-lasting changes in individuals and organizations. They call these leaders "transformational." Leaders change culture by rendering a goal more important for followers. They do this by appealing to a broader range of their followers' needs. They build their followers' confidence as they work toward a goal that the leader has clearly defined. Transformation happens when leaders give followers a chance to ally their own interests with that of the group.

INCLUSIVENESS IN LEADERSHIP

Developing inclusiveness, or recognizing and valuing all group participants, is a critical leadership skill. By considering the contributions of all group members, leader can more successfully weigh options, thus reducing the risk of making a wrong decision. Including all members can also quell hostilities among group members, even at high levels of management. An inclusive approach also promotes a high level of group satisfaction in solving problems and achieving goals (Gardner, 1991).

Inclusiveness is especially important to public sector leaders. Because public sector stakeholders have different needs and goals, public leaders need to acquire skills for juggling diverse viewpoints. In groups that have members with varied expertise and experience, each person has the potential to control agendas and resources. Leaders are therefore catalysts for creating a common vision and then implementing it (Bryson & Crosby, 1992).

In gaining inclusive skills, leaders must understand and recognize cooperative variables. These variables include the willingness of the members to rectify biased information, how much power members share, and how involved members are with outside interests.

VARIABLES IN POWER SHARING

Several variables influence how power is shared among group members. These variables include: motivation and rewards; task requirements; the structure of an organization; interpersonal communication styles; and situational influences.

Motivation and Rewards. As previously discussed, leaders gain their followers' compliance by offering incentives. Followers share power to the extent that their leaders incorporate follower interests into the goals of the project, and to the extent followers trust leaders.

Public leaders often invoke feelings of "public spirit" to invite support among stakeholder groups. Take, for instance, this scenario:

A city manager receives numerous resident complaints on a dangerous intersection near a highway on-ramp. The city manager works with the director of highway safety to identify those in the neighborhood who would be affected. These stakeholders include businesses, residents, and a civic group. After meeting with each group, the manager and director of highway safety generate a list of redesign plans.

Of these ideas, they favor one submitted by a resident who is a civil engineer; a plan that would not only reduce construction costs, but also give additional access to the neighborhood. The manager and director discuss the plan with other groups and make design adjustments according to such needs as noise reduction. In this way, the manager and director gather support for the new plan not only by offering "something for everybody," but also by pointing out that the discussion process benefited the city's interest in efficiency as well.

Task Requirements. Leaders can promote follower cooperation by clarifying task objectives, demonstrating individual accomplishments, and providing sufficient resources. By doing this, leaders reduce the chances that followers will compete for leader attention or for scarce resources. Moreover, by inviting follower suggestions, the leader increases the chances of solving problems. The following example illustrates the importance of task requirements.

In a state agency, two departments manage similar contracts. Department A develops contracts with other governmental agencies and nonprofit organizations. Department B does the same with private firms. Usually, the two departments do not share information and have little employee–employee interaction—except when problems affecting both departments erupt.

In one situation, the problem centers on a client from the government who has made a contract with private vendors. Both Department A and Department B claim control over the contract. In meetings, the department heads trade insults and dredge up old conflicts. The division director meets with each department head separately. The director helps them identify options for how each can use its resources to meet the needs of the client. Once the department heads agree on the best way to assign tasks, the division head writes a contract specifying each department's responsibilities. This contracting process enables the departments to complete these tasks successfully.

Structure of an Organization. In bureaucratic organizations, certain positions have greater status, power, and influence than others. "Top" officials, for instance, have greater prestige than "mid-level" managers, who in turn have greater influence than do "front-line" supervisors. Professionals in specialized positions that are crucial to the agency's primary mission, moreover, wield great power. In addition, the use of power and status in bureaucratic organizations often distorts information and prevents open discussion. The *Challenger* disaster at NASA illustrates this.

Although individuals having similar attributes such as race, gender, age, and socioeconomic class may sometimes think and act similarly, the on-the-surface similarities mask real differences. For instance, organizations typically reward so-called masculine characteristics of leadership, such as aggression, decisiveness, and risk taking (Hofstede, 1991). Because many top organizational leaders value these characteristics on the notion that they are requisite for organizational productivity and because such leaders embed their values in the organization's culture (Schein, 1997), organizations uphold the "masculine model" of leadership. Yet, even when the model is practiced, it does not of itself result in necessarily high productivity. The most effective models are those that combine "masculine" and "feminine" characteristics depending on the needs of followers and situational variations. The adherence to the belief that "masculine" characteristics are superior in achieving organizational goals in spite of individual or circumstantial differences produces error and low productivity. It also results in denigrating individual value, motivation, and productivity.

Interpersonal Communication Styles. Individuals vary in their openness to communications feedback and willingness to disclose thoughts and feelings to others. Individuals who take time to examine their own biases in interpersonal relationships and who learn to share their insights about individuals of diverse characteristics and backgrounds develop human interaction competencies. These competencies are important to leaders, particularly in establishing a relationship of trust with followers. Leaders who develop these competencies create a climate that tolerates openness. Followers are free to question assumptions in others without fear of reprimand. They may also discuss their own ideas with leaders, no matter how different the ideas may be.

Situational Influences. Situations that are out of the ordinary often produce uncertainty and even fear. As leaders and followers confront crises, events that did not happen as expected, or uncontrollable losses, for instance, they may seek cues for understanding in stereotypical or "pat" explanations. This may lead people to blame individuals or members of particular groups for the uncertainties. Animosity may also mount, and those who are blamed may become scapegoats for the uncertainty and fear.

Freyerheim (1994) found that two government leaders who had to explain detrimental effects of an air pollution crisis to constituents were able to avert constituent fear and blame by appointing an interorganizational task force. Meeting for over a year, the task force solicited a wide range of ideas and strategies and developed a common understanding of the crisis. To test their understanding, the task force divided into sub-groups, developed alternative scenarios for how different constituents would react to the crisis, and selected strategies they believed would create a shared meaning. By allowing open, independent, and decentralized discussion, the government leaders enabled a large number of diverse constituents to develop a comprehensive view of the crisis. This gave them a feeling that they could do something about the seemingly overwhelming situation.

SUMMARY

Diversity of individual characteristics and backgrounds can greatly enhance the quality of public programs, products, services, and overall performance. Differing viewpoints provide new ways to solve complex problems that confront government. To gain skills in using diversity, leaders can first understand the richness of diversity. Diversity includes not only inherited characteristics, but also qualities that make up individuals' social identities, such as education, occupation, and socioeconomic class. *Diversity* also refers to differences in interests, needs, and goals that exist, even among followers from similar backgrounds. Leaders can also develop skills to remove obstacles to harmonious follower relationships. Conditions that divide followers include attributional bias, formation of in-group ideologies, authoritarianism, dissimilar cultural norms and practices that lead to infrequent social contact, ethnocentrism, and a belief that people succeed or fail largely on their own efforts.

Underlying many of the obstacles is prejudice: the unwillingness to think of others as unique. In the workplace, prejudice adversely affects work relationships and satisfying work experiences. Some notable outcomes include low interpersonal trust, diminished work motivation, tendencies to behave according to expected role stereotypes, creating and heightening boundaries between individuals and groups, and approving policies and practices that "keep one in one's place." Because prejudice is learned socially, leaders can introduce and reinforce norms and behaviors that produce inclusiveness. *Inclusiveness* refers to the acknowledgment of individual differences, but assumes such differences give uniqueness to individual identity and produce potential benefits to the organizations. Leaders can influence follower adoption of inclusive norms, values, and actions by practicing critical thinking, engaging in social dialogue, and ensuring equal participation. The skills for managing diversity and achieving inclusiveness among followers will be integrated with other skills for problem solving and decision making in Chapter 8.

QUESTIONS FOR THOUGHT AND DISCUSSION

1. What was the last meeting you attended? What was the occasion, and who were some of the people present? Did you become aware of any membership differences (other than obvious ones, such as gender, race, and age)? How did the known differences affect the quality of the meeting content and process?

2. What are some practical ways that leaders can encourage group inclusiveness? Can inclusiveness lead to conflicts?

3. What are some ways laws, regulations, and rules can reflect institutional bias? Can you think of some relevant examples of this from your own experiences? What are some ways that agency leaders can monitor and deal with the existence of institutional bias in their organizations?

CASE DISCUSSION

THE SELECTION PANEL DECISION

TIME: APPROXIMATELY 1 HOUR

DIRECTIONS

Read the following case scenario silently and rank each of the five candidates in terms of whom the selection panel should select. Meeting in a small group, share your rankings. Appoint a selection panel chairperson to lead the group to consensus. At the end of a 30-minute discussion, the chair will report the group's decision and give explanations for the decision.

SCENARIO

You are a member of a selection panel of a federal agency and are meeting to rank the top five candidates for a GS-13 position in program analysis. The position is non-supervisory, and involves making detailed analyses and recommendations independently on complex program evaluation reviews and reports. The reports are re-viewed by the department director and are prepared for the agency head. A bachelor's degree is not required, although the incumbent may substitute years of experience and other educational credentials in lieu of a degree. The incumbent must demonstrate sufficient skills, knowledges, and abilities to perform the tasks at the level.

Five candidates from a pool of 54 applicants were selected as finalists for the position.

Jan Schmidt is a single, 45-year-old Anglo female who just retired from the U.S. Marine Corps. She received several decorations and awards for out-standing performance of duty. Although Jan has no degree, she has taken some college courses through base education and has completed several years of technical military training in program analysis and management. Jan began her career as a clerk typist and worked her way up to supervisor of a large military planning unit before retiring.

Peter Clark is a 28-year-old Anglo male and recent graduate of a master's degree program in management. He had worked for 5 years as a bank accountant, but took a temporary job with the agency this summer when the bank was merged and he lost his position. Peter recently married a financial analyst who is completing her master's degree in another city.

Ray Schupe is a 39-year-old Anglo male who has been employed as a GS-12 program analyst with the agency for 10 years. Ray earned a bachelor of science in horticulture while working part-time at the agency and is taking graduate courses in management at a nearby university. He has received several outstanding performance of duty awards. Ray lives in a committed relationship with a partner of 16 years.

Manny Gonzales, a 32-year old Hispanic male, is a naturalized citizen who has been employed with the agency for 6 years as a programmer/analyst. During this time, Manny earned a degree in history and political science and has been active as a community organizer in his neighborhood. He has served on the agency's prestigious quality assurance and ethics task force, and has earned several performance awards. Manny is married to a law student and has no children.

Rayna Kirby is a 37-year-old African American female and single mother of three school-age children. She is active in church activities, school committees, and volunteers at a local shelter. Rayna earned three outstanding performance awards and is completing a bachelor's degree in statistics at a local university. She has completed several short-term management development programs the agency offers and plans to attend graduate school next year.

CASE STUDY

THE ELDERLY OUTREACH PROGRAM: A ROLE PLAY EXERCISE IN DIVERSITY

TIME: APPROXIMATELY 1 HOUR

DIRECTIONS

In this exercise, you will identify some forms of diversity in a simulated case study exercise. You will also practice some techniques and skills for increasing the use of diversity in group problem solving and decision making.

Read the case study and divide into small groups consisting of seven persons. If there are "extra" players, have them serve as "spotters" for observing the group process and providing constructive feedback. In the group, decide who will play

which roles. On a separate sheet of paper, write a script of words or phrases each character might say. Play these roles in arriving at a group consensus response.

BACKGROUND

The elderly care outreach program is a cooperative program between the state and local governments to provide cost-effective, centralized social service programs. The program began 3 years ago as the result of the campaign by the current governor to reduce costs associated with duplicate programs of recreational programs for elderly poor in small towns and rural areas of the state. After the election, 25 municipalities and rural areas formed a partnership with the state agency. The program is headed at the state level by a director, who reports to the politically appointed department head. Reporting to the director is the deputy director, Chris Petersen. Petersen is responsible for coordinating the programs and services among the agency and local organizations and for supervising a staff of three professionals and five technical and administrative staff.

Just before the last election, the governor formed a coalition with the opposing majority party. Most of these legislators were "fiscal conservatives" who want to cut taxes and reduce government spending. Although the program has saved tax dollars, the fiscally conservative legislators believe it could do more. This year, they are considering reducing expenses by "contracting out" the services to a private sector organization.

To demonstrate that the program has been successful, despite the cuts earlier this year, the governor has called on the agency head to appoint a task force to review and assess the costs and benefits. The purpose of the task force, for this meeting, is to develop a strategy for collecting and analyzing the data. The task force consists of the following people:

Chris Petersen, deputy director of the state department of human services. Chris chairs the task force.

Pat O'Donnell, a program and budget analyst with the state agency. Pat is in charge of analyzing the expenditures and costs of the elderly outreach program and has access to all planning documents, budget expenditures, and performance measures of program outcomes.

Lyn Browne, a health care social worker at the state agency. Lyn has been with the agency for 15 years and had worked for a small town recreational services agency as a social worker supervisor for 9 years prior.

Jackie Thomas, a recreational services manager at the state agency. Before coming to the state agency three years ago, Jackie worked as an intake specialist with one of the community agencies. At the state agency, Jackie has won several performance awards for individual outstanding performance, customer service, innovation, and community leadership excellence.

Casey Long, a community agency social services manager. Casey is responsible for managing the elderly care program, including budgeting and staffing duties, at a local government human services agency. A 24-year employee of the agency, Casey has extensive contacts with various business, civic, and nonprofit groups and organizations having relationships with the elderly care outreach program.

Lee Stickney, a recreational services intake manager with a local government agency. Lee has recently completed a community survey of needs, projected enrollment in the program for the next three to five years, and costs of administration with a local government agency.

Leslie Greenberg, a special assistant with the governor's public relations staff. Leslie has detailed information regarding elderly care services provided by profit, nonprofit, civic, and religious organizations in the state. Leslie has spent 12 years as a news reporter and marketing and public relations professional.

Robin Morales, a professional recreational services employee of a rural community services organization. Robin has worked closely with elderly clients for the past 8 years and understands their needs, the needs of rural social groups, and resources that may be used to augment governmental assistance.

SOME QUESTIONS TO CONSIDER AND DISCUSS

1. What documents need to be reviewed? How can they be accessed and included in the discussion?

2. Who are some key external constituents? What roles might they play in the data collection and analysis?

3. How will the report balance different types of information (such as positive with negative)? How will they be included in the data-collection and analysis strategy?

4. How can the group set goals within the time limits set for the exercise?

5. What roles and responsibilities will group members adopt in the strategy formulation?

QUESTIONS FOR ASSESSING THE GROUP PROCESS

1. What pieces of information were particularly helpful in developing a data-collection and analysis strategy? Who provided the information?

2. What forms of diversity did you encounter? How did diversity help achieve a resolution to strategy formation? How did differences pose obstacles? How were they handled?

3. What role did the leader play in facilitating the strategy formulation discussion? Did the leader provide for inclusiveness in the discussion? If so, how? If not, why not?

4. How much did you feel your own ideas and suggestions were acknowledged and used?

5. Were you satisfied with the overall group strategy? with the ways in which the group worked together?

8

TEAM LEADERSHIP IN THE PUBLIC SECTOR

SYNOPSIS

This chapter points out that using teams is central to developing collaborative leadership, particularly in view of the growing interest in public sector productivity and competition with private corporations. Following a distinction between teams and groups, Chapter 8 describes common task and interpersonal roles leaders play in collective settings. This chapter also describes stages of team evolution and pitfalls typical at each. Identifying conflict as one of the most pervasive impediments to team development, this chapter describes seven types that frequently disrupt teams. Chapter 8 concludes by discussing skills leaders need to manage conflict and enable team members to produce high-quality results.

OBJECTIVES

- To describe differences and similarities in teams and groups
- To describe task and relationship requirements of teams
- To discuss key characteristic stages of team development
- To describe obstacles to team formation and work
- To diagnose team conflict and state strategies that address each

KEY TERMS AND CONCEPTS

group cohesiveness

holding environment

leadership task responsibilities

line teams

staff teams

synergy

team development variables

team orientation stage

types of team conflict:
> *commitment related*
> *goal related*
> *legitimacy related*
> *performance related*
> *personality related*
> *resource related*

INTRODUCTION

Skills for team leadership have become essential. Leaders must be aware of the personalities, motivations, and skills of all involved. They must achieve multiple goals while satisfying multiple stakeholders. In this sense, public sector leadership is more like conducting an orchestra than performing solo. This chapter describes team leadership skills. It discusses the conditions both inside and outside a corporation that promote effectiveness. We will explore key topics such as differentiating groups from teams, promoting behavior favorable to teams, and analyzing team development. Additionally, the chapter provides self-assessment tools and interactive exercises to help readers to apply their skills.

TEAMS AND PUBLIC SECTOR ACCOUNTABILITY

The TQM revolution in industrialized, Western societies, transformed both private and public organizations into "leaner and meaner" enterprises. Team-based models of customer service have become more common as organizations strive to meet current and expected demands. In addition to reducing the cost of services for their clients, public sector organizations must also strive to improve accountability to taxpayers.

This burgeoning interest in team-based productivity, especially in the public sector, has placed heavy demands on leaders. Employee-centered quality improvement teams have been introduced at federal, state, and local levels of government. Public leaders have worked with boards and commissions, and have used ad hoc task groups to resolve problems. This use of teams, however, is a significant change for many public leaders. The scope of their work has widened to the point where they must not only manage their own projects, but must also work with groups to provide public services. A few examples follow.

SELF-MANAGED TEAMS

One example is the use of self-managed teams in Windsor, Connecticut (Rusaw, 1998). In 1990, Windsor began two pilot projects of self-managed teams to integrate customer service and empowerment concepts. Self-managed teams consist of employees responsible for providing holistic services to a particular clientele. The Family Services Unit, for instance, is responsible for providing individuals and families with day care, individual and group counseling, case management, leisure activities, and emergency financial support. The unit does not have a manager, but does have a service unit leader. This person oversees budget and cost accounting of services and coordinates information with the town council, other agencies, and with citizens. The 23-member service unit meets weekly in small, function-specific groups with the service unit leader to plan services, make operating decisions, and discuss needs and opportunities for training (Swift, 1991).

JOINT MANAGEMENT—UNION PROBLEM SOLVING

Phoenix, Arizona initiated the Participative Association of Labor and Management Team (PALM) in 1996 to save tax dollars and avoid a hiring freeze in the city's Water Services Department (Anonymous, 1998). Using reengineering techniques, the PALM team saved $3 million in the first 2 years in reduced chemical and electrical costs with fewer employees. The team consisted of Water Services Department management and representatives of two unions. PALM began with an analysis of work structures, competitiveness assessment, and reengineering planning. In the reengineering phase, the joint labor—management team came into being and developed implementation strategies. Implementation took place in the third phase.

NATIONAL PERFORMANCE REVIEW (NPR) INNOVATION LABORATORY

The U.S. Agency for International Development (USAID) asked its overseas missions for volunteer participation as Country Experimental Laboratories (CEL) during USAID's NPR initiatives. The multidisciplinary teams developed and implemented financial management policies and procedures (Weber, 1997).

GROUPS AND TEAMS

SIMILARITIES AND DIFFERENCES

Although groups and teams are similar on the surface, there are important differences. Both groups and teams are collections of persons possessing varied interests who work toward a single goal. Both demand healthy communication skills, and may have formal or informal leader—member relationships.

However, there are important differences between the two terms. Perhaps the most striking difference is that a team exhibits a strong sense of unity. Although groups may identify purposes and develop plans, teams make a singular effort by coordinating the abilities of each member. Working as a team means working interdependently; that is, relying on the talents of others who will share responsibility for reaching joint goals (Cohen & Bailey, 1997).

Teams also have the distinguishing characteristic of synergy. *Synergy* is the ability of a team to work as a whole unit rather than as a loose collection of individuals. *Synergy* also refers to a leader's ability to let followers assume leadership roles and accept responsibility for the decisions that are made. Synergy allows teams to accomplish a specific goal while maintaining a unique identity. Groups, by contrast, are merely divisions of a larger organization, focusing on a product that will be credited to individuals, not a unified team (Katzenbach & Smith, 1993).

STAFF AND LINE TEAMS

Although all teams have a singular purpose, we can break them down into categories. Sundstrom, DeMeuse, and Futrell (1990) identify four different classifications: (1) advice and involvement teams, (2) production and service teams, (3) project and development teams, and (4) action and negotiation teams. Cohen and Bailey (1997) group these into two broad categories based on staff and line responsibilities. *Staff responsibilities* are those taken on by managers who give advice and make supervisory decisions. *Line responsibilities,* by contrast, belong to those who make their own decisions and plans. In the public sector, examples of staff teams include quality improvement teams and task forces. Line teams are self-managed entities.

TEAM LEADERSHIP SKILLS

LEADERSHIP SKILLS: TASK AND RELATIONSHIP REQUIREMENTS

To endow workers with the ability to realize a unified goal, leaders need skills in two essential areas. The first area, *task requirements,* simply means that the leader must identify how a team will reach a goal. The second category, *human requirements,* calls upon a leader to assess how members will react to goals, expectations, and the needs of others. A successful leader satisfies both these requirements.

COMMON TASK REQUIREMENTS AND LEADERSHIP SKILLS

Leaders help realize goals. To this end, leaders must articulate specific goals, and even set subgoals or milestones. They must also assign individual tasks and provide members with sufficient authority to act on their own. In order to satisfy task requirements, leaders need to have a wide range of skills:

Vision. Leaders need to know how a task fits into the broader mission of the organization.

Goal Translation. Leaders must be able to articulate the vision to all members so they understand how their individual efforts will contribute to an overall purpose.

Analyze Ideas and Information. Leaders help members identify problems and provide resources for developing solutions.

Agenda Building. Leaders present problems for team consideration and define the steps needed to solve them.

Solution Finding and Agreement. Leaders teach critical-thinking and problem-solving skills. They involve members in research and decision making, and establish a common ground for reaching consensus.

Focus on Task at Hand. Leaders keep team members' attention riveted on their goals. Leaders also review members' contributions to task goals to prevent them from straying to side issues. An important leadership skill is giving members a sense that they have completed subgoals on the route to a larger goal.

Stimulate Discussion. Leaders solicit members' opinions, encourage idea sharing, and provide the specific information members need to solve problems.

Clarify Information. Leaders reduce confusion by asking members to elaborate on their ideas. They prompt them to restate arguments, define terms, and combine ideas to form a more unified, comprehensive vision.

TYPICAL RELATIONSHIP GOALS AND LEADERSHIP SKILLS

Because teams have to coordinate individual efforts toward a single goal, members must have the ability to work well with others. Healthy working relationships result when people learn to define standards for acceptable conduct. In such a setting, workers learn to support each other and resolve personal conflicts. They celebrate successes, profit from mistakes, and establish trust.

Although good relationships encourage success, team members may be ineffectual unless they derive satisfaction from working together. Leaders must spend a great deal of time building these relationships. Members must develop trust for the leader, for the organization, and for each other. The leader therefore plays a central role in the early and late stages of team development. Leaders help prevent the confusion and conflict that can derail a team's purpose. Some important leadership skills in this area are as follows.

Promoting Cohesiveness. Leaders foster a sense of team identity by focusing on a goal that members find meaningful. They encourage the involvement of each member, and promote mutual respect.

Resolving Conflict. Leaders recognize disagreements among members and channel these disagreements into creative solutions. Leaders also identify individual interests that hinder overall team success. Leaders actively resolve conflicts by removing potential obstacles to achieving the goal.

Satisfying Individual Needs. Leaders accept that people join teams to meet their own needs. Persons may be motivated by a need to derive satisfaction from their job, to advance their careers, or to gain recognition. In helping individuals to reach personal goals within team contexts, leaders help foster trust, commitment, and a sense of community.

STAGES OF TEAM DEVELOPMENT

In reaching common goals and coordinating members' efforts, teams pass through several stages of development. The stages evolve as teams resolve conflicts, develop healthy work relationships, and contribute to the completion of tasks (Henderson-Loney, 1996). Although the descriptions and numbers of stages vary in previous leadership studies (Luft, 1984), some common areas of stage development follow.

Stage 1: Orientation. As teams form, they require specific information from the leader on what is expected of them, why the team was selected, and how to coordinate tasks interdependently. At the same time, leaders are expected to relieve tensions associated with forming new relationships. Members may initially distrust a new coworker and wonder what policies will help them work together. In the first stage, people depend heavily on the leader. Leaders need to provide much information, encouragement, and rewards to workers. They must stimulate motivation through vision and mutual trust.

Stage 2: Conflict. In their working relationships, team members may experience a variety of conflicts. Many are marked by a competition for resources, such as information, materials, and technology. Members may also vie for power and influence as they claim their stakes. Moreover, conflicts may erupt within groups, as factions and coalitions form to assert or defend ideas. Finally, conflicts may arise with people outside the team, such as departmental leaders or political groups.

Stage 3: Coming to Terms. Team members may realize that conflict prevents them from reaching individual and corporate goals. To resolve differences, members may impose their own form of law and order. Thus members adhere to a set of informal rules. Although these rules may be tacit, a leader often helps resolve a conflict by establishing a written contract. This way, leaders can help members evaluate their earlier agreements when new conflicts arise.

Stage 4: Synergy. When team members resolve conflict through unspoken or written agreements, they are free to work toward a common goal. Because conflict no longer consumes their energy, team members concentrate on the purposes for which they were assembled. The new focus is often sharing resources to achieve mutual ends. The leader's role is to renew a common vision and to provide team members with resources. In realizing that collaboration encourages desirable results, team members take on projects with greater energy and productivity.

Stage 5: Unity and Parting. When team members realize that collaboration has brought mutually satisfying success, they develop affinity. Friendships deepen when members cease regarding themselves as individuals with independent goals, but rather as comrades with a single purpose. After the goal has been reached, however, workers may experience tension. Departing from associates to life outside the team may be difficult. To help them adjust, leaders can remind members of their success and reward them. Members may also continue relationships, even after the task has ended.

PREDICTABLE TEAM CRISES

Drexler, Sibbet, and Forrester (1990) point out that as teams pass through stages of development, they encounter fairly predictable crises. These turning points are questions that team members have, which, if left unaddressed by the leader, produce conflict and regression (see Table 8.1 p. 146). The leader must understand these typical issues and help team members recover purposes as well as inspire them to advance. By understanding the concerns of team members at each stage of development, leaders can prepare for possible obstacles to the team's functioning. Certain conditions trigger conflict. Often, conflicts arise from cycles of fear and mistrust: Fear leads to mistrust, mistrust to fear. Depending on the type of problem confronting the team, fear and mistrust can inhibit progress toward both task- and relationship-based goals.

CONDITIONS BLOCKING TEAM PROGRESS

Some key conditions that block team progress are described below.

Fear. Individuals may resist participation because they are fearful. They may not wish to disclose personal information, or may have experienced rejection in the past, especially from certain members. In addition, they may feel uncertain to how others will respond to their ideas.

Leaders may help members overcome fear by using both task- and relationship-oriented skills. If members are apprehensive because they do not have a clear goal, leaders can clarify it. A leader must do this

. TABLE 8–1

STAGES OF TEAM PERFORMANCE

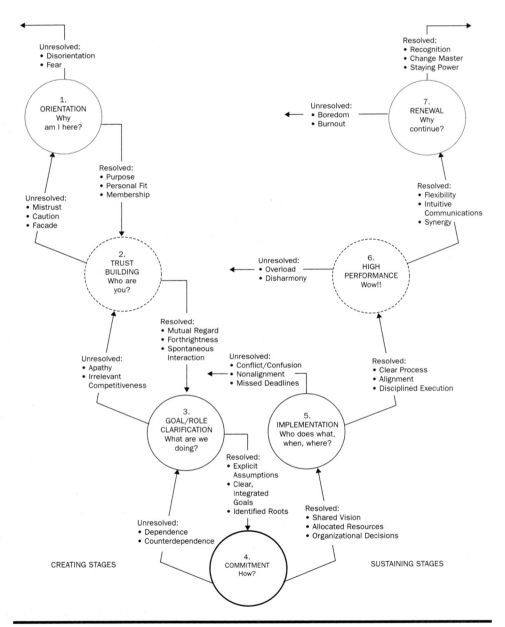

SOURCE: A. B. Drexler, D. Sibbet, and R. H. Forrester (1988). The team performance model. In W. B. Reddy (Ed.), *Team building*. San Diego: University Associates, p. 49. Used by permission.

Drexler/Sibbet Team Performance™ Model.

frequently because objectives can become clouded when workers focus too narrowly on specific tasks. Moreover, leaders can reassure fearful members by identifying and rewarding their skills. If members lack special skills for a task, leaders may teach them the skills through group or individual coaching.

Mistrust. Developing trust among members is an ongoing process. People need to believe that they will not be discouraged, abused, or tricked when working with others. Mistrust can raise latent conflicts to the surface at any stage of team development. Unless leaders continually reinforce mutual trust, team members can become locked into a holding pattern of conflict.

Leaders can build trust by making members feel they belong to the team. Leaders give individuals support and recognition. They also conduct mini training sessions throughout the development of the team. These sessions should encourage giving constructive feedback, learning to support one another, and a "leveling" of doubts. Early in team formation, leaders can help team members to get to know one another by using thorough but nonthreatening exercises. The exercise, "Team Building at Headquarters," at the end of this chapter shows how leaders can help members reduce their anxiety and open up to others.

SIX TYPES OF TEAM CONFLICT

We can identify six types of conflict that arise from fear and distrust:

1. goal related
2. commitment related
3. resource related
4. performance related
5. legitimacy related
6. personality related

These types of conflict may appear simultaneously. For example, goal-related conflict may result from individuals not having clearly defined objectives. Leaders may then encourage the team to work together to set goals. However, if antagonistic members dominate this process, a leader may step in to resolve disputes. Some types of conflict are discussed in detail below.

GOAL-RELATED CONFLICT

Goal-related conflict arises when members lack clearly defined roles and when there are cross-purposes in how to do a task (Yank, Barber, & Spradlin,

1994). This tension may result in forming coalitions, competitiveness, or withdrawal. It may also lead to suppressing information, delaying decisions, diverting the main discussion to trivial details, and violating the chain of command.

Leaders may resolve goal-related conflict through clarifying assignments and tasks. Specifically written descriptions help. Moreover, leaders must often mediate when conflicts erupt. Important mediation skills include revealing hidden assumptions, listening for common interests, and facilitating compromise.

COMMITMENT-RELATED CONFLICT

The ability of a team to assume responsibility for its success rests on several commitment-related conditions. First, when team members feel their needs for recognition and self-fulfillment are not met, they may put little effort into a task and perform poorly. Second, team members may believe their work is futile, especially if they feel their efforts are being ignored. Third, the team may lack commitment; that is, they may feel overwhelmed or unprepared to meet management's expectations. They may also feel pressured by people outside the team, thus losing sight of their own objectives.

Leaders can encourage members to become more deeply committed to task- and relationship-based goals using several techniques. One of the most important is involvement, which enables team members to share their values and goals. In so doing, they often exceed their own expectations, finding creative solutions to a variety of technical problems (Lawler, 1986). Further, the personal discretion used in decision making allows the team as a whole to address social problems confronting it (Walton, 1985).

Leaders can also reinforce the purpose and importance of the team's efforts. Communication—formal or informal—should be an ongoing process. One important way to sustain communication is through frequent meetings. In these meetings, a leader must give new information, seek opinions, and describe potential problems with the project. Another way to communicate is by understanding team members' interests, and satisfying these as adequately as possible. Still another is by reminding team members of the benefits that will accrue for their efforts.

RESOURCE-RELATED CONFLICT

Team members may balk at a project because they lack material or technological resources. Material resources can include funding, information systems, or even space availability. Technological resources can be the knowledge or skills needed for a task. When resources are deficient, serious problems arise. For example, insufficient funding can cause competition and conflict. These types of conflict can result in poor performance, discouragement, or overdependency on leaders.

Leaders may generate resources to help team members to set and meet challenging goals. It may be necessary to train team members in basic problem-solving skills. Leaders themselves may also use creative problem-solving methods to optimize limited resources. Further, leaders can give advice and support to outside organizations in exchange for resources. Also, leaders may request in writing that team supervisors adjust work assignments according to resource availability.

PERFORMANCE-RELATED CONFLICT

One of the fundamental goals of a team is to instill self-leadership. This means that team members would learn to assume responsibility for achieving goals by supporting each other despite personality differences. If team members do not develop such responsibility, several problems can result. Some members who feel overloaded may eventually "burn out." Other members may become too reliant on the leader or other team members. This may lead to coalitions that sabotage a leader's efforts. It may also produce friction between teams, stifling creativity and performance.

Leaders can encourage team members to take responsibility in several ways. One is by consistently and fairly rewarding each member's contributions—even minor ones. Further, leaders may praise the team as a whole for meeting important milestones in the project. Leaders can acknowledge these achievements and use them to encourage progress toward the final goal.

Leaders can also create what Heifetz (1994, p. 104) calls a "holding environment." A holding environment is a relationship that will "hold the attention of another and facilitate adaptive work." Heifetz defines "adaptive work" (p. 22) as the skill of adapting to others who have different values, and a way to "diminish the gap between the values people stand for and the reality they face." Leaders build this kind of environment by teaching team members to value their own contributions and apply this confidence to future projects. Pointing out the value of their work helps members to derive satisfaction in having contributed to a worthwhile goal. In all, holding environments are based on trust. At the same time, they encourage members to manage their own skills to benefit the whole.

LEGITIMACY-RELATED CONFLICT

Legitimacy refers to the authority needed to make and implement decisions. A common stumbling block for teams is having the ability to choose a course of action without having the authority to carry it out. That is, managers often reject a team's recommendation. A similar stalemate occurs when legislation gives team members the proper authority, but denies them the ability to make an informed decision. For instance, regulations may be so convoluted or contradictory that team members make inadequate decisions.

To minimize these frustrations, leaders should get clear definitions from legislators on where authority lies. Leaders can then set reachable goals that help members to focus their energy in a productive direction. Additionally, leaders may research legislative regulations so that team members will have crisp guidelines for interpretation.

PERSONALITY-RELATED CONFLICT

Team members may clash with one another because of personality differences. There may be various "difficult" people on the team. For example, a member may dominate discussions or refuse to accept criticism. The opposite type, those who say very little, may be overly sensitive to remarks that are not intended as critical.

Difficulties arise from other personality types as well. Highly agreeable people, for instance, who appear warm and supportive, may harbor latent anger. They often withhold valuable criticism so as to fit in with the group. This characteristic, sometimes called "groupthink," appears in Janis and Mann's (1977) study. Dominating members were able to steer others into accepting their ideas through subtle intimidation. Those who could have disagreed but did not feared ostracism. They therefore took a safer path by agreeing to the consensus. A summary of Janis and Mann's "groupthink" characteristics appears in Table 8.2.

Leaders may use a variety of tactics to handle specific types of difficult people. Domineering types require assertive techniques. Leaders need to lay down clear rules approved by the entire group. Leaders must also intervene

▪ TABLE 8–2

"GROUPTHINK"

Characteristics	Ways to Reduce Groupthink
1. invulnerability	1. assure neutrality of planning group
2. discounting rational warnings	2. establish several outside planning groups
3. belief in inherent morality of the group	3. deliberate findings with own hierarchical unit
4. group holds stereotypes that reduce anxiety	4. invite outside experts
5. group pressures doubters	5. play "devil's advocate"
6. avoid self-censorship	6. survey rivals' intentions: construct alternative scenarios
7. share illusion of unanimity	7. appoint separate subgroups to discuss alternatives
8. "mindguards" protect leader from adverse information	8. examine residual doubt

FROM: I. L. Janis and L. Mann, *Decision making: A psychological analysis of conflict, choice, and commitment.* New York: The Free Press, 1977.

before this type has taken over. Further, leaders may encourage silent types to speak up and by soliciting their opinions, rewarding them for contributing, and assigning them tasks they can do well.

SUMMARY

With an increasing variety of teams in government, leaders require skills that will ensure they meet public expectations. Leaders must also use these skills to foster growth and satisfaction in team members. Leaders recognize that teams are not loose collections of people, but rather a collection of interdependent persons working to reach a unified goal. Each team member, including the leader, has the responsibility not only to reach a certain goal, but also to help other members gain satisfaction from the work.

In addition to self-leadership, two types of skills are necessary for the team's success: task and relationship skills. Task skills include identifying a unified goal and translating this vision into specific objectives. Task skills also entail carefully analyzing information, assessing problems, and creatively seeking solutions. Leaders also help members to reach goals by focusing their attention on their work. They also stimulate problem-solving discussions, and clarify information to help members make informed decisions.

Personal relationships play an important role in a successful team. Leaders encourage these relationships while fostering a team identity by pointing out mutually meaningful beliefs. Further, leaders recognize that fear and mistrust breed conflicts that can thwart the team's efforts. Conflicts centered in fear and mistrust manifest themselves in the following ways: tensions relative to reaching goals, commitment levels, resource availability, performance, amounts of authority, and personality differences.

Conflict can appear at any stage of team development. These stages emerge as members attempt to resolve a number of questions. In the early life of a team, for instance, members seek to understand the motives and talents of other members while gauging their possible threat to the team's goal. In later stages, after the members discuss these concerns—how possible threats can affect other members, and how those threats can be defused—they are free to perform. Disburdened of conflict, team members perform with synergy. This helps them to perform up to their expectations, and even to outstrip them. While each team member remains an individual worker, they recognize a unique team identity as well. This identity often lingers, even after the team disbands.

In mastering skills for developing teams in the public sector, leaders play a unique role. This role requires a variety of skills, including task and personal skills.

First, a leader must have a vision and the ability to communicate it. Leaders translate this vision into reality and a given reality into a guiding vision. The success of this depends not only on leaders' judgment, but also on their followers' needs.

Second, leaders encourage commitment through involvement. Leaders provide resources that team members can use to achieve superior results. In order to create a smooth workflow, leaders must exploit the skills of each member while tapping hidden resources in their organization. Leaders clarify information to help members bring a goal to fruition. Leaders keep members informed and mentor them in preparation for challenges. Moreover, leaders seek out feedback from both team members and those affected by the team's decisions.

Third, leaders foster a sense of community. When leaders perceive that members feel a sense of futility, disillusionment, or burnout, leaders offer encouragement. This reminds workers of the importance of their roles, and gives meaning to their efforts.

Finally, leaders make the team more accountable by keeping records of their accomplishments and giving them feedback. They use information not only to track their progress, but also to fulfill obligations.

QUESTIONS FOR THOUGHT AND DISCUSSION

1. Think of a successful team experience you have had either recently or when you were growing up. What goals did the team have? How were they set? What (or who) helped you achieve the goals? What obstacles did the team encounter? How were they managed?

2. What are some benefits of teamwork in government?

3. What, in your opinion, must leaders do to enable teams to accomplish abstract, complex, or long-range goals?

4. Can teams improve public organization productivity? If so, what are some "necessary" and "sufficient" conditions for this? What leadership roles and responsibilities need to be brought to bear in this effort?

5. What are some ways that organization conflict may be resolved using third-party interventions? What are some examples of effectiveness that you know and can share? In your opinion, what made the interventions successful?

CASE STUDY

TEAM BUILDING AT HEADQUARTERS: A SIMULATION

BACKGROUND

Relationships between the Department of X and field offices had always been tense. But things came to a head in the headquarters training division office shortly after Dale Smith, a GS-15, took over as director.

In Dale's 15-year tenure, Dale knew the familiar complaints. Field offices saw headquarters as issuing directives without fully understanding particular local conditions. Headquarters, however, viewed the field offices as lacking a "big picture" perspective; they just didn't understand the national scope of legislation. Emotions flared between the two, sometimes culminating in traded slings and charges of incompetence. Dale had a file filled with war stories. Some came from Dale's 10 years as a field employee; others occurred after her arrival at headquarters 5 years ago. Dale knew both sides, and, following a series of promotions at headquarters, was determined to make a difference in the relationships.

Dale's chance came after Dale and staff had developed a management training program for all department managers and supervisors. Dale thought the finished piece was impressive, and was eager to show it off as the new director. It contained state-of-the-art, computer-based simulations, video clips, and special exercises that would really spark dialogue between headquarters and field managers. Dale distributed the training program and was ready to implement it department-wide.

Dale and staff flew to Atlanta for the pilot. But the Atlanta line manager, who was responsible for implementing the training, was not impressed. After he had shown Dale and the headquarters staff the newly renovated Atlanta office and treated them to lunch at one of the city's finest restaurants, he brought them back to the office. With only 90 minutes before Dale's plane was to leave, Dale pressed the manager about the training program.

"Dale," the manager said, "you have done a great job. But we don't have the fancy stuff you have here in Atlanta. Besides, our people see things a bit differently. So I developed my own training pro-gram and we'll kick it off next week. That way, I know it will be successful. I also talked with the other field officers, and I think they'll all tell you the same thing."

Still shocked on the flight back to Washington, but realizing headquarters could not compel the field offices to use the materials despite its quality, Dale decided that a headquarters–field office retreat was urgently needed.

DIRECTIONS

As members of Dale's staff, your task is to plan the retreat. To accomplish this, complete the "Cognitive Style Inventory" and divide into small groups according to individuals' preferred cognitive styles. At least one group should consist of one dominant style, while at least one other group should consist of mixed styles. Each group will have approximately 30 minutes to develop a plan for the retreat. Each group should select a spokesperson to summarize the group's plan in a report to the larger group.

QUESTIONS FOR REFLECTION

1. How did the groups vary in terms of the designs they produced? Were cognitive styles evident in the designs? Did the designs reflect a dominant style, or were different styles evident?

2. How easy (or how difficult) was it to make decisions in your group? How were different cognitive styles integrated? How did differences affect the team's relationship and task goals?

3. What are some ways that you, as a public leader, can use different cognitive styles in some team activities with which you are familiar?

THE COGNITIVE STYLE INVENTORY

Lorna R Martin

DIRECTIONS

For each of the statements in this inventory, refer to the following key and decide which number corresponds to your level of agreement with the statement; then write that number in the blank to the left of the statement.

KEY: 1 = STRONGLY DISAGREE, 2 = DISAGREE, 3 = UNDECIDED, 4 = AGREE, 5 = STRONGLY AGREE

_____ A   I get a "feel" for a problem or try to "see" it before I attempt a solution.

_____ B   I analyze a problem or situation to determine whether or not the facts add up.

_____ C   I create pictorial diagrams/visual images while problem solving.

_____ D   I have a classification system ("pigeonholes") where I store information as I solve a problem.

_____ E   I catch myself talking aloud as I work on problems.

_____ F   I solve a problem by first "spotlighting" or focusing on the critical issues.

_____ G   I solve a problem by first "floodlighting" or broadening the scope of the problem.

_____ H   I attack a problem in a step-by-step, sequential, and orderly fashion.

_____ I   I attack a problem by examining it in its entirety before I look at its parts.

_____ J   The most efficient and effective way to deal with a problem is logically and rationally.

_____ K   The most efficient and effective way to deal with a problem is to follow one's "gut" instinct.

_____ L   I carefully solve a problem by ordering, combining, or building its parts in order to generate a solution for the whole problem.

_____ M   I carefully solve a problem by examining it in its entirety, in relationship to its parts, before I proceed.

_____ N   All problems have predetermined, "best" or "right" answers in a given set of circumstances.

_____ 0   All problems are open ended by nature, allowing for many possible answers or solutions.

_____ P   I store volumes of data in my memory, much like a computer, by compartmentalizing each entry for easy recall.

_____ Q   I store a lot of data in my memory by adding to the image that is already there and then determining how the information "fits" (like the relationship between a jigsaw puzzle and its individual pieces).

_____ R   Before solving a problem, I tend to look for a plan or method for solving it.

_____ S   I generally rely on "hunches," gut feelings, and other nonverbal cues to help me in the problem-solving process.

_____ T   I generally rely on facts and data when problem solving.

_____ U   I create and discard alternatives quickly.

_____ V   I generally conduct an ordered search for additional information and carefully select the sources of data.

SOURCE: From _The 1989 annual: Developing human resources_ (pp. 123–140). Used by permission.

_____ W   I consider a number of alternatives and options simultaneously.

_____ X   I tend to define the specific constraints of a problem early in the problem-solving process.

_____ Y   When analyzing a problem, I seem to jump from one step to another and back again.

_____ Z   When analyzing a problem, I seem to progress from one step to another in a sequential way.

_____ AA   I generally examine many sources of data, letting my eyes "play" over the information while searching for guiding clues.

_____ BB   When I work on a problem involving a complex situation, I break it into a series of smaller, more manageable blocks.

_____ CC   I seem to return to the same source of data several times, deriving different insights each time.

_____ DD   I gather data methodically, at a chosen level of detail, and in a logical sequence.

_____ EE   I generally sense the size and scope of a problem to produce the "whole picture."

_____ FF   When I solve a problem, my approach is detailed and organized; as a result, arriving at a solution is generally a time-consuming process.

_____ GG   I am able to solve a problem quickly and effectively; I do not spend a great deal of time on the problem-solving process.

_____ HH   I have an excellent memory and a good aptitude for mathematics.

_____ II   I am comfortable with uncertainty and ambiguity.

_____ JJ   I would describe myself—and so would others—as predictable and reliable.

_____ KK   I have an abundance of ideas and an inquisitive nature.

_____ LL   It is my nature to avoid "making waves" with change.

_____ MM   I would describe myself—as would others—as a risk taker.

_____ NN   I am comfortable with the status quo; "new ways" are not always better ways.

SCORING SHEET

Instructions: Transfer your inventory responses to the appropriate blanks below. Add the numbers in each column, and record the totals in the blanks provided.

_____ A	_____ B
_____ C	_____ D
_____ E	_____ F
_____ G	_____ H
_____ I	_____ J
_____ K	_____ L
_____ M	_____ N
_____ 0	_____ P
_____ Q	_____ R
_____ S	_____ T
_____ U	_____ V
_____ W	_____ X
_____ Y	_____ Z
_____ AA	_____ BB
_____ CC	_____ DD
_____ EE	_____ FF

_____GG		_____HH	
_____II		_____JJ	
_____KK		_____LL	
_____MM		_____NN	

_____Total Intuitive Score   _____Total Systematic Score

INTERPRETATION SHEET

Place an "X" in the appropriate block to indicate your degree of cognitive specialization.

Your Systematic Score:
High	> 81	_____
Medium-High	71–80	_____
Medium-Low	61–70	_____
Low	< 60	_____

Your Intuitive Score:
High	> 81	_____
Medium-High	71–80	_____
Medium-Low	61–70	_____
Low	< 60	_____

Instructions: Scan the numbers listed below, one style at a time, until you find a style that lists your degree of systematic specialization as well as your degree of intuitive specialization. The style that lists both is your own cognitive style. For each style, the more extreme degrees of that style are listed at the top.

Systematic Score	**Intuitive Score**
Systematic Style:	
High > 81	Low < 60
High > 81	Medium-Low 61–70
Medium-High 71–80	Low < 60
Intuitive Style:	
Low < 60	High> 81
Medium-Low 61–70	High> 81
Low < 60	Medium-High 71–80
Integrated Style:	
High > 81	High > 81
High > 81	Medium-High 71–80
Medium-High 71–80	High > 81
Undifferentiated Style:	
Low < 60	Low < 60
Medium-Low 61–70	Low < 60
Low < 60	Medium-Low 61–70
Split Style:	
Medium-High 71–80	Medium-High 71–80
Medium-High 71–80	Medium-Low 61–70
Medium-Low 61–70	Medium-High 71–80
Medium-Low 61–70	Medium-Low 61–70

DESCRIPTIONS

Systematic Style. An individual identified as having a systematic style is one who rates high on the Systematic Scale and low on the Intuitive Scale. According to findings in the Harvard studies, an individual who typically operates with a systematic style uses a well-defined, step-by-step approach when solving a problem; looks for an overall method or programmatic approach; and then makes an overall plan for solving the problem.

Intuitive Style. An individual who rates low on the Systematic Scale and high on the Intuitive Scale is described as having an intuitive style. Someone whose style is intuitive uses an unpredictable ordering of analytical steps when solving a problem, relies on experience patterns characterized by nonverbalized cues or hunches, and explores and abandons alternatives quickly.

Integrated Style. A person with an integrated style rates high on both scales and is able to change styles quickly and easily. Such style changes appear to be subconscious and take place in a matter of seconds. A result of this "rapid-fire" ability is that it appears to generate an energy and a proactive approach to problem solving. In fact, individuals with an integrated style are often referred to as "problem seekers" because they consistently attempt to identify potential problems as well as opportunities in order to find better ways of doing things.

Undifferentiated Style. An individual who rates low on both the Systematic and the Intuitive Scale is described as having undifferentiated cognitive behavior. Such an individual appears not to distinguish or differentiate between the two style extremes and therefore appears not to display a style. In fact, in a problem-solving or learning situation, he or she may exhibit a receptivity to instructions or guidelines from outside sources. Undifferentiated individuals tend to be withdrawn, passive, and reflective, and often look to others for problem-solving strategies.

Split Style. An individual who rates in the middle range on both the Systematic and the Intuitive Scale is considered to have a split style involving fairly equal (average) degrees of systematic and intuitive specialization. At first glance the Split Style appears to differ from the Integrated Style only in the degree of specialization. However, persons with a split style do not possess an integrated behavioral response; instead, they exhibit each separate dimension in completely different settings, using only one style at a time based on the nature of their tasks or their work groups. In other words, they consciously respond to problem solving and learning situations by selecting the most appropriate style.

Due to the fact that an assessment score identifying a Split Style generally indicates an equal degree of both dimensions, it might be assumed that both dimensions would be equally exhibited. However, actual observational findings have not produced this result. As a rule, in stressful situations, one dimension appears to dominate, generally as a result of habit. It has been significant that many individuals exhibiting this particular cognitive style have indicated that they were in the process of a cognitive transition; they were moving into a new area of cognitive specialization and were "trying out new behaviors and skills."

Descriptors of Style	Language Patterns	Nonverbal Patterns
Systematic Style: Convergent thinker Concrete Highly structured Logical Rational Ordered Linear Step-by-step approach Concentrates on facts, figures, and data Reduces problems to workable segments Product focused Deductive Very conscious of approach Uses a well-defined method or plan for solving a problem Uses a highly sequential process Handles a problem by breaking it down into a series of smaller (often hierarchical) and manageable components	"Let's examine the facts" "The data indicate" "The specific objectives must be measurable" "Here are my points: A, B, C,..." "What's your rationale?" "Where's the logic in that?" "Do the following: 1, 2, 3,..." "I have to figure this out carefully before I can come to a conclusion"	Creates an endless list Establishes a chronological ordering of steps to be taken Spends a great deal of time on detail Often belabors a point or step of the process before proceeding to the next step

	Descriptors of Style	Language Patterns	Nonverbal Patterns
Intuitive Style:	Divergent thinker Global Visual Spontaneous Concentrates on ideas and feelings Emotion based Process focused Inductive Not consciously aware of approach, but does use a method that is generally driven by experience Keeps the overall problem in mind Frequently redefines the problem Looks at the "the big picture" or the entirety of the problem	"Somehow my gut tells me…" "I have a sense that…" "Let's look at the whole picture" "You're not looking at the big picture" "The solution is simple" "Common sense dictates" "I see the answer, but I don't know how I got it"	Very visual in approach "Plays" with (pours over) data Can appear to be disorganized Thinks with eyes; has to see the problem Frequently draws or graphically displays the problem or alternative solution continually
Integrated Style:	Has highly developed, dual cognitive specialties Is highly flexible and adaptable; alternates easily and quickly from one specialty to another Exhibits high degrees of internal locus of control Looks for a vision of the future.	"I'm just as concerned about the process as I am about the product" "Before we establish measurable objectives, we should develop a philosophy" Looks for a vision of the future "Our objectives should be consistent with that philosophy." "I have the answer, but I need to determine how I arrived at it"	Active Alert High participation and involvement Frequently acts as facilitator or interpreter of language in groups Appears to be comfortable with disorganized "organization" Creative, innovative Proactive

(continued)

	Descriptors of Style	Language Patterns	Nonverbal Patterns
Undifferentiated Style:	Receptive Is not a problem-solving specialist; does not exhibit a specific specialty Passive Reflective Relies heavily on rules, procedures, instructions, suggestions, or guidelines Reacts to the problem or stimulus and does not impose a process on the problem Exhibits high degrees of external locus of control Has difficulty making decisions Procrastinates; delays action	"I don't need to know the whys, whens, and wherefores. Just tell me what you want me to do" "I don't ask questions; I just do what I'm told" "Tell me exactly what you want to have done"	Passive, mostly nonverbal Reflective Low involvement Confluent Waits patiently for specific directions
Split Style:	Has approximately equal degrees of systematic and intuitive style that are average/medium in terms of degrees of intensity Styles are used as completely separate entities Styles are not at all integrated and are consciously selected for each specific situation Out of habit, one style is used more often than the others	Pattern changes according to the style being used at the time of observation Generally an individual with a split style is in the process of a cognitive transition involving building new strengths and skills in the dimension that is perceived to be the weaker of the two (systematic or intuitive)	Pattern changes according to the style being used at the time of observation Generally an individual with a split style is in the process of a cognitive transition involving building new strengths and skills in the dimension that is perceived to be the weaker of the two (systematic or intuitive)

9

LEADING CONFLICT RESOLUTION IN PUBLIC ORGANIZATIONS

SYNOPSIS

Expanding on the use of conflict resolution strategies leaders may use in team building, this chapter describes in greater depth the concept of conflict and relates it to establishing collaborative relationships in nonteam settings. This chapter emphasizes the management of conflict among a myriad of external public organization stakeholders and constituents. In particular, Chapter 9 describes stages and levels of conflict. It also discusses typical responses. Using techniques from Fisher and Ury's (1991) principled negotiation strategy, this chapter describes some ways leaders may achieve ends that benefit both their interests and those of stakeholders.

OBJECTIVES

- To describe stages of conflict
- To describe conflict sources in individual, interpersonal, organizational, and societal contexts
- To state five preferred responses to conflict
- To describe the process of principled investigation in resolving conflict
- To evaluate situational conditions surrounding choices of conflict resolution

KEY TERMS AND CONCEPTS

cognitive dissonance

principled negotiation

responses to conflict
 accommodating
 avoiding
 collaborating
 competing
 compromising

stages of conflict
  aftermath
  felt
  latent
  manifest
  perceived

"wicked" problems

INTRODUCTION

Managing conflict in public organizations is a critical leadership skill that demands an understanding of diverse elements. A leader must not only have insight into the motivations of disputants, but also must adapt to each circumstance in resolving conflict. Many public policies are based on the democratic idea of conflict. New programs, policies, or agencies are the result of extensive debate and compromise at all levels of government. Conflict is common in government because power rests with diverse people and agencies. Resolving conflict becomes difficult for leaders because they lack direct control over programs or policies.

In this chapter, we shall define *conflict* and see how the complexity of the public sector breeds conflict. We shall examine some approaches public leaders may use in resolving conflict. A case study and a summary of resolution styles provide further understanding of conflict management.

WHAT IS CONFLICT?

When people hear the word *conflict,* they often have unpleasant thoughts; they may associate conflict with stress, anger, rivalry, fear, or competition. Conflict creates an uneasy feeling that things are different from the way we would expect or want them to be. Conflict, as Deutsch (1994) notes, occurs whenever incompatible activities collide, making us feel injured or undermined.

Finding a universal definition of *conflict* can, however, be difficult. Part of the reason for this is that people have varied perceptions of the word *tension.* Schwenk (1990) found differences in how nonprofit managers regarded conflict differently from profit managers. Profit managers saw conflict as damaging to the quality of products and decisions. Nonprofit managers found it useful (although unpleasant) for clarifying goals among diverse groups.

Conflict is difficult to define, moreover, because it may exist on several levels simultaneously. Conflict may be felt on an individual level, such as tension that workers with different views feel. It may also result from workers feeling pushed into performing contradictory tasks. It may emerge from a discrepancy between needed and available resources. Tension may also arise from problems that are deeply rooted in socioeconomic backgrounds. Conflicts may spring from stress in a worker's personal, professional, or economic circumstance.

STAGES OF CONFLICT

Although conflicts often lie dormant, they may be triggered by certain events. This event may be an unexpected change in work conditions, a crisis, a personal loss, or the sudden deprivation of resources. Pondy (cited in Rahim, 1997) recognized that conflict could be both latent and active when he identified its five stages of development:

1. **Latent.** Conflict not yet risen to the surface, although conditions have set the stage for it.
2. **Perceived.** People begin to sense that conflict exists, although they may attempt to downplay or deny it.
3. **Felt.** Conflict emerges when individuals begin to feel its effects—tension, anxiety, or anger.
4. **Manifest.** The stage of open warfare. People or groups try to thwart one another in a win/lose competition. Two outcomes are possible: The conflict may continue, resulting in disaster, or the conflict may be resolved, channeling disagreement toward a constructive end.
5. **Aftermath.** Disputes are over, and a resolution has been reached.

LEVELS OF CONFLICT

In addition to passing through stages of development, conflict may appear in various forms, ranging from individual, interpersonal, organizational, political, and societal.

INDIVIDUAL CONFLICT

On a personal level, one may experience conflict consciously, but also internally. That is, it may be disguised as uneasiness, or a feeling of tension between how one wants to act and how one is expected to act (Bazerman, Tenbrunsel, & Wade-Benzoni, 1998).

Points of view also affect the level of conflict. Persons with varying perspectives see circumstances differently. For instance, two employees may react differently to a request to work overtime. A worker who has already logged 80 overtime hours in a month, and sacrificed weekend family time, may resent the request. Another, needing extra cash, may view it as an opportunity to erase credit-card debt. This form of unexpressed conflict often resides within us.

INTERPERSONAL CONFLICT

Conflicts may also erupt openly between persons. These conflicts are often disputes with family or peers. At work, a person may engage in conflict with managers, employees, and clientele.

Experiences may also affect the level of interpersonal conflict. Past relationships with authority figures—a parent or teacher perhaps—may influence how people manage conflict. Background affects an individual's perception of others in the conflict, what he or she expects to gain from it, and how to resolve it. One's method of managing interpersonal conflict often provides insight into other forms of conflict as well.

Many interpersonal conflicts arise from *cognitive dissonance;* that is, the feeling that another's opinion simply does not make sense (Devine, Tauer, Barron, Elliot, & Vance, 1999). When people become aware of this difference of interpretation, conflicts may break out. This form of conflict often depends on how individuals present their argument, and how others, in turn, react to it (Drake & Donohue, 1996).

ORGANIZATIONAL CONFLICT

On the level of an organization, conflict may occur among an agency and outside groups, among departments, and even among the different branches of government. Organizational conflict usually stems from the way the agency is set up—the work it performs, its clients, or the amount of available resources.

Coe (1997) sees organizational conflict as the result of intermittent and short-term attempts at government "reinvention." He notes that it occurs when "repeated, worthy, and well-intentioned efforts" try to reengineer how work is organized. Organizational conflicts emerge when these efforts create mutually exclusive conditions. For example, cutting red tape may actually complicate matters because separate procedures are needed to avoid mistakes. Similarly, it would be counterproductive to give the power of decision to an entire team while holding each individual accountable for the outcome.

Organizational conflict affects the performance of groups and individuals. Rogers and Molnar (1976) note that several conditions in an organization affected individual conflict:

- Multiple sources of funding
- Authority to spend unbudgeted money and to alter responsibilities
- Other organizations blocking access to resources
- Reorganizations and mergers
- Pressure from outside groups

Shrum (1990, p. 508) also observed conflict in government officials who faced a "web of restrictions brought about by mandates and professional obligations." These officials were therefore "unable to use their resources."

POLITICAL CONFLICT

Conflict can also result from dynamic interaction among groups, organizations, and social factions. Political conflict may manifest itself when individuals, groups, or institutions attempt to gain power and influence through appeals to or use of legitimate authority.

Vizzard (1995), for instance, describes a conflict between organizations on the issue of gun control. In 1968, the Gun Control Act was passed to deal with unlicensed firearm sales. It not only sought to control firearm licensing, but it also proposed criminal penalties for falsifying sales records or knowingly selling firearms to felons. Implementation of the act, however, was a struggle between groups such as the National Rifle Association; Congress; and the Alcohol, Tobacco, and Firearms Division of the Treasury.

SOCIETAL CONFLICT

Societal conflict occurs when people, groups, or organizations become aware of problems affecting the welfare of the citizenry. Usually, these conflicts are what Stubbart (1987) calls "wicked" problems. They have no simple, universal solution and require the concerted efforts of several diverse groups. Homelessness, overpopulation, environmental pollution, and unemployment are examples.

Funding for public schools illustrates societal conflict. Johnston (1998) analyzed Kansas's public school policies in relation to a court mandate that required states to fund programs for all schools equally, even if local districts were unable to pay. The Kansas legislature had created a highly centralized system that seriously constrained local funding decisions. The result was conflict. Many local school districts faced a loss of funding, and residents feared state intrusion into other facets of school administration.

To address these concerns, the state set up a Local Option Budget (LOB), in which local districts could use up to 25% of state funds for meeting their needs. Although the LOB helped restore local control over funds and improved the quality of education, it also forced smaller and poorer districts to pay more money.

RESPONSES TO CONFLICT

Since differing perspectives make conflict hard to diagnose, how do people respond when it happens? Responses vary with the circumstances and the personalities of those involved. One must examine one's usual methods of managing conflict, and assess their suitability in a given situation. Thomas (1992) describes five main types of conflict management styles and how people apply them: (1) avoidance, (2) accommodation, (3) compromise, (4) competition, and (5) collaboration. We shall summarize these styles and note circumstances in which they are effective. You may assess which style you prefer in the conflict resolution exercise at the end of this chapter.

AVOIDANCE

Some people try to avoid conflict altogether, or only certain types of conflict. These individuals tend to repress emotional reactions, ignore the problem, or remove themselves physically from the situation. Avoidance strategies have value in instances where exit is possible. Avoidance is prudent, for example, if the conflict has trivial consequences, if involvement would fail to yield positive results, or if there is no chance for retaliation. The tactic of nonviolent protest, in which a minority avoids face-to-face confrontation with a more powerful majority, is an effective way to preserve integrity and resources.

ACCOMMODATION

When presented with confrontation, people may decide to accommodate others. In doing this, they subjugate their own needs to those of others. Accommodation allows people to preserve relationships or store up favors for later use. People who use accommodation value the formation of interpersonal relationships. Caro (1982) describes how Lyndon Johnson used accommodation to gain support in the U.S. Senate. Johnson, Caro notes, would determine which senators were important to the outcome of an issue—who might gain further support and who was undecided. After this thorough preparation, Johnson would use his aides to rehearse the possible responses each senator could make. He would then "accidentally" run into the senator in a corridor to convince him to support a position.

COMPROMISE

People may use compromise as a trade-off solution. Compromise is often used as a settlement among diverse interests. This method yields a middle ground where each party gets part of what they want, usually through negotiation. Public officials use compromise to a great extent, especially to gain support from diverse groups. As an example of compromise, consider the following scenario:

When the city council hears a developer describe plans to build a mall near a historic landmark, the members must also listen to objections from landmark preservationist groups, environmentalists, business owners, and residents. The council may reach a compromise decision. They may allow the developer to build the mall somewhere outside the historic district, perhaps in a growing area on the outskirts of the city. In this way, preservationists' goals would be met and environmentalists would be satisfied that forests would not be cut down. Businesses and citizens would celebrate the new jobs, and the historic district would not have to contend with traffic congestion and lowered property values.

The developer, however, may be unwilling to accept the compromise because a mall outside of the historic district would not produce as high a return on his investment. If the developer then withdraws the proposal to build the mall, those groups in favor would lose out.

COMPETITION

People who achieve their own ends—not those of others—use competition as a means to resolve conflict. Competition may be used when people want to fulfill their goals quickly. In a social situation where people have limited resources, they are forced to use some form of competition. However, if people feel that the resources are merely apparently limited, they may use a win/lose strategy. For instance, budget cuts in a university may require departments to share copying services. This results in delayed services, disputes over who has priority for use, and overall frustration.

COLLABORATION

If people are concerned about meeting their own goals as well as those of others, they resolve conflict by seeking solutions that would benefit both parties. Fisher and Ury (1991) view collaboration as a win–win solution that comes about through negotiation. This involves finding the cause of the conflict and sharing it openly with others. Careful listening skills are necessary for negotiation in order to generate consensus and a mutually satisfying strategy.

PRINCIPLED NEGOTIATION

Fisher and Ury (1991) developed a "principled negotiation" approach to resolving conflict, based on extensive research in the Harvard Negotiation Project. They contend that people negotiate every day, from modifying their daily work schedules to getting a seat on a crowded commuter train. Negotiation enables people to get what they want while allowing others to do the same. Yet, negotiation is potentially draining, especially when people use "hard" tactics to meet their goals. In this case, the rival often submits without struggle. "Principled negotiation," however, ensures that the final decision is mutually beneficial. If people find they cannot agree on a solution, they can establish a set of objective principles that allow them the merits of working together. The use of objective principles, rather than flatly insisting on one's own position, promotes fairness in resolving conflicts.

The "principled negotiation" approach consists of four components: (1) separating people from the problem, (2) focusing on interests rather than positions, (3) inventing options for mutual gain, and (4) insisting on objective criteria. Fisher and Ury (1991) contend that each party, in meeting these requirements, will achieve their goals while building mutual trust.

SEPARATE PEOPLE FROM THE PROBLEM

To understand another's needs, one must clarify the other's perceptions and reasoning. One must encourage mutual participation, identify one's desired outcomes, and allow emotional "venting."

FOCUS ON INTERESTS, NOT POSITIONS

When one takes a position it is inspired by a particular interest. However, since every interest could manifest in a variety of positions, it is important to express one's original motivation. This works because a single position can often satisfy multiple interests simultaneously. To persuade people, one must express the reasoning behind the point of view.

INVENT OPTIONS FOR MUTUAL GAIN

To create options, one must brainstorm strategies, avoid premature judgments, and assume that resources are not fixed. One must also offer an opponent something in exchange. An opponent will be prone to accept a proposal if there is chance of a gain.

INSIST ON OBJECTIVE CRITERIA

In solving a problem, it is necessary to base a decision on principles, not pressure. In so doing, one should search for objective criteria: market value, professional standards, efficiency, costs, moral standards, or tradition.

Principled negotiation has great merit in the public sector, especially when leaders must use only a few resources to satisfy many different people. Consider the following example.

In a Connecticut town during the 1990s, citizens often attended town meetings to protest the way legislators proposed spending tax money. Citizens repeatedly voted down a proposed budget before approving one. In one city, however, such frequent referenda never happened. Instead, the city council conducted surveys of local resi-

dents to get a feel for their desires. They also met with leaders of interest groups to understand their goals. The council took this information and identified points that everyone involved could agree on. This became the blueprint for the budget proposal.

SITUATIONAL APPROACHES TO CONFLICT RESOLUTION

Although resolving conflict by building trustful relationships is important, Savage, Blair, and Sorensen (1989) hold that other strategies should be used. The approach one should adopt, they state, depends on circumstances: expected goals, desired depth of relationships, or possible benefits. The resolution strategy may satisfy everyone involved. Depending on circumstances, therefore, strategies of win–win, win–lose, and even mutual avoidance should be considered. The authors assert that one should consider the following conditions in selecting a strategy:

1. **Relative Power of Those in Conflict Situations.** Which parties can force compliance through control of resources?

2. **Degree of Tension or Hostility.** Leaders can compare the differences between points of view. If the level of hostility is not too high, leaders can help followers reduce tension and reconcile differences.

3. **Personal and Organizational Interests of Those in Conflict.** This is best exemplified by looking at city employees. In talking with customers, employees tend to develop good communication skills. These abilities, in turn, benefit the organization by channeling accurate and timely information to patrons.

In considering these three conditions, leaders can use four main types of resolution strategies:

1. **Collaborative**—Useful when both relationships and results are important, and when workers are interdependent. Building trust is the key to resolving issues fairly.

2. **Subordinate**—Useful when the leader has little to gain from resolving issues, but when the relationship with the other party is important.

3. **Competitive**—Useful when the product is important, but when relationships are not. A competitive stance is suitable for conditions of mutual distrust and hostility.

4. **Avoidance**—Useful when relationships and the product are both unimportant. A leader should stand apart from squabbles where the result would be inconsequential.

Leaders can vary these strategies depending on the interests of those involved, and the importance of an agreeable resolution. If leaders feel that both the product and personal relationships are important, they may use a collaborative approach to resolve matters. If, however, those involved in the conflict are not prone to reconcile personal differences, they may take advantage of a leader's show of faith. To prevent this, a leader may use a strategy similar to Fisher and Ury's (1991) principled negotiation.

For example, in resolving a scheduling conflict with a union representative, a manager should base the decision on corporate policy. If the union has a different interpretation of policy, the representative may try to get the manager to change the scheduling decision. This could cause a stalemate and aggravate hostilities. To prevent damage to the manager's authority and his relationship with the union, the agency may call in an objective mediator (an ombudsman) to find common links between the two sides.

Kaufman (1991) notes that the context of the conflict determines which resolution strategy is appropriate for public sector problems. Kaufman suggests that deliberation and consensus are important strategies for making decisions in individual, departmental, or political conflicts. However, when organizations handle conflict with external assistance, a combination of strategies is useful. Negotiation should be tried first. If discussions end in deadlock, however, parties should use arbitration.

Elangovan (1995) cites five conditions that affect the type of intervention strategy a leader can use:

1. The importance of the dispute to personal or organizational survival
2. Time pressure
3. The nature of the dispute—whether it centers on differing interpretation of policy or merely a challenge to the values of the status quo
4. The quality of the relationship between the parties
5. The likelihood that the parties can reach a settlement on their own

Depending on the combination of variables in each conflict, a leader may choose a strategy that would allow others to control the resolution, or a strategy that insists on letting everyone control it. For instance, consider a circumstance where workers do not depend heavily on a leader's decision-making power. The workers are also highly committed to any decision once it is in place, and personal relationships are built on trust. In this situation, the best strategy would be to give extensive control to employees over resolving the dispute. However, in low-commitment, high-dependency, and poor-relationship situations, a third party should be used to mediate the conflict.

SUMMARY

Conflict produces tension that people perceive between themselves and others. It passes through several stages of development, from a latent hostility to outright clashing. People become more aware of the tension as it affects their lives, relationships, and productivity.

People respond to conflict using several types of strategies. For example, they may *avoid* confrontation if they feel the outcome is unimportant to their own needs. People may *accommodate* different opinions if doing so would build a stronger relationship—and if the relationship is important. They may choose to *compromise* to meet their own needs while maintaining a positive relationship. At other times, using outright *competition*—or satisfying one's own needs over the other—may be critical to survival. Finally, people may wish to *collaborate,* thus reaching their own goals while benefiting others.

Fisher and Ury (1991) assert that people may use a "principled negotiation" strategy to build collaboration. This involves articulating one's own interest, as well as that of others. People using this approach must also adhere to mutually acceptable standards of resolving the conflict. By focusing on objective principles rather than on subjective opinions, people can avoid an emotional confrontation, and resolve matters calmly.

Public sector leaders may benefit from adapting approaches to each situation.

Situational approaches enable leaders to tailor their styles of resolving conflict to the interests of those involved. This adaptation also helps in working under the constraints of public sector regulations.

Situational approaches call for the leader to evaluate several variables before crafting a resolution strategy. Some important variables include:

- The relative power of people in conflict situations
- The degree of tension
- Personal interests
- The importance of the relationship
- How critical the conflict is to individual and organizational expectations
- The level within the organization where the conflict occurs
- The degree of time pressure
- The likelihood that workers can reach a settlement without direct leader involvement

Leaders can master the complexity of managing public sector conflict by analyzing the situation, considering present and desired relationships, assessing the importance of the conflict, and how much good leader intervention would do. Selecting the best strategy comes by way of experience and knowing all possible options.

QUESTIONS FOR THOUGHT AND DISCUSSION

1. Recall a recent interpersonal conflict in which you were involved. How did the conflict start? Did emotional issues become entangled? How did parties resolve the conflict? How did you feel about the resolution?

2. In your opinion, what are some of the ways for public leaders to take a proactive stance when dealing with "wicked" problems that seem to divide stakeholders?

3. Inadequate resources and the manner in which people perceive their distribution often trigger conflicts. In public institutions, this can produce divisions and even alienation. Think of an example of disputes over resource inequality. In your opinion, how can public leaders create environments that allow for these types of conflicts to be resolved? What particular leadership skills are effective?

4. What is your preferred conflict-resolution style? In your own experiences, when has this style been effective in enabling you to achieve your objectives? When has it been not effective? In the latter situations, did you use another style? If so, what were the outcomes?

CASE STUDY

NIMBY IN DUNN, NORTH CAROLINA

DIRECTIONS

This case study reveals the type of multiple conflicts that public sector organizations often face. The study is concerned with the attempts to locate a biomedical waste incinerator in a community that is opposed to it—even though it could spark some much-needed economic development. As a case of "Not in My Backyard Syndrome" (NIMBY), it details the opposition of residents and others who are concerned for the way a new program might lower the quality of life in the neighborhood. As you read the case, examine the interests of all parties in the conflict: city and county officials, residents, community groups, regulatory agencies, and the private firm. Also, identify and analyze possible strategies that could be used to resolve the conflict. Then, working in small groups, decide what you believe the city council should do.

BACKGROUND

Dunn is a town of approximately 10,000 residents located in Harnett County in eastern North Carolina. Dunn has an elected mayor, a five-member town council, and an appointed city manager. The town has a wide mix of industry and business, and is also taking advantage of the consumer trade brought in by its proximity to a major highway, Interstate 95.

In November of 1989, Scott St. Claire, President of Thermetics Incorporated, a private firm located in Charlotte, North Carolina, announced his intention to build a biomedical waste incinerator. The incinerator would be located just outside Dunn's city limits, but within the city's corporate zone. Pending state approval of the company's compliance with land and air quality regulations, a 22-acre tract was contracted for purchase by Thermetics from Doug Goldwin, a local farmer and industrialist.

Thermetics proposed building an incinerator that would cost over $5 million and burn up to 75 tons of medical waste per day, a far greater load than the 1–2 tons of medical waste created daily by the two hospitals in the county. It was obvious that Thermetics was choosing to build its facil-

SOURCE: Adapted from Martin P. Sellers (1993). NIMBY: A case study in conflict politics. *Public Administration Quarterly, 16*(4), 460–477. Used with permission.

ity near Dunn because of its proximity to the interstate highway and its rural location. Dunn could expect that a large quantity of medical waste from other states would be transported into the city's industrial zone should the facility be built there.

The siting process became public when St. Claire of Thermetics contacted Tom Mesa, head of the County Economic Council, to set up a meeting with city and county officials for Thermetics to present its plan. The local newspaper publisher was also contacted, and both he and Mesa were very positive about the prospects of a multimillion-dollar investment coming to Dunn. The county's economic growth pattern had stabilized over the past 5 years and this would be an economic "shot in the arm."

Harnett County Commissioner Mayo Smith and other county officials showed more than a little support for the idea. Hoping to increase the scope of Harnett County's mix of industry and business, John Shaw, Vice President of United Carolina Bank and Chairman of Harnett Industrial Development Commission, was also an early supporter. Abe Elmer, a former mayor of Dunn (and candidate for the state senate) favored the project. He said that the public should take a wait-and-see attitude, gather facts, and support the plan if a biomedical waste incinerator could prove to be beneficial to Dunn.

A meeting was scheduled for 5 December for these and other officials to gather and hear the plan. The meeting ended with all parties feeling positive about the plan.

A week later, the Dunn Area Chamber of Commerce (DACC)—a very powerful interest in Harnett County, consisting of business owners and large landowners—met in opposition to the plan. This meeting was very emotional. However, no one from Thermetics was present to explain the firm's position. A number of board members and town council members felt it unwise to speak out against the incinerator because it might broadcast to other industries that Dunn was hostile toward certain types of businesses. The overall sense of the meeting was that locating the incinerator in Dunn was a bad idea because of possible negative consequences.

The DACC met again on 5 January. Debbie Johnson, a concerned homeowner who lived across from the proposed incinerator site, left the meeting as chairperson of a newly formed citizen group: Harnett County Concerned Citizens (HCCC). Mrs. Johnson, now a lightning rod for growing opposition, began arming the group for battle. A petition against the project listed nearly 5,000 signatures. Meetings were scheduled with citizen groups, such as the Lions and Moose clubs, to solicit their support. At these meetings, there was no participation of Thermetics or experts on incineration or biomedical waste disposal. The influence of one lone opposing voice, it seems, is stronger than the silence of many supporters.

The HCA's biggest complaints about the incineration of medical waste were that (1) air emissions are uncontrollable and misunderstood, (2) ash storage would add to an already problematic situation for the county's landfills, and (3) on-site storage of waste and its transportation are not regulated. They claimed that business growth, population growth, and property values would all take a nose-dive if Dunn became known as a waste dump. Having the support of signed petitions, HCCC called for the Dunn City Council to adopt an ordinance requiring a $100,000 application fee as well as a $100 per-day fee for any incinerator established in the city planning zone. Moreover, HCCC requested that a public hearing be scheduled to air sentiments on the issue.

DISCUSSION

The county commissioners have scheduled a public hearing for early February. They have invited representatives from the Dunn Area Chamber of Commerce (DACC) and the Harnett County Concerned Citizens (HCCC) as well as Thermetics to discuss the issue. Following the hearing, the commissioners will meet and decide how to proceed. If you were leading the commission at the public hearing, what strategy of resolving conflict do you think would be most effective, assuming arguments on both sides were strong? Consider the effectiveness of each technique in terms of (1) acknowledging each speaker's interests, (2) expected outcomes of resolution options, and (3) long-term relationships with the constituents, Thermetics, or other potential industrial firms.

CONFLICT RESOLUTION EXERCISE

DIRECTIONS

The following two-part exercise will enable you to practice your conflict-resolution skills.

PART I: CONFLICT RESOLUTION STYLE

In Part I, you can assess your preferred conflict-resolution style by checking the response that most nearly matches what you would do. Using the scoring key, determine your preferences for styles of resolving conflict.

PART II: ROLE PLAYING

Practice your skills in negotiation by role playing the four scenarios with others in a small group. Working in groups of four, participants select two of the four scenarios to enact preferred styles of conflict resolution. For the first scenario, one participant plays the role of employee, and one plays the manager. Each participant should read the scenario, determine his or her interests, and use his or her preferred style throughout.

Those participants not role playing should act the part of "consultants." During the role play, consultants observe the chosen strategy of conflict resolution and its effects on the manager and employee.

One consultant should observe the manager and the other the employee.

At the end of 5 minutes, the role play is stopped and participants discuss their reactions to the style of conflict resolution. After the discussion and consultant feedback, participants enact the second scenario by switching roles. The employee and manager players become consultants, and the consultants, the employee and manager. After 5 minutes, time is called and feedback is again given.

SCORING KEY

Read each of the four scenarios, then select the response you would MOST LIKELY choose and rank it a 5 and the one you would LEAST LIKELY choose, rank 1. For the remaining choices, rank them in order of preference from 4 (LIKELY), 3 (SOMEWHAT LIKELY), and 2 (NOT TOO LIKELY). In the blank space beside each choice, write the number corresponding to your most likely response. Following the ranking, transfer the scores to the appropriate response numbers and total the scores for each five choices.

SCENARIO 1: I DON'T DO WINDOWS

Robin is a hardworking case manager who spends much overtime working on "crisis" projects. Robin's office looks like a tornado has hit it: Files are scattered on the floor, desk, cabinets, and chairs. Robin's director visits her office and notes the disorder. Robin maintains that cleaning offices is the responsibility of the cleaning crew. She does not feel it is appropriate for a professional to dust, tidy up, and put away files. Besides, she knows where everything is. The director points out that some of the files might contain sensitive information and could fall into the hands of unscrupulous people, or simply be misplaced. Robin becomes irritated and says that her heavy overtime prevents proper filing. The manager reacts defensively.

CHOICES

You are called in to halt the emerging conflict. Which strategy would you suggest the manager use?

_____1. Suggest the issue is not important and let Robin continue "as is."

_____2. Suggest the manager refer to the filing regulations and hold Robin accountable.

_____3. Agree with Robin—the janitor should ensure that the area is kept orderly.

_____4. Ask Robin to file documents according to regulation and the manager to tolerate Robin's untidiness.

_____5. Set up a meeting with Robin and the manager. Seek a mutual agreement on how to ensure confidentiality and a professional-looking work area.

SCENARIO 2: A SUPERVISOR IN WAITING?

The branch manager of a record management section of a large governmental agency is meeting with Pat to discuss his possible promotion. Pat has worked in the unit for 12 years and has consistently received superior performance reviews. Pat seems eager for the promotion, believing technical competence, hard work, and longevity are important assets for the job. The branch manager, however, knows that Pat can sometimes belittle coworkers, telling them the "best" way to do their jobs. The branch manager has not spoken to Pat about this in the past because Pat has not been considered for a supervisory position. The branch manager intends to discuss this in the meeting with Pat. Because Pat is unaware of the branch manager's feeling, he will likely react negatively.

CHOICES

You are a consultant. What strategy of conflict resolution would you suggest to the branch manager?

_____1. Be forthright with Pat. You think Pat lacks the "people skills" for a supervisor's position and will therefore not consider the issue further. Downplay the negative perceptions of Pat and focus on the facts.

_____2. Because Pat has done a competent job in the past, his expertise can be used to train less qualified people. This will enable the unit to increase output in the future.

_____3. Give Pat a temporary supervisory assignment and observe how he handles people.

_____4. Point out that Pat can learn people skills after being promoted. Encourage the branch manager and Pat to honestly examine the facts. Tell them to look at their expectations and the qualifications necessary for the job.

_____5. Reach an agreement on whether Pat should apply for the supervisory job.

SCENARIO 3: THE COST-CUTTING COPIER DISPUTE

Jan is the director of a social and human services department. Reporting to Jan are two managers: Chris Jones, of the youth program; and Dale Smith, manager of elder care services. Recently, a shortfall in local tax revenue has caused city council to cut funds for new equipment purchase. Jan had planned to buy a new copier for the expanding elder care services, but has to cancel the purchase. This means 10 people from the youth program and 14 from elder care must share the use of only two copiers. Because the machines are old and overworked, they frequently break down. Lengthy repairs during the downtime add to frustration, sparking numerous daily disputes over copier "rights." Jan has scheduled a meeting with Chris and Dale to attempt to find a solution.

CHOICES

If you were Jan, you would:

_____1. Help Dale and Chris come up with a creative way to share the copiers.

_____2. Tell Dale and Chris to make out a schedule for using the copiers, and be sure people sign up ahead of time.

_____3. Be honest. Employees should adjust copier use on their own, based on workload and deadlines.

_____4 Ask Dale and Chris to listen to their employee's dissatisfaction to ease emotional tension. This way, employees will feel they have been heard and complaints should diminish.

_____5. Work out a system of "odd" and "even" days of use. Chris's employees would use the copier on odd-numbered days and Dale's, on even ones.

SCENARIO 4: DETAILS, DETAILS, DETAILS

Kerry supervises Tracy and Lynn, who are counselors in a state employment agency. Both have earned superior performance ratings for their quality of work at the agency. However, both counselors have difficulty communicating with the other. Conflict has lately become acute when they are not with clients. Lynn serves as the intake counselor, gathering basic eligibility information from clients and—depending on the determination of need—

sends the clients to Tracy. Tracy, who insists that even minor details in a case should be documented, says Lynn does not give sufficient information on clients. This causes Tracy to make hasty decisions, and worsens her irritation with Lynn's habits. Lynn, however, wonders why Tracy would be upset now. Tracy has not mentioned it to Lynn in the 4 years they have worked together. Kerry has called you in for advice.

CHOICES

As a counselor, you would suggest:

_____1. Kerry should tell Lynn to consider the level of detail needed for the reports and adjust to this level. Detail is important not only in preventing costly mistakes but also for auditing purposes.

_____2. Because Tracy and Lynn have worked together for a long time, they know each other well enough to find a mutually beneficial solution. Kerry need not intervene.

_____3. Invite Lynn and Tracy to discuss their ideas. Help them formulate a plan for balancing the level of detail with sharing information openly and honestly.

_____4. They should compromise. Kerry should encourage Tracy to be more assertive in conveying thoughts and feelings to Lynn. Also, Kerry should tell Lynn to provide the level of detail Tracy requires so that Tracy can perform her duties well.

_____5. Kerry should reassign the two counselors to work in groups where their personality styles will be more compatible with others.

SCORING

Transfer your rankings to the corresponding numbers below. Note that the numbers are not in order. Add up the numbers. The highest number is your PREFERRED style. If you had two identical scores, you have style FLEXIBILITY or can use alternate styles, depending on situational conditions.

	Avoid	Accomodate	Compete	Compromise	Negotiate
Scenario 1	1 _____	3 _____	2 _____	4 _____	5 _____
Scenario 2	2 _____	4 _____	1 _____	3 _____	5 _____
Scenario 3	4 _____	3 _____	2 _____	5 _____	1 _____
Scenario 4	2 _____	1 _____	5 _____	4 _____	3 _____
Total:	_____	_____	_____	_____	_____

	Avoid	Accomodate	Compete	Compromise	Negotiate
Highest Score: _____					

Notes:

10

RATIONAL AND NONRATIONAL PROBLEM SOLVING AND DECISION MAKING IN THE PUBLIC SECTOR

SYNOPSIS

Asserting that problem solving and decision making are intertwined and occur on a continuum, this chapter examines both rational and nonrational approaches. Rational approaches, which concentrate on purposeful methods to achieve specified ends, are based in economic theories that proscribe one "best" way to manage. Processes include problem identification, developing and weighing alternative solutions, selecting the optimal choice, and implementing the alternative. Nonrational approaches include incrementalism, satisficing, "garbage can," cybernetic, and heuristic. Chapter 10 cites and assesses examples of each in the public sector. This chapter also discusses techniques that enhance creative thinking.

OBJECTIVES

- To state relationships between problem solving and decision making
- To define rational and creative dimensions of thinking
- To describe processes that occur in rational problem solving
- To discuss uses and limitations of rational and nonrational models of problem solving and decision making as they are used in the public sector
- To discuss key approaches to nonrational decision making
- To discuss ways to encourage participation in public sector decision making arenas

KEY TERMS AND CONCEPTS

Cybernetic Model

decision making

Delphi Technique

Free-Market Choice Model

"Garbage Can" Model

heuristic approach

incrementalism

mixed scanning

Nominal Group Technique

paradigm

problem solving

satisficing

strategic planning

INTRODUCTION

Public sector leaders face many challenges in having to solve problems and make decisions. Complex problems such as terrorism, AIDS, or overpopulation defy simplistic solutions. This complexity demands creative approaches. Leaders must find novel ways to garner widespread support among varied interests. They must enable their followers to implement strategies, and remain optimistic that their leadership will make a difference.

In examining concepts of problem solving and decision making, we shall argue in this chapter that the two processes are intertwined. We shall describe some specific aspects of both problem solving and decision making in the public sector. We will see how public sector problems differ from those of the private sector. Further, we will discuss common techniques of problem solving and decision making. The exercises will provide additional insight into the leadership skills used in solving public sector problems.

THE CONTINUUM OF PROBLEM SOLVING
AND DECISION MAKING

Although some people may differentiate problem solving from decision making, they are closely related processes. This is especially true if problems are complex, deep rooted, or open ended. Further, both processes involve logical and emotional mindsets. They include logical, social, psychological, and sometimes political elements. They are, in this sense, holistic; that is, they encompass a wide range of concerns. Hunt and Magenau (1984, p. 119) express this in the following passage:

> Decisions both result from and affect the flow of events. They are selections of courses of actions, but decisions are not identical with the actions themselves. Decisions are 'inside' people, so to speak. They are mental, or as we shall say, cognitive events that intervene between informational inputs and subsequent behavioral outputs.

Accordingly, we may observe that models of problem solving and decision making have focused on rational thought, an approach that relies on careful goal setting to achieve high-quality results. The nonrational approach, however, centers on the notion that subjectivity affects problem solving and decision making. In both models, participation and creativity grant certain advantages. To understand these advantages, we shall look at the framework of both approaches and describe their shortcomings.

RATIONAL AND NONRATIONAL METHODS

As noted, problem solving and decision making include a range of rational and nonrational methods. At the rational end, people carefully form and execute plans. They follow a logical path of identifying problems, analyzing information, and using this information to explore possible solutions. After deciding which alternative will produce the best results, they implement it.

Conversely, nonrational approaches rely on intuitive methods that foster consensus. People using this approach consider the interests of those working on the project as well as those affected by their decision. The nonrational method follows unpredictable patterns of analyzing data and making smaller choices on route to the final decision. For a comparison of rational and nonrational problem-solving, decision-making models, see Table 10.1.

. TABLE 10-1

RATIONAL PROBLEM-SOLVING AND DECISION-MAKING PARADIGM: A COMPARISON OF KEY FEATURES

Rational Approach	Nonrational Approach
Identification of problem	Emergence of problem
Identify decision objectives	Identify members' goals and interests
Analyze problem	Elaborate on problem
Generate solution	Construct solution
Evaluate alternatives	Evaluate plausible compromises
Select optimal solutions	Select most acceptable solution
Implement and follow up	Follow up and implement

In solving problems and making decisions, there are varying degrees of rational and nonrational methods. The mix depends on factors such as resource availability, extent of participation, and the degree of strategic impact. In municipal planning, for instance, rational methods would take place in designing a new highway intersection. Planners would consider the cost of building and maintaining the intersection, the current and projected volume of traffic, and how noise and congestion would affect the neighborhood. Before legislators approve the plan, however, planners may use a nonrational approach by considering various people involved: residents, environmental groups, and regulatory agencies. We examine these two models in detail below, and explore some contemporary examples.

RATIONAL PROBLEM SOLVING

The rational model of decision making separates the following tasks: defining problems, identifying unknowns, formulating possible solutions, and selecting the strategy most likely to yield desirable results. The model has its roots in economic theory. Some important ideas include the following.

1. People develop strategies deliberately in solving problems and making decisions.
2. Strategies consist of milestone decisions, or steppingstones that contribute to a desirable end.
3. The ends yield the maximum economic payoff at minimal costs.

Mintzberg, Raisin-ghani, and Theoret (1976) identify three distinct phases of rational problem solving and decision making:

1. **Identification Phase.** Individuals recognize problems or opportunities for change. They diagnose causes and develop possible solutions.
2. **Development Phase.** Having diagnosed the problem, people research it to see if others have found solutions. If so, they may adopt that strategy or modify it to their circumstances.
3. **Selection Phase.** People choose the best course of action based on individual judgment, experience or intuition, ranking alternatives, and bargaining and trade-offs.

Irving and Janis (1977) observe that people pass through five stages in solving problems and making decisions:

Stage 1: Appraising the Challenge. Individuals remain complacent until they perceive a possible loss. In response to this disturbing prospect, persons decide whether their complacency poses a serious risk to their project.

Stage 2: Surveying Alternatives. When individuals lose confidence in old policies, they seek alternatives by soliciting advice and reflecting on their own experiences. This phase sees a rigorous search for all possible solutions.

Stage 3: Weighing Alternatives. After concluding that all alternatives have been explored, people rank them according to potential gains and losses. They then select the best alternative after much deliberation.

Stage 4: Deliberating Commitment. Having selected the best alternative, individuals decide whether to include other persons in its implementation. This stage can be stressful because people often feel they must commit to a course of action despite their own doubts.

Stage 5: Adhering Despite Negative Feedback. Although people may feel satisfied with a solution, they may encounter conflict in receiving negative feedback. At this point, individuals must decide if they should return to Stage 1 or continue and hope their solution works despite the objection.

FREE-MARKET CHOICE MODEL
AS A VARIANT OF THE RATIONAL MODEL

In the public sector, we see a variant of the rational model in the *Free-Market Choice Model*. For many years, legislators and citizens have sought ways to make the government work efficiently and effectively. The recent trend to give public functions to private contractors is inspired by the economic idea that free-market competition ensures a high-quality product. In this arena, governmental agencies compete with private organizations in response to consumer needs. Since the quality of the service must beat out this competition, this recent "privatizing" has reinvented the way public organizations conduct their affairs.

Osborne and Gaebler (1992) contend that a government that "steers rather than rows" can use this consumer-driven system in innovative ways to solve major social and economic problems. In their best seller, *Reinventing Government*, the authors illustrate this concept with numerous case examples. Osborne and Gaebler describe how a recreation department reduced membership fees for a softball team by acquiring community sponsors. Another example shows how a California city sold land to private developers to help fund additional projects. Several states have adopted similar "enterprise funds" to improve their services.

STRATEGIC PLANNING

Strategic planning, or the comprehensive development of long-term goals, is being used more and more by government. Berry and Wechsler (1995) surveyed state agencies and found that 60% had adopted some form of strategic planning since the mid-1980s. Of these agencies, most had retained the system. In fact, many had set up offices to coordinate the process, using both staff and outside interests to set further goals. The agencies, inspired by the success of other organizations, used a strategic planning that was guided by the vision of an agency head. Other reasons for this boom in strategic planning included public pressure for administrative reform, the resolution of resource problems, and the need to coordinate budget and programming goals.

Berry and Wechsler (1995) note that many state agencies adapted the Harvard Policy and Stakeholder Model in forming strategic plans and tying them to the budget. The Harvard Policy and Stakeholder Model involves scanning the organization to identify the concerns and problems of all involved. Armed with this data, administrators invite these people or groups to help set long-range goals. As a result of this process, the authors identified six main outcomes:

1. Clarification of the agency's direction and goals

2. Assistance in policy and budget decisions

3. Enhancement of relationships with clients

4. Improvement of management, especially in teamwork and staff morale

5. Reorganization of the agency's programs

6. Improvement of services

Leadership played a key role in success. Since most strategic planning grew out of individual effort rather than company policy, leaders helped establish methods for taking purposeful action. These leaders, Berry and Wechsler point out, asserted their "leadership vision [by using] strategic planning in symbolic as well as substantive ways" (1995, p. 166).

SHORTCOMINGS OF THE RATIONAL MODEL

As we may observe, the rational model separates decision making from problem solving. Decisions are made after analyzing data and devising solutions. Selection of the best approach, however, often uses abstract criteria that are irrelevant actual resource levels, political issues, or other unstable conditions. Rational decision making succeeds when people agree on goals and have personal discretion in obtaining resources.

Although the Free-Market Model seems to foster economic effectiveness, in the government, it is dogged by two persistent problems: politics and red tape. People, especially in a market-driven system, erect their own sets of bureaucratic barriers. Moe (1994) shows that citizen groups that are not subject to a central authority often organize themselves. Many times, this means using short-term political leadership, makeshift committees, and outside contractors who have limited understanding of the agency's goals. Frederickson (1996) points out that this fragmented authority leads to diffused accountability, as it encourages the notion that any enterprise can deliver the government's services. Poor coordination can also produce incoherent policy (Peters & Savoie, 1996), vying for political control of public resources (Thompson & Ingraham, 1996), biased interests, and lack of equity in program development (Stewart & Ranson, 1988; Walmsley, 1990).

NONRATIONAL APPROACHES

Rational approaches fare poorly in environments where people have different goals, are unable to plan for long-term changes, or have access to complete and unbiased information. Nonrational models acknowledge that people often fail to assess circumstances, formulate alternatives, and select the best option. In a nonrational method, people identify various personal preferences, possible outcomes, and available resources. These subjective considerations shape the decisions of those using this approach. Subjectivity affects how they identify the problem, how they analyze the data, and how they develop solutions. Nonrational methods focus on the here-and-now, the workable, and the tailoring of solutions to problems.

FORMS OF NONRATIONAL PROBLEM SOLVING AND DECISION MAKING

Nonrational approaches work best when there are scarce resources and when dissent exists among group members. Nonrational approaches to problem solving and decision making can appear in five forms: (1) incrementalism, (2) "satisficing," (3) "garbage can," (4) cybernetic, and (5) heuristic.

Incrementalism. Operating under constraints of time, budget, or resources often hinders making good decisions. At best, these circumstances allow what Lindblom (1959) calls "limited, successive comparisons." Each piece of data demands a decision on how to use it. When this decision is made, the range of alternatives is reduced. The solution that emerges is narrowed down to what the majority can accept in principle and what is likely to work in practice. According to Lindblom, the incremental form carries five central assumptions:

1. It achieves goals by taking small steps to change conditions or policies. It does not change underlying structures.

2. It is not comprehensive. It considers only the limited range of choices given to the problemsolver–decisionmaker.

3. It considers choices made in sequence over time, never absolute or irreversible choices.

4. It considers outcomes that are merely sufficient (not optimal) given limited resources.

5. It considers the multifaceted nature of groups.

"Satisficing." Herbert Simon (1976) maintains that people solve problems and make decisions to meet a minimum of acceptability standards. These subjectively defined standards constitute a "bounded" rationality: Persons evaluate solutions according to whether they will meet requirements within cost and time constraints. Hence, individuals solve problems and make decisions to "satisfy" their intuitive sense of what they want, and "suffice" for what they need.

"Garbage Can." March and Olsen's (1984) "Garbage Can" Model is appropriately named because the problem's definition and the solution both emerge from an unstructured group discussion. The goal is often tacked on *after* groups have met. This approach starts when strategies are developed during crises or when goals are unclear, leaving group members to improvise solutions. A type of anarchy can emerge as people form alliances in the scramble for a solution. In this environment, many strategies are tossed into a "garbage can." When more accurate or timely information presents itself, people dredge up these strategies and recycle them to suit a new circumstance.

Cybernetic Model. Kravchuk and Schack (1996) asserted that changing environmental conditions, particularly in multilevel, bureaucratic organizations, make using rational models impractical as well as limited. To develop effective, objective criteria, leaders require setting up feedback loops to send and receive information from contexts. This permits not only adjusting to new situations, but also heading off potential problems in an uncertain environment. The authors maintain that the Cybernetic Model is particularly appropriate for developing performance measurements to improve productivity.

Heuristic Approach. Another approach that uses variables to create choices in decision making is what Hendrick (1994) describes as a heuristic approach. As used in policy analysis in particular, the heuristic approach explores conditions within and outside the policy area to examine potential consequences of choices. Like the Cybernetic Model, it enables decisionmakers to assess the effects of their decisions and make changes to select an alternative appropriate to different conditions.

SHORTCOMINGS OF NONRATIONAL APPROACHES

Nonrational approaches to problem solving and decision making often treat the symptoms of a problem without curing its root causes. Without changing underlying conditions, it is likely that these same problems will resurface. This increases not only costs, but also frustrations, as people may feel that circumstances are beyond control. Further, nonrational approaches require compromise, denying many what they want or need. Compromises placate, but rarely satisfy everyone. Moreover, nonrational approaches can become mired in conflict. This not only alienates those affected by a project, but it also makes it difficult to respond effectively to a pressing situation.

PARTICIPATION AND CREATIVITY
ENHANCING QUALITY

In both rational and nonrational approaches, people concern themselves with how well results meet expectations. To increase the chances of success, leaders encourage participation and creativity. Participation is defined as when group members have an influence on each other in working toward a common goal.

PARTICIPATION

An ingredient necessary to democratic problem solving and decision making is citizen participation. The forms vary, but in essence, participation is the ability to discuss information voluntarily so that everyone has a say and can offer his or her own expertise to benefit the group as a whole. Participation fosters useful and innovative strategies. It also encourages the responsibility and commitment of the citizens.

Participation in government occurs in many forms. One form can be seen in citizen groups. A group, for instance, may express their thoughts openly on a new shopping mall being considered for their neighborhood. Participation may appear in another group of citizens who volunteer for committees to advise legislators. A third form would be to serve as auxiliary members of fire departments, libraries, and schools. Finally, citizens express their views through voting. Referendums enable voters to affect legislative processes.

In the public sector, participation involves incorporating a range of interests, corporations, and other governmental or nonprofit organizations. Some chief aims are to gather comprehensive and timely information, to survey the needs of those affected by the decisions, and to affect results that will benefit as many people as possible. By nature, participation rests on consistent authority in solving problems and making decisions, while benefiting those involved.

Roberts (1997) described a form of participatory problem solving that combines stakeholder input with generative learning. She describes its use in the example of an innovative education task force in Minnesota. Under the direction of the governor-appointed chair, Ruth Randall, the task force defined a strategic issue, developed an agenda of shared goals that produced voluntary commitment, and created a single mental model based on a diversity of individual contributions. Through generative learning, the task force produced a single, agreed-on strategy from several competing expectations.

CREATIVITY

The wide exposure of public service sets it apart from the private sector. As such, public servants require a more creative approach to solving problems and making decisions. Public agencies serve diverse clients while working under several layers of legislative control. They must deal with problems for which there are no clear-cut solutions. The law grants public leaders the authority to represent the citizenry while restricting their freedom to act independently. This restriction sets public leadership apart from private leadership (Bozeman, 1987). However, the responsibility to act on behalf of citizens places pressure on public leaders to seek creative paths. Moore (1995) contends that using imagination and calculated risk adds great value to the services such leaders can perform.

CREATIVITY TECHNIQUES

Creativity techniques improve the quality of problem solving and decision making in the public sector. Creativity finds ways to accomplish difficult assignments, provide innovative and customized services, and incorporate diverse ideas and interests. Two creative problem-solving and decision-making techniques that have been used effectively in public sector organizations are the Delphi Technique and the Nominal Group Technique.

The Delphi Technique. The Delphi Technique is a structured way of creating innovative solutions to complex problems using an anonymous panel of experts. It thus combines rational problem solving with participation and creativity. In the Delphi Technique, a leader identifies those who have expertise in a particular area. The judges, who do not meet face to face, submit their ideas anonymously. Leaders collect the information and feed it back to the judges. After several discussions, the leader may use the information for solving a complex technical problem or reaching a decision outside his or her specialty (Hampton, Summer, & Webber, 1987).

Nominal Group Technique. Nominal Group Technique combines participation with creativity by using a structured form of brainstorming to solve problems and make decisions. The leader-assembled group may meet face to face, but do not speak to one another. Instead, they each develop their own list of strategies without fear of censure. Other group members examine these lists and rank the options according to importance. The group leader tallies the votes and announces the top choices. In successive ranking, group members pick the solution they believe best fits the need at hand.

STEPS IN THE NOMINAL GROUP TECHNIQUE

1. Silent generation of ideas in writing
2. Round robin feedback from group members, who record each idea using a summary word or phrase
3. Discussion of each recorded idea for clarification and evaluation
4. Individual voting on priority ideas, with the group decision being the average ranking

SOURCE: Based on A. L. Delbecq, A. H. Van de Ven, and D. H. Gustafson (1975). *Group techniques for program planning.* Glenview, IL: Scott, Foresman.

Nominal Group Technique is thus a means of generating innovative solutions while developing consensus among group members. It is also an important means for finding common ground, so each group member can accept and build on the solution or decision. A summary of the Nominal Group Technique appears in Table 10.2.

LEADERSHIP USING BOTH RATIONAL AND NONRATIONAL MODELS

Although we have seen two forms of problem solving and decision making—the rational and nonrational—we may observe that they often meld together in actual practice. Public administrators use various combinations of these methods every day. For example, Schneider, Jacoby, and Coggburn (1997) observe that state agencies using optional Medicaid health care have wide latitude in making important decisions. They find that administrators use incrementalism during the earliest stages of decision making. As they meet difficult constraints, however, they use innovative problem-solving and decision-making methods to adjust. The authors point out that the state administrators had to provide "expensive benefits with difficult resources ..." (p. 247). The administrators were usually obliged to

> justify their actions to legislators and to the federal government, the provider of their funding.... Therefore, they found it expedient to start with options that provide the most widely needed and highly visible returns—precisely those services that have the broadest impact within the Medicaid recipient community.

The blending of rational and nonrational methods helps public leaders sort through an entanglement of social problems. This combination can also help leaders identify, with participatory input, which problems can—and should—be addressed using available resources. Fiorino (1990, p. 82) notes that public leaders must choose objectives "from a near infinity of targets." Administrators must weigh competing priorities and solve problems with limited resources. Addressing the difficulty of these choices, Fiorino asks:

> How does an ecological risk, such as the destruction of a wetland, compare to a health risk, such as an increased incidence of lung cancer around a chemical plant? Should society devote more attention to the long-term risks of formaldehyde in building materials than to the low probability but potentially catastrophic consequences of an emergency chemical release? Does the contamination of an aquifer in a lightly populated area warrant as much of society's resources as damage to an estuary that threatens commercial fishing (p. 82)?

MIXED SCANNING

Public leaders cope with questions like these by employing what Etzioni (1986) terms, "mixed scanning." Mixed scanning is a model of decision making that blends data processing with implementation. Someone using this method scans for broad problems, and then points to particular areas where others can focus their attention. In essence, it finds information that workers can use to unravel social problems. Mixed scanning combines incrementalism (seeking precedents that can inform decisions) with innovation (using creative methods when no precedents can be applied to circumstances).

SUMMARY

Leadership is a process of envisioning the best outcome of a project, and crystallizing that vision into reality. In solving problems and making decisions, leaders can use a rational or nonrational approach. Commonly, they use both methods at once. Each affords certain advantages, depending on human and material resources. In general, leaders use these methods to map unknown territory. In the public sector, visionary leaders often see their ideals fulfilled by inspiring followers from diverse backgrounds. A leader gains commitment to a cause when followers share goals, values, and a willingness to put effort into what they see as an important project.

In the public sector, policy making follows a winding course between rational and nonrational methods of problem solving and decision making. Leaders not only initiate the vision, but also put it into a form that many different factions can understand. Further, leaders must adapt their approach depending on circumstances. At each turn, leaders sort through abstract theories to interpret their vision and put it into practice. In making sense of conditions, leaders involve others and tap their creative talents. A solution that works is the result of applying various forms of rational and nonrational methods.

QUESTIONS FOR THOUGHT AND DISCUSSION

1. Think of an example of how people solve problems and make decisions in a group or organization with which you are familiar. What rational and nonrational approaches do they use? Do they combine these approaches in any way? If so, under what circumstances?

2. It is difficult, for several reasons, to initiate long-range planning in many governmental organizations. One of the chief obstacles is lack of centralized (i.e., legislative and executive branch) goals. In your opinion, is this less difficult in countries that have more centralized (or nationalized) structures? Explain why or why not.

3. In what ways can public leaders promote flexibility in problem solving and decision making to include a variety of stakeholder interests, needs, and purposes?

4. What are some purposes and benefits of stakeholder involvement in problem solving and decision making? When are some times that leaders should *not* use participation?

CASE STUDY

RATIONAL VERSUS NONRATIONAL DECISION MAKING IN A POLITICAL MILIEU

TIME: APPROXIMATELY 2 HOURS

GOALS

In the following case study and role-playing exercise, you will be able to

- describe conditions where rational and nonrational decisions are made in practice,
- examine use of rational and nonrational decision-making concepts in a situation with limited resources, high political stakes, and diverse group goals, and
- develop skills for creating consensus among diverse clientele.

DIRECTIONS

After reading the background, form small groups of 9–10. In each group, select roles that each person will play. The roles should include at least two spotters who will provide feedback. After selecting roles, write down some key points in support of your positions.

The participant playing Mayor Jackson in each group begins the discussion. The mayor acts as a facilitator–recorder during the discussion, jotting down ideas for resolution of the management problem. On a separate piece of paper, he or she writes down alternative funding sources. Mayor Jackson will read the group's solution when the larger group is assembled at the end of the role-playing session.

BACKGROUND

Piccadilly Manor is a public housing complex that sits in the middle of Springvale, a northeastern city of 800,000. Nearly 40% of the complex that houses people over age 40—a three-story complex with a capacity of 700—is empty. Of the 280 occupied units, 174 (or about 62%) have single tenants age 65 and over. The remaining tenants are households headed by a single parent. Nearly all residents receive public assistance, usually less than $7,000 per year.

HOUSING FUNDING

Springvale and the U.S. Department of Housing and Urban Development (HUD) signed a cooperation agreement that outlined federal funding for specified public housing. The federal funds are based on formulas that match, dollar for dollar, the amounts raised with local funding, including tenant rent. For this fiscal year, HUD has allocated $7 million for Piccadilly Manor. Funds are to be used to subsidize rents as well as to maintain structures. No funds may be used for renovation.

The $7 million is a significant drop from the $12 million peak in the early 1980s. In fact, for nearly two decades, federal subsidies have deteriorated. To meet the decline in funding, Springvale's City Council has postponed expensive upgrades to the units, postponed maintenance, and enlisted residents to help with upkeep. Springvale pays these residents minimum wages from other fund sources. To offset the expenses, moreover, Springvale has waived residents' normal real estate taxes, but requires dwellers to pay the city 10% of the rent in lieu of taxes.

According to the cooperation agreement, Springvale must provide usual services and utilities, such as fire and police protection. In addition to the problem of dwindling revenue, the city has encountered problems with public safety personnel. Because of the high crime rate in Piccadilly Manor, public safety employees are reluctant to answer resident calls. This slow response makes residents feel even more isolated from mainstream Springvale, and more vulnerable to fires and crime.

PICCADILLY MANOR ADMINISTRATIONS

Mayor and City Council. Primary responsibility for administering Piccadilly Manor is shared by a city council of nine members and an at-large mayor. To find alternatives for funding, the council has focused on Piccadilly Manor for the past 4 years. Various ideas have been explored, such as forming alliances with businesses or nonprofit organizations. The mayor and council members serve 2-year terms, and often concentrate on issues that will get them reelected. Or, they may be voted out altogether. Five of the nine council members were reelected last November. In any case, this brief term of service has made planning for the long run difficult.

Housing Authority Board. When Springvale built Piccadilly Manor in the early 1950s, the city council appointed a Housing Authority Board to oversee administration of government funds. This board also provides security services and day-to-day maintenance. The board determines tenant eligibility, participation, and rent. The board's current director, Kelly Wilson, is appointed by Mayor Jackson and reports to the city council.

The board also employs technical and professional workers to carry out specialized services, including: (1) maintenance and custodial work, (2) purchasing and inventory, (3) finance and accounting, (4) processing tenant applications, (5) personnel and training, (6) security, and (7) social services.

Although these employees are hired under Springvale's civil service laws, most Piccadilly Manor employees are residents who receive minimum wages. The technical and professional workers often argue with the employee–residents over work roles and responsibilities—"turf battles" have divided the two groups and have lowered morale and performance. Moreover, employee–residents decry the fact that they have virtually no benefits and can be terminated without notice. They resent the fact that the city workers receive benefits because of their union.

RESIDENT COMPLAINTS AND FUNDING ISSUES

Resident complaints have escalated over the past 2 years. The most recent was an angry letter to the mayor and city council describing many residents' frustrations. In it, residents complained of rats in the buildings; faulty electrical systems; leaking toilets; drug dealers having gun battles on the streets; and inadequate public transportation to shopping centers, medical offices, or vocational training facilities.

DEALING WITH COMPLAINTS

It is now January and the new city council members have begun their 2-year terms. Topping their agenda is the angry letter from Piccadilly Manor residents. The council finds frustration, too, at having inadequate funds for improving conditions there. A meeting, which Mayor Jackson has called, is the first step in dealing with the problem. Those at the meeting are a task force consisting of Mayor Jackson, one incumbent and two new council members, Housing Authority Board Director Wilson, and two Piccadilly Manor residents. Mayor Jackson hopes the task force will find creative ways to address the administrative crisis. Frustrated with past strategies that misfired, Jackson wants to reinvent the way Piccadilly Manor is managed. By involving residents with those who can help turn decisions into action, Mayor Jackson is confident the new council will take creative measures.

TASK FORCE MEMBERSHIP

The task force is comprised of the following members.

Mayor Terry Jackson. The mayor would like to accommodate the varied interests of the board. Because Jackson will begin campaigning for reelection later this year, he wants to cultivate the support of both residents and other interest groups associated with housing. The mayor believes that this can be achieved by offering several financial incentives, such as tax breaks to businesses and nonprofit organizations. The mayor is eager to show voters that financial management is sound and has improved the well-being of residents.

Council Member Taylor Jones. Jones is a newly elected liberal who believes that the housing project should be moved from the inner city to the suburbs. The reasoning is that tax receipts will be higher there, services more abundant, and the quality of life will be improved, especially for families with school-age children. Jones proposes financing the move through a variety of means, such as grants, nonprofit funds, and fundraisers. Jones was friends in college with a person who is the head of a popular rock group and knows the person will donate concert proceeds to help fund the relocation.

Council Member Tracy Smith. Smith, a returning council member, is a pessimist. Moving tenants to the suburbs will solve nothing. In fact, it will create *more* problems. Suburban property values will tumble, the crime rate will increase, and "white flight" will escalate. Smith believes that existing housing is structurally sound, based on recent studies, and that tenants oppose moving. Some upgrading is necessary, but Smith can't count on major sources of revenue. Smith believes that the money that *does* come in would be best used for self-help programs that would teach tenants how to manage their units.

Council Member Cam Brown. Brown, a local businessowner and first-time council member, strongly believes that inefficient management should be eliminated. The solution is to contract essential services. This could be done at lower cost than is currently provided for under civil service policies. The council would be responsible for directly overseeing the contracted work and would pinpoint deficiencies quickly. Brown does not believe the council should invest more money in the existing system because that system does not work.

Pat Davis. Davis is a Piccadilly Manor employee–resident. Davis has been active in getting support for public housing from medical, religious, and charitable nonprofit organizations. Davis is rumored to have had ties with militant groups in the late 1960s and has a style that is direct and confrontational. Davis believes that other council members are insensitive to the needs of housing tenants. She believes that other members are perpetuating racial, ethnic, and economic biases by denying further resources to tenant management.

Chris Gomez. Gomez, like Davis, is a Piccadilly Manor resident. Gomez voices the frustrations of many other tenants: There is escalating rent and inadequate plumbing, heating, medical, and protective services. Gomez also favors additional council aid, but is less militant than Davis. Gomez would like to have tenants trained in leadership and community organization skills as well as in maintenance. Gomez believes that a strong community can take care of itself and is committed to creating awareness and support from within.

Housing Authority Board Director, Kelly Wilson. Before adjourning last May, the city council appointed Wilson to replace Corky Corcoran. The *Springvale Times* implicated Corcoran in a real estate scandal involving use of federal housing funds. Corcoran resigned and took a job as finance director in another city. Wilson—formerly a political science professor and director of a nonprofit organization—is knowledgeable on administrative reform and is eager to lead the board to providing first-rate services. Wilson wants to expunge the political influences from the board and promote more participation, which would include a mix of citizens, residents, and civic and community leaders in determining policy.

SPOTTERS' ROLES

Spotters make observations of individuals interacting during the role-playing. Following the role-playing session, spotters give each member feedback and invite reactions.

QUESTIONS FOR LARGE GROUP DISCUSSION FOLLOWING THE ROLE PLAY

1. What different points of view emerged among the players? How did participants manage the differences in viewpoints?

2. How did different task force members solve problems creatively? What words or behaviors encouraged this? discouraged this? How did the interaction among members set the stage for the type of decision model (rational or nonrational) that the task force adopted?

3. In making decisions, what were some criteria task force members used? What values were prominent in the decision-making process?

**QUESTIONS FOR INDIVIDUAL GROUP
MEMBERS FOLLOWING THE ROLE PLAY**

Each group member also should answer
the following questions:

1. What type of decision-making model
   did members use? What conditions
   affected the type of model used?

2. How did you generate options for
   solving the administrative problems?

3. What criteria did you use to evaluate
   the options suggested? How were
   these criteria established?

4. How did differences in member interests affect the process
   of decision making?

5. How did the membership differences affect creating novel
   strategies?

6. How were political differences
   resolved?

7. How satisfied were you with
   the recommendations chosen?

11

PUBLIC LEADERSHIP AND INNOVATION

SYNOPSIS

This chapter points out that innovation is more difficult in the public than the private sector, but can be achieved under certain conditions. It defines innovation as changes in services or products resulting in something new to industries, organizations, or individuals. Chapter 11 discusses several forms of innovation in the public sector, such as reinvention, reengineering, and Total Quality Management (TQM). It enumerates conditions for successful innovations and depicts skills leaders need.

OBJECTIVES

- To define innovation
- To describe conditions that enhance innovation in the public sector
- To discuss examples of innovation in government
- To demonstrate skills in leadership innovation

KEY TERMS AND CONCEPTS

change agent

charisma

creativity

empowerment

entrepreneurialism

feasibility assessment

innovation

National Productivity Review Achievement Award

public partnerships

"small wins"

Total Quality Management (TQM)

transactional leadership

transformational leader

visioning

INTRODUCTION

Many movements in the past have strongly urged innovation in government. In the nineteenth century, the Pendleton Act set up standards for civil employment based on merit rather than political affiliation. Later, Woodrow Wilson declared that administration was distinct from politics, an idea that has become the core of public administration. The Hoover Commission outlined great reforms in the management of governmental personnel. Further, all presidents since Nixon have sought to make government more responsive to public interests. Callahan and Holzer (1994, p. 201), working from contemporary sources, state:

> Government has never been under such pressure from the public to be more productive and effective, nor has government appeared more willing to change.

Bounds, Yorks, Adams, and Ramsey (1994), state that organizations evolve in three phases: normalcy, anomaly, and replacement. They say that the old bureaucratic model of maintaining the status quo, or "normalcy," is ineffectual. When governments evolve into anomalies, they lack the tools to fulfill their mission. On diagnosing this condition, however, agencies search for new principles to guide their work. Innovation is therefore necessary for survival.

The requirements of public service, however, make innovation difficult. Light (1994) identifies some limitations of the government: frequent leadership changes, failure to integrate innovations into the agency's mission, and lack of funding from elected leaders for developing new ideas. Roessner (1977) also outlines some criticisms that suggest government is less innovative than the private sector.

- Bureaucrats form budgets according to the needs of their bureaus, not overall efficiency.
- Agencies have limited external pressure to improve performance and receive negative feedback when they try.
- Public organizations lack executive control.
- Public agencies lack the incentive of profit.

- Government lacks clearly defined goals.
- Because of the high leadership turnover and lack of executive control, leaders must produce immediate results.
- The government lacks competition.
- There is an imbalance between tax revenue and services rendered.
- The government is driven by routine standards rather than consumer demands.

Roessner (1977), however, states that productivity in government is based on effective measures used in service industries. Further, government faces competition in many ways, especially in the widespread contracting to private companies. Innovation is also apparent in new forms of incentive— flexible time schedules or allowing each team to make decisions on how best to serve clients. He notes that it is important to "hold on to a vision, to tolerate disorder, and to keep exploring ways to realize what employees— in either the private or the public sector—believe is possible to achieve" (1977, p. 8).

In order for innovation to succeed in government, several conditions must be met:

- A methodical process of creatively envisioning a desirable future
- Generating breakthrough ideas that work within the frame of an agency's objective and the scheme of decentralized government
- Supporters with diverse resources from many public and private groups
- Organizations with enough flexibility to function in changing conditions

Leadership, which coordinates and implements innovation, requires the creativity and persistence of many people. To meet the challenges of public sector innovation, leaders must cultivate the skills necessary to orchestrate change. Chapter 11 is designed to help leaders develop these skills by describing the process of innovation. To further develop these abilities, we look at examples of innovative programs in the public sector. Because leaders assume various roles in innovation, this chapter also outlines behavior that would yield success.

WHAT IS INNOVATION?

In general, we may define *innovation* as any change in service that produces something new to an industry or organization. Innovation hinges on the type of mission an organization has and how it seeks to fulfill it. It also depends on how people working on the project use their resources to implement ideas.

The definition has several related concepts. Creativity is a form of innovation. Several scholars, however, distinguish innovation by saying it is *applied creativity*. Innovation differs from similar concepts of creativity: entrepreneurialism, invention, reinvention, and reengineering. We shall briefly explore these concepts.

INNOVATION

Bingham (1976) defines innovation as the first use of an idea by a group whose members have similar goals. However, Elden and Sanders (1996) view *innovation* as an offshoot of something invented elsewhere; to create something that didn't exist before is invention, not innovation. Rogers (1985) says that innovation results from the diffusion of new ideas to organizations that adapt them to their needs.

INVENTION AND ENTREPRENEURIALISM

Invention is conceptually akin to entrepreneurialism since they both create a unique idea, service, or product. Roberts and King (1992, p. 176) define *entrepreneurs* as "social actors who are involved in the creation, design, and implementation of innovative ideas in public sector practice." They see entrepreneurs as those who work outside the formal boundaries of government to initiate policy. Schneider, Teske, and Mintrom (1995) note that entrepreneurs engage in "arbitrage," which can mean a novel recombination of existing elements or using a product for a new function.

REINVENTION AND REENGINEERING

Reinvention continues in the entrepreneurial spirit by introducing changes that replace old ideas with radically different concepts. Yet, reinvention and reengineering, according to Elden and Sanders (1996), are done *to* organizations rather than *with* them. That is, both reinvention and reengineering imply a drastic change rather than a sustained development.

In order to change government creatively, both innovation and radical change are necessary. It is not sufficient merely to supplant old ideas and introduce new ways of thinking. Ideas must be adapted to specific conditions. In government, these conditions involve a constellation of interest groups, regulatory bodies, clients, and businesses. Tailoring novel ideas to a variety of organizations demands innovative leadership skills. In the same way, converting creativity into useful tools depends on sustained learning (Senge, 1990). Public leaders, in particular, need skills for cultivating organizations that can continually adapt to the special demands of their employees and clients.

WHAT IT TAKES TO BE CREATIVE IN GOVERNMENT

Creativity in government requires thinking in a way that completely breaks with past practices. It is important to think differently about how the government runs. In the absence of novel approaches, new ways of doing business will revert by default to old ways. However, this thinking must recognize the fragmented nature of government. Power to change rests in a variety of elected officials at all levels of government. It also rests in a large number of organizations that have legal or economic influence over elected bodies. Unlike private entrepreneurs, public innovators find creative solutions by working with a variety of public officials and voters. West and Berman (1997) maintain that while individuals are important, administrative creativity is viewed as a *group* process. The process demands that the group suggests, evaluates, and accepts new ideas.

ORGANIZATIONAL STRUCTURES

The structure of a governmental agency influences the generation of creative ideas. Some of these structural elements, identified by research studies, are as follows.

Turbulent Environment. Creative ideas emerge when organizations are pressured to solve problems. Crisis propels a search for cues. In the economic and political devastation following the 1904 hurricane in Galveston, Texas, citizens demanded a more effective emergency response system. From their demands, the concept of an independently appointed city manager came into being. Organizations that experience no such turbulence become resistant to change.

Interdependence. Interdependent organizations rely on each other for ideas, raw materials, funds, and/or technological resources. They contribute services and products to a common purpose. In order to offer innovative services, interdependent agencies must seek creative and reliable contributions from internal and external sources. Parochial, or independent, agencies rarely invite creative ideas (Delbecq & Mills, 1985).

Organizational Size and Resource Availability. Large organizations often support innovation more than small ones for several reasons. Large organizations have greater material and financial resources. They also have more support from elected officials, appointed committees, and public interest groups. Having ample resources enhances creativity (Kingdon, 1995; Koberg, 1987). Further, large organizations often have a great number of professionals who contribute diverse viewpoints to solving problems.

Decentralization and Flexible Structures. Decentralized organizations— ones that rely on the work of small teams—often delegate authority and encourage workers to come up with innovative ways to solve problems. If creative ideas are filtered through layers of management, it becomes difficult for top-level managers to appreciate the need for reform.

ORGANIZATIONAL LEADERSHIP

CLIMATE A climate open to innovation depends not only on the structure of an organization, but also on a leader's values and attitudes. In general, innovation flourishes where managers value the improvement of work. Managers must also foster workers' satisfaction and communicate an interest in experimentation and risk-taking.

Delbecq and Mills (1985) studied organizations with high and low innovation. They sought to identify qualities that encouraged the generation and implementation of creative ideas. They found that managers often:

- had ambivalent support for novel suggestions;
- gave inadequate resources in early phases of a project, and forced those with creative solutions to justify their requests for resources;
- allowed other departments to compete for resources; and
- made decisions based on political connections rather than unbiased assessments of novel alternatives.

PERSONAL CHARACTERISTICS Several research studies have found that most innovators have certain personal qualities. Among the most prominent personal traits include the level of education, the degree of psychological flexibility, a cosmopolitan attitude, and a willingness to take risks (Schneider, Teske, & Mintrom, 1995).

Because of the differences between public and private organizations, Roberts and King (1992) believe that public entrepreneurs—that is, those able to bring about change through innovation—have particular personal qualities. To test this, they studied five public entrepreneurs: the director of a think tank, the head of a lobbying group, the president of a nonprofit organization, an author/educator, and an elected official. Through careful observing and interviewing, the authors analyzed their subjects' thinking patterns, character development, and maturity of outlook toward problems. They found six main qualities of the entrepreneurs:

1. A high degree of personal involvement in projects
2. A strong orientation toward achievement
3. A self-view as an instigator of constructive social activity
4. High leadership and management potential
5. High imagination
6. Critical and analytical thinking skills

Roberts and King (1992) also discovered that public entrepreneurs differed from their private sector counterparts. They stated that the differences centered mainly on the fact that public entrepreneurs have little control over resources, forcing them to rely on their influence to achieve collective ends. In looking at these differences, they found the following.

Attitude. Public entrepreneurs generally had a respectful and tolerant view of others. Private entrepreneurs were often manipulative, vengeful, ethically dubious, and self-promoting.

Power. Public entrepreneurs relied on the power of their personal resources: ideas, relationships, influence, and hard work. Private entrepreneurs used positional power and controlled vast resources.

Values and Ideals. Public entrepreneurs acted out of a sense of values and duty. Private entrepreneurs also possessed a set of values, but self-interest often prevented them from acting on their beliefs.

TRANSFORMATIONAL LEADERSHIP

The innovative leaders are often transformational leaders who motivate followers. A transformational leader must define and implement goals that will benefit the whole social order, and not merely a small section of it. We can therefore define a *transformational* leader as one who uses inspiration and education to convert the interests of followers into a motivation to achieve socially beneficial ends.

Transformational leadership differs from *transactional* leadership in that transactional leadership is based on an exchange or contract between leaders and followers. Transactional leadership includes the careful calculation of: (1) the amount of effort needed for a particular task; (2) the amount of resources needed to succeed; (3) the possible outcomes given limited resources; and (4) the payoff, or the ability to satisfy those affected by the task.

Transformational leadership is often marked by *charisma,* what Weber (cited in Shafritz & Hyde, 1987) calls "special gifts." Weber observed that these unique abilities spring to life when groups are confronted with danger or crisis. He noted that during crisis, a leader without charisma fails to give followers a feeling of security, a vision of a better future, or the skills to affect a desirable conclusion.

Charisma brings distinction to transformational leadership. Leaders with charisma usually set high expectations and have a strong need for power. However, they also have great conviction in their views and confidence in themselves and others. These leaders offer an unconventional vision that is not yet attainable. Charismatic leaders often use symbolic language to punctuate the importance of goals and to inspire followers (Conger & Kanungo, 1988). They also seek to enhance the values that improve the way followers feel about themselves. These values allow followers to excel and to achieve recognition and status. It helps followers to find meaning and fulfillment, to serve a humane cause, regain what they have lost, or to recover from disastrous circumstances (Shamir, Zakey, Breinin, & Popper, 1998). Followers solidify these values by joining groups that support them, and by using slogans or songs that express them.

However, Bass (1985) observes that transformational leadership can exist without symbolic speech, compelling visions, or even endearing personalities. Some forms of charisma—as we see in the magnetism of popular actors—do not always alter character. Whereas charisma has the ability to inspire followers, it also glorifies the leader. Therefore, charisma may not involve genuine talent or even exemplary action. What matters is that followers *perceive* a positive influence—real or imagined—and act on it. Charisma rests in the eye of the follower.

Waldman, Bass, and Yammarino (1990, p. 383) define *charisma* as "exemplary acts that followers interpret as involving extraordinary abilities, determination, and confidence. [Charisma instills] the desire to identify with the leader." With this identification, followers adopt the values of charismatic leaders, and become committed to the same goals.

Behling and McFillen (1996) assert that charismatic leadership produces three main follower responses.

1. **Awe.** In this condition, leaders project self-confidence and followers give them unconditional acceptance. Problems and relationships are seen in terms of the present and not the past. Leaders give their followers their full attention, courtesy, and trust. Followers work effectively in the absence of constant approval and recognition. Leaders succeed by creating self-portraits that invoke mythical heroes.

2. **Inspiration.** Leaders inspire others by being sympathetic. They are sensitive to the needs and fears of followers. Followers are also inspired when leaders demonstrate a moral justification for their actions. Leaders also inspire by showing constant commitment to achieving a goal.

3. **Empowerment.** Leaders reassure followers. They make followers feel competent by exuding their own confidence and mastery over a situation. Additionally, leaders give followers a chance to see how their abilities can help a project succeed.

WHAT IS THE LEADER'S ROLE IN INNOVATION?

In bringing innovation to government, leaders play several roles, including personal guidance, team facilitation, and the overall management of organizations. These roles are the result of a combination of factors: the leader's individual needs and skills, opportunities in the organization, relationships with those inside and outside the organization, and the ability of followers to solve problems and learn new things.

ORGANIZATIONAL ROLES

Proactive Change Agent. To facilitate innovation, public leaders must actively seek opportunities to improve present and future conditions. Change in bureaucratic organizations frequently comes about after a crisis or when a situation becomes unbearable. This kind of *reactive* change often addresses the symptoms, and not the causes of a problem. Innovative leaders, however, see problems as opportunities and take early action to keep them from becoming crises.

Power Broker. Innovative public leaders understand both the formal structure of organizations and the informal ways to get things done. This means that leaders know who has power and influence in an agency. Leaders also know when to introduce change, and when to wait for more receptive occasions. Innovative leaders are able to gain support for projects, and have command over many bases of power.

Resource Finder. Because of limited financial and material resources in government, innovative leaders learn where to find information and support. For instance, a leader may contact employees, clientele, political allies, or private sector leaders.

Champion–Negotiator. Innovative leaders work both individually and with teams to generate ideas, policies, and strategies for change. Listening to the thoughts and feelings of others fuels imagination. Sponsoring those who offer novel approaches encourages follower support and produces greater productivity.

SKILLS OF INNOVATION

To enact the above-mentioned roles, innovative leaders must master many skills:

- Creative thinking and problem solving
- Visioning and strategic planning
- Agenda setting
- Policy making
- Employee empowerment
- Organizational development
- Communication skills
- Use of teams

Although much has been written on the skills innovative leaders need, we will focus on those important to public leaders (summarized below). Readers may practice these skills by completing the exercises at the end of this chapter.

IDEA FINDING

Kingdon (1995) notes that innovative leaders identify problems and act to resolve them in several ways. Often, problems are revealed through a "focusing" event, such as a crisis or a personal experience. Problems also surface when leaders realize a disparity between current conditions and their idea of an ideal state. Finally, leaders discover problems when analyzing their followers' approaches or thought patterns that could affect their performance. When people are unable to make sense of a situation, they often look to leaders to resolve these discrepancies.

Bingham (1976) conducted an extensive study of innovation in public libraries, school districts, and public housing. His findings indicate that motives for innovation spring from several sources in addition to simply recognizing a problem. He found that the most influential variable affecting bureaucratic innovation was the amount of economic resources available to leaders. Moreover, innovative ideas increased if there were "spillover" resources; that is, innovations in one area that benefited other areas, such as use of computer technology in libraries. Other ways to stimulate innovation included gathering information from professionals, the use of process grants, and the use of feedback.

CREATIVE THINKING

Kanter (1988) says that a crucial skill in creative problem solving is the ability to think "kaleidoscopically." This kind of thinking, she says, means shaking up the world we often take for granted, and forcing ourselves to see new patterns in it. As a kaleidoscope presents different colors and shapes, creative thinking requires seeing things from many points of view. Innovative leaders often reflect on their experiences and try to view people and events through different frames of meaning (Schneider et al., 1995). Leaders also participate in communities outside their own, where people create new symbols and offer new cultural meanings. Innovative leaders often find themselves moving among a variety of educational, civic, or professional organizations—in short, people at the forefront of change in their fields. This cross-disciplinary contact inspires new ideas and innovation.

VISIONING

Although creative thinking contributes to innovation, it is only part of the process of envisioning a desirable future. Visioning involves seeing the whole process of innovation—from idea to action—in an encapsulated form. Vision is what drives leaders to share creative ideas with people who can implement them. Vision often emerges when leaders see a chance to transform a persistent problem or crisis into a public advantage (Altschuler & Behn, 1997; Goss, Pascale, & Athos, 1993).

AGENDA SETTING

In the public sector, putting ideas and visions into action means establishing an agenda with elected officials and potential citizen stakeholders. One of the first steps in this process is assembling those involved and analyzing the needs of the organization (Goss et al., 1993). By involving the main stakeholders in defining goals and solving problems, they gain an understanding of both the vision and the need for action (Emery & Purser, 1996). In addition, innovative leaders focus on critical, timely, and persistent issues appearing in the media (Kingdon, 1995).

CREATING DIALOGUE

In addition to focusing on specific goals, innovative leaders must spur dialogue to ensure their followers' commitment. The various perspectives become a widening net of discussion. Leaders establish forums for public debate (Bryson & Crosby, 1992). These forums, in turn, generate new ideas for policy making (Moore, 1995). In transforming debate into policy, innovative leaders establish new meanings and symbols that diverse followers value. From these ideas, innovative leaders construct a common vision.

CREATIVE PROBLEM-SOLVING TECHNIQUES

Public leaders use a variety of creative problem-solving techniques to produce innovative strategies. Among the most fruitful is the Nominal Group Technique (Delbecq, Van de Ven, & Gustafson, 1975) described earlier in this book. This technique uses brainstorming to include all participants, and enables people with diverse points of view to come to an agreement on a strategy.

CONDUCTING FEASIBILITY ASSESSMENTS

Once followers have agreed on a strategy, public leaders may wish to conduct a study to see how feasible it would be. The leader would not only assess the technical feasibility, but also the possibility of future constraints, such as budget cutbacks or public rejection (Kingdon, 1995). Some common pitfalls, according to Delbecq and Mills (1985) include overestimating demand and setting unrealistic revenue goals, overly complex designs, and an underestimation of the training needed to bring the services to a large number of clients.

PILOTING IDEAS AND STRATEGIES

In the public sector, a sweeping change is difficult because of decentralized political power, fragmented organizations, and diffused accountability. What works, however, are incremental changes, or "small wins" (Weick, 1984). These pilots, or tests, allow innovators to examine how new ideas are received. Based on this assessment, they can continue or retract the program. Workable pilot projects must be concrete and compatible with organizational goals. They must also have the potential for high visibility (Kingdon, 1995). Implementers must be committed to the project, and have the assurance of proper funding and technical support before beginning (Delbecq & Mills, 1985). Without this up-front support, even the best-conceived project will fail.

EMPOWERING USERS

Innovative leaders demonstrate to others the relevance of their creations to the needs and values of their followers. Leaders empower others to adopt or adapt innovations. Conger and Kanungo (1988) assert that empowerment is not the same as delegating authority to employees, but rather a way to promote autonomy. They note that empowerment is

> a process of enhancing feelings of self-efficacy among organizational members through identification of conditions that foster powerlessness and through their removal by both formal organizational practices and informal techniques of providing efficacy information (p. 474).

How can leaders empower others? One way is to create open channels of communication (Rogers, 1985). Leaders may also redesign the organization to encourage interaction among departments. They can reward managers for actively seeking out ideas and using critical thinking skills (Thompson & Ingraham, 1996). Further, leaders can empower employees by including them in regular planning sessions or task forces (House, 1988). Lastly, leaders can reeducate or train employees to be more innovative and confident (Thomas & Velthouse, 1990).

ASSESSING INNOVATIONS AND FEEDBACK

To ensure success, innovative leaders must assess whether an innovation has met the expectations of those using it, and plan for improvements if needed. Assessing the progress of the innovation includes formal and informal evaluation tools. Methods often include surveying users of the product, interviewing relevant personnel, and observing trends in financial and personal documents. In general, innovations rely on a variety of objective measurements that are based on overall organizational performance (Kopczynski & Lombardo, 1999). This often means using a ratio of costs to expected benefits.

Poister and Streib (1999) feel that leaders should incorporate innovations into strategic planning and management. They note that strategic planning

blends futuristic thinking, objective analysis, and subjective evaluation of goals and priorities to chart future courses of action that will ensure the long-run vitality and effectiveness of the organization (p. 309).

However, Poister and Streib add that strategic management is mostly concerned with developing strategies and periodically updating them. Strategic management encompasses managerial decisions that determine long-range performance. This requires four actions:

1. Continual monitoring of external trends and forces likely to affect agency
2. Shaping and communicating a clear vision of what the government is striving to become
3. Creating strategic agendas to drive decisions at other levels of the organization
4. Guiding all management processes in a cohesive way to enhance strategic agendas

Innovative leaders can affect profound changes in government by integrating new policies into management, planning of services, and relationships to outside groups.

EXAMPLES OF INNOVATION IN GOVERNMENT

The current interest in governmental innovation has produced numerous changes in thinking and practice. The categories of innovation seen in the public sector today are described below.

NATIONAL PRODUCTIVITY REVIEW (NPR) ACHIEVEMENT AWARDS

The National Productivity Review (NPR) has spawned several movements to improve productivity through innovative leadership. For instance, Thompson and Ingraham (1996) describe 135 laboratories operating in federal agencies initiated through NPR. Callahan and Holzer (1994) describe some recipients of the annual Exemplary State and Local (EXSL) Awards. These agencies were recognized by the National Center for Public Productivity at Rutgers University for significant cost savings, increased productivity, and improved products. Some examples of these improvements in 1992 include the following.

1. An automated fingerprint identification system that has helped to solve crimes, save time, and cut costs in nine western states.

2. The Diversity Commitment program in San Diego, California, which has started over 200 diversity awareness projects. To affect this change, this agency used strategic planning, discussion, education, and problem solving.

3. Friends for Life in Albuquerque, New Mexico, established a base of community volunteers who augmented juvenile services by providing companionship, mentoring, and surrogate family relationships.

4. Personnel Pilot Project in the State of Florida division of Worker's Compensation. They increased productivity, quality, and consumer satisfaction under a pilot program authorized by Florida Senate Bill 2302. Under the provisions of the law, the division streamlined its classification and pay plan, developed employee incentive programs, and created innovative training and career development projects. In fiscal year 1991–1992, the division saved $687,034.

TOTAL QUALITY MANAGEMENT (TQM)

Governmental agencies have begun to use the system of Total Quality Management (TQM). TQM is a comprehensive process of change that combines problem solving, productivity improvement, and organizational development. Berman and West (1995) surveyed local governments that used TQM and find that most of these agencies gave rewards for using TQM and committed substantial resources to it. The most successful uses of TQM had certain characteristics in common: They involved high levels of professionalism and training, occurred in large cities, and worked under council–manager governments. Quality interventions were most common in police, recreation, and personnel departments.

Origins. Many projects resulted from internal budget pressures and the need to increase employees' productivity. Several were responses to public complaints and voter demands.

Implementation. Implementation strategies stemmed from transformational leadership—that is, leaders who introduced new visions, goals, and processes. Most of the programs, moreover, encouraged employee empowerment and involvement through a reward system. Support came from a variety of sources: elected officials, municipal managers, community members, and influential private figures.

Organizational Factors. Successful organizations incorporated TQM innovations into policies and human resource programs. They improved communication between departments, team problem solving, employee participation, and training programs.

MULTIPLE PARTNERSHIPS

Many innovative programs have taken place because of partnerships among federal, state, and local governments, businesses, and citizens.

FINANCIAL MANAGEMENT PARTNERSHIP Perlmutter and Cnaan (1995) describe using private money for public programs in Philadelphia. The partnership included local residents, city officials, and businesses.

Philadelphia, facing insufficient tax revenues, sought alternative funding through business partnerships. The partnership resulted in a joint effort to redesign fiscal management, an example of long-term, proactive planning.

USING MUNICIPAL, BUSINESS, UNIVERSITY, AND CUSTOMER RESOURCES Wethersfield, Connecticut, instituted an innovative program that combined TQM, strategic planning, citizens groups, and the largest employer in the community (Rusaw, 1997). The program began with the vision of town Manager, Lee Erdmann, to revitalize the economy, involve citizens in government, and encourage more efficient use of dwindling financial resources among employees. Following a seminar in TQM, Erdmann sent city managers to a year-long training program at the University of Connecticut.

Management Training. As part of the program's completion requirements, the managers applied TQM concepts to their own operations by initiating small projects. These projects consisted of identifying who provided and received services, mapping workflow, analyzing strengths and weaknesses, and developing a strategy for making incremental changes. After evaluating client needs and feedback, the managers identified obstacles to reaching the goal and recommended changes to reach it efficiently.

Using Customer Feedback. Wethersfield used several methods for enabling employees to identify and prevent potential problems. Some of these methods included citizen surveys, service audits, and the appointment of community liaisons. The town also took steps to create forums for discussing mutual needs. Members of all departments wanted to listen sympathetically to the citizens' ideas so they could apply them to everyday operations. This process yielded creative ideas for improving services. It also produced an examination of stereotypes in an effort to reduce obstacles to communication.

Creation of "Small Wins" Laboratories. The extensive customer service training program created an opportunity to design novel problem-solving strategies as well as techniques of affecting small changes that were low risk but, in the long run, profitable. The success of these numerous small improvements quickly spread throughout the organization. As it did, the overall climate became one of trust, support, commitment to improvement, and openness to taking risks.

Strategic Planning. In the maelstrom of downsizing and cutbacks, Wethersfield created a method of envisioning a better cultural and economic future for the community. Erdmann's participatory plan inspired and coordinated incremental changes. This document, while it gave the town a glimpse of a brighter economic future, also became the guide to help Wethersfield adapt to changing circumstances.

EMPLOYEE EMPOWERMENT

Rago (1996) describes the barriers and struggles in trying to change the Texas Department of Mental Health and Retardation from an agency based on management to one based on leadership. With the goal of becoming more customer-oriented, the department embarked on a project to empower customers, employees, and the organizational culture. The effort succeeded largely because the managers adhered closely to the agency's mission statements. This created a sense of involvement for the employees—they took greater responsibility for decisions and therefore felt they had contributed to the program's success. Rago concludes that five conditions must exist for a large-scale empowerment program to work:

1. Leadership must maintain a constant purpose and effort.

2. Reform uses many of the commonly accepted norms and values of the old culture. This is because it is more difficult to introduce completely different norms and values in an existing organization.

3. The agency's vision and goal must be clearly communicated to all levels of the agency. Leaders must be noticeably involved in the change effort.

4. Training must have practical applications for the participants. Supervisors must expect employees to apply the training to current practices.

5. Employees must overcome their personal struggles with change. Change can create a mental state that pits the worker against the organization.

CULTURE CHANGE

Leadership styles often follow the same approach as the organization. In a prison, high-ranking officials usually define this approach. Yet, in the California Department of Corrections, officials made progress toward changing their leadership to a participatory style (Battalino, Beutler, & Shani, 1996). The need to change was evidenced by several conditions: the influx of 1,700 prisoners, an increasingly hostile environment, the threat of legislative inquiry, workers' compensation claims, and court actions.

EMPHASIS ON HUMAN VALUES The structural innovations of trial projects in the California prison resulted in three major changes: (1) a new health care division; (2) automated record-keeping; and (3) the "Treatment of People" program, which sought to transform the organization into one that values the contributions of each member.

In the latter program, two consultants worked with the director and chief deputy to begin changing the system in 1993. The top officials appointed an advisory council of diverse people who discussed and planned a reform approach. Central to this was the development—with staff input—of five core values. The director and deputy approved these values and communicated them through bulletins, newsletter articles, and speeches. The values became the basis for a continuous quality improvement. To reinforce change, managers held team-building retreats to test new projects. The successful results enabled the department to set up additional advisory committees of staff to oversee the projects.

The projects included a skills-based training program, audits, and the development of performance assessments.

OBSTACLES TO CHANGE The changes, however, found some difficulties. The "Treatment of People" program was designed to change attitudes and foster reform. However, it was not fortified with strategic thinking, analysis, planning, or assessment of resources. Further, the new system had trouble adapting to existing procedures. In addition, the efforts were viewed as added responsibilities that required much work before they could be started. The lessons learned from the pilot projects, moreover, did not diffuse through the whole department. This might have been different, the authors conclude, if a parallel system had been in place to support the change.

SUMMARY

This chapter introduced the main concepts of innovation in the public sector. It explored the driving forces and the constraints of innovative leadership. Factors that affected the rise of innovation included rapidly changing conditions outside organizations and the interdependent relationships within them. Both these conditions require careful management. Successful leadership depended on how much commitment workers held for the organization's goal. It also hinged on personal qualities that enhanced innovation, such as creativity or dedication.

Innovative leaders bring about change by playing roles: proactive change agent, power broker, resource finder, and champion–negotiator. To assume these roles, leaders need the following skills:

- Creative thinking
- Strategic visioning
- Generating a variety of possible problem-solving strategies
- Analyzing feasibility studies and trial projects
- Careful assessment of an innovation's progress
- Empowering innovation users

This chapter also gave examples of how innovation has transformed contemporary government. We discussed the innovative ideas in some exemplary practices and programs. Innovations underscored many projects associated with Total Quality Management, public–private partnerships, employee empowerment, and culture change. As greater public interest centers on government reinvention, the need for innovation in leadership will escalate.

In Chapter 12, we shall examine the ethical challenges that confront public leaders who seek to transform government.

QUESTIONS FOR THOUGHT AND DISCUSSION

1. From your own experiences with public organizations, what are some impediments to innovation? How do these barriers affect follower motivation? stakeholder perceptions of public sector responsiveness and effectiveness? In your opinion, are these conditions unique to government? Explain why or why not.

2. What are some incentives public leaders may use to promote creativity among followers? What are some particularly effective tangible rewards in this regard? intangible rewards?

3. In your opinion, how might leaders facilitate innovation through organizational change to foster greater productivity and follower satisfaction? Discuss some particular strategies leaders may use to bring about small wins.

4. Recall some contingency leadership skills and techniques and some interpersonal communications strategies discussed earlier in the text. In particular, describe some ways leaders may empower followers to provide innovative service. What are some barriers that affect empowerment? How can leaders use personal power skills to overcome these?

INNOVATIVE ORGANIZATIONAL AUDIT

DIRECTIONS

Respond to the following statements as you feel they apply to your organization. Rate how true the statements are by ranking them on a scale of 1 (LEAST TRUE) to 5 (MOST TRUE). Enter your ratings on the rules of the Audit section. When you have completed the audit, in the Scoring section, enter the scores from the Audit section in the rules supplied for each, total each score, and interpret the results.

AUDIT

1. _____ People are rewarded when they challenge standard operating procedures.

2. _____ The organization prepares employees to meet the challenges of rapid change in their work.

3. _____ Managers make decisions based largely on an understanding of the client's needs.

4. _____ Employees may use discretion in deciding how they will carry out novel situations.

5. _____ There is not much duplication in the work this organization does.

6. _____ Employees visit other organizations to identify possible practices to adapt.

7. _____ The organization has measurable work standards for professional work.

8. _____ The organization regularly gathers information from people it serves and uses it to change how things are done.

9. _____ Employees have numerous opportunities to develop new skills on the job.

10. _____ The organization gives adequate financial rewards for work improvement ideas.

11. _____ Managers help employees try out new ideas.

12. _____ Managers resolve "turf wars" between departments through negotiation.

13. _____ Most workers have daily contact with key constituents.

14. _____ Employees regularly attend training sessions to learn new skills.

15. _____ Employees use professional judgment in deciding ethical matters in their work.

16. _____ The organization adapts to rapid change among our clients and customers.

17. _____ Managers usually use different approaches to motivate employees.

18. _____ Employees are encouraged to learn from failure.

19. _____ Most groups work together in accomplishing the major work of the organization.

20. _____ It is easy to discuss ideas with managers here.

21. _____ Employees use agreed-on standards of quality in performing their work.

22. _____ The organization has a vibrant employee recognition program.

23. _____ The organization uses teams to develop new approaches to solving problems.

24. _____ The organization has many professionals who came from other organizations or the private sector.

25. _____ Team leadership roles rotate among members.

SCORING

This assessment measures nine characteristics of an organization that promote innovation. To analyze them, write the score for each item in the blank spaces and add the total score for each of the nine characteristics. The numbers in parentheses refer to the ratings you entered in the Audit section.

1. **Risk Taking.** Employees are challenged and rewarded for coming up with novel ways of doing things and are encouraged to learn from past mistakes. Standard operating procedures are guides, not rules, for making decisions.
   (1._____ 11._____ 18._____)
   Total: _____

2. **Rewards.** People receive tangible and intangible rewards for trying out new ideas. Employees receive top-level recognition for their contributions so that they feel a sense of pride and achievement in their work.
   (10._____ 17._____ 22._____)
   Total: _____

3. **Empowering.** Employees are trusted. They are encouraged to use professional judgment in making nonroutine decisions. They are encouraged to learn and take part regularly in educational events on and off the job.
   (4._____ 9._____ 14._____)
   Total: _____

4. **Objective Measurements.** Employees have valid and objectively defined standards that measure their work. These standards are derived from the organization's mission and assessments of the organization's main programs, products, and services.
   (7._____15._____21._____)
   Total: _____

5. **Feedback.** The company has well-established communication with people inside and outside the organization. It uses information to monitor the quality of service and make corrections before problems escalate. Employees know their customers and clients directly.
(8._____ 13._____) Total: _____

6. **Turbulence.** Organizations are flexible enough to respond to problems. They communicate with employees and customers to enlist support in solving problems.
(2._____ 16._____) Total: _____

7. **Interdependence.** Although the organization has checks and balances to control waste, fraud, or abuse, these controls do not interfere with a seamless flow of work. Managers defer their own interests to the overall mission of the organization.
(5._____ 12._____ 19. _____)
Total: _____

8. **Decentralization.** There is little difference in social status between managers and employees. The organization absorbs a variety of ideas from all personnel to find creative solu-

tions and to boost commitment to reaching goals.
(20._____ 23._____ 25._____)
Total: _____

9. **Cosmopolitan.** In making decisions, managers focus on the "big picture" of customer and client needs. They encourage the influx of new ideas by analyzing feedback and soliciting the skills of "outsiders." They enjoy learning about organizations that use "best" practices.
(3._____ 6._____ 24._____)
Total: _____

TOTAL SCORE (*a total of all the total lines above*): _____

High: 125 points

Low: 45 points

Key: 45 – 65 = low innovation

66 – 85 = low average

86 – 105 = high average

106 – 125 = high innovation

Note: If scores are below 85, this may suggest areas where you, as a leader, may institute some new ideas and practices. If scores are above 85, reinforce those positive qualities. Improvement is continuous.

CASE STUDY PROBLEM

A COMMUNITY POLICING EXPERIMENT

TIME: 30 MINUTES

DIRECTIONS

Read the case problem below. After reading the case, divide into small groups and complete two tasks.

1. Imagine you have been appointed the Chief of Police to recommend a strategy that will be presented to the city council. Discuss how you would solve the problem creatively. The goal is to determine a strategy that

all team members can agree to and are committed to doing. Appoint a recorder/spokesperson to summarize and report your strategies at the end of the exercise.

2. Using skills of innovation, write how you would "sell" your ideas to the city council, the officers, the residents, and organizations interested in the welfare of Hilldale (10 minutes). When you have finished, dis-

cuss your plans. The spokesperson should be prepared to present your plans to the class.

PROBLEM

In Mega City, the police department faces a continuing problem: Few officers are willing to provide service in the Hilldale section because the high incidence of murder, drug abuse, domestic violence, and prostitution poses great personal risk. In the past, the chief of police, with concurrence of the city council, has given police force volunteers extra pay, additional technical support, and reinforcements to work in high-risk areas such as Hilldale. However, even with these incentives, the city has failed to attract sufficient numbers of volunteers.

The city council is considering a number of options to solve the problem, from using a lottery or pool to supplement volunteers to instituting a community policing pilot project. Under this concept, officers set up substations in neighborhoods and focus on listening to residents' complaints as well as their ideas for improvements. As the Chief of Police, you feel the community policing idea would not only better motivate officers to serve Hilldale, but would also reduce risks by enabling residents to assist officers reduce crime.

12

THE ETHICS OF PUBLIC LEADERSHIP

SYNOPSIS

Because roles of public sector leaders have been changing to adapt to a myriad of new demands for innovation, responsiveness, productivity, and accountability, ethical standards for evaluating leadership behavior have become more complex. In this changing context, this chapter examines foundational concepts of ethics and discusses particular implications for public leaders. Chapter 12 also analyzes conditions affecting ethical development, and organizational, social, economic, and political attributes that facilitate ethical climates in public organizations.

OBJECTIVES

- *To define ethics in the context of public sector leadership*
- *To define key concepts and terms associated with ethics*
- *To distinguish normative and nonnormative views of ethics*
- *To discuss Kohlberg's Stages of Cognitive Moral Development Model*
- *To discuss contributors to ethical development*

KEY TERMS AND CONCEPTS

civism

deontic principles

ethics

nonnormative ethics
normative ethics
particularist ethics
teleological ethics

Kohlberg's Stages of Cognitive Moral Development

laws

universalist versus particularist

moral courage

moral sensitivity

moral understanding

professional responsibility

responsibility

"street-level" bureaucrats

teleology

INTRODUCTION

Public leadership is in a quandary of ethics. Recent scandals and intense media scrutiny of public officials has caused much turmoil and weakened our trust in government. The values of public service have suffered because of the rapidly changing and often conflicting roles that leaders must assume. Kathryn Denhardt (1988) points out that because these roles have changed, new theories of ethical administration should be developed. She notes that several conditions have altered leadership roles:

1. the need for more innovative leaders, especially as catalysts of change,
2. more distinct roles as policymakers,
3. the growth of government and the distancing of legislators from the public who demand more accountability, and
4. increased professional expertise as public bureaucrats move into advocacy arenas.

Ferlie, Pettigrew, Ashburner, and Fitzgerald (1996) state that a public leader's duties are in conflict. That is, they must balance the democratic values of justice, equality, and fairness with market competition.

In this chapter, we will examine ethics in relation to public sector leadership. We shall introduce the main concepts and terms in the field of ethics and relate them to leadership. In addition, we will discuss conditions that affect the personal development of ethics, such as maturity levels, individual traits, and cultural elements. Then we shall discuss how ethical leadership can be cultivated within the changing social, economic, and political landscape.

DEFINITION OF *ETHICS*

In general, the word *ethics* refers to reasoning based on a set of beliefs or principles and their application to a particular situation. Cooper (1982, p. 4)

notes: "Ethics involves substantive reasoning about obligations, consequences, and ultimate ends." He adds, "[D]oing ethics...involves thinking
more systematically about values which are embedded in the choices we
make."

Ethics have two primary origins: (1) reasoning from "universalist" or
higher-order principles that prescribe proper personal or social conduct,
and (2) reasoning from "particularist" principles that are formed through
experience, blending personal and social norms. Prominent in the philosophy of Emmanuel Kant, "universalist" ethics make claims of truth with no
metaphysical support. Claiming universality, they hold that people act ethically because of idealistic character traits (O'Neill, 1996).

"Particularist" ethics, on the other hand, are action-oriented. Based
largely on Aristotle's philosophy, "particularist" ethics embody principles
that emerge from actual social norms. "Particularist" ethics claim validity
based on unique features of time and local context. Principles derived from
such conditions do not apply to all situations.

TELEOLOGICAL ETHICS

Teleological ethics combine reasoning with action. *Teleology* means "end-
seeking." Therefore, this form of ethics is oriented toward objective ends
and practical moral ideals. Teleological ethics are informed by principles
that justify actions by demonstrating that they are instrumental in achieving
a moral objective. Also called "consequentialist," these ethics evaluate decisions according to the morality of outcomes. There are three common forms
of teleological ethics.

1. **Egoism**—the view that everyone ought to promote his or her own
   self-interest
2. **Act Utilitarianism**—judgment based on the expected versus actual
   good or harm
3. **Rule Utilitarianism**—use of moral principles derived from experience

DEONTIC PRINCIPLES

Ethics enable people to develop socially acceptable relationships by providing practical reasoning strategies. This sets up an exchange of mutual rights
that can be applied to a number of situations. The rules are *deontological,* or
"binding." Deontology says that there are certain universal principles that
people are obligated to understand and abide by (Denhardt, 1988). Deontological principles are *requirements* rather than mere recommendations.

Deontic relationships form the basis of rights and obligations. In a relationship, one party has an obligation to meet the needs of another. The other
person is the recipient of the action. However, the obligation to perform an
act can be two-way. Some recipients have the right to request an action,
whereas this right is discretionary for others. For instance, O'Neill (1996)

states that the concept of "justice" involves obligations with rights. As a concept of reciprocal respect (May, 1996), "justice" draws attention to problems of inequality and oppression. Justice obligates those who have the power to address such problems to exercise it. In this sense, justice is both owed and required.

RESPONSIBILITY

Responsibility demands a discretion based on authority. Harmon (1995) defines *responsibility* in terms of being bound to principles external to the agent. That is, responsibility entails being accountable to a higher law, usually defined by legal authority. Responsibility allows an application of judgment based on sensitivity to particular situations. It is based on a perception of "otherness" in moral actions (McDonough, 1982). Responsibility, according to May (1996), has two roots: (1) "giving a response" or being accountable, and (2) "being responsive for," or responding to the need of someone in a specific situation.

PROFESSIONAL RESPONSIBILITY

Responsibility involves recognizing universal rights, while serving as a guide for discretion. For instance, the right to liberty is considered universal. But institutionalized liberty rights are restricted to certain domains. One cannot, for example, exercise full liberty rights of dumping industrial chemical wastes in rivers. Those granting liberty rights bear "distributed obligations" (O'Neill, 1996, p. 130), by specifying for whom the rights are intended. Agents not only use the law as authority, but also shape rights by deciding how the goods or services are delivered.

PUBLIC LEADERSHIP RESPONSIBILITY

Public leaders act ethically when they adopt professional standards of behavior (Van Wart, 1996). Professional standards entail discretion and are based on various values (Jos, 1990). Rohr (1986, p. 65) maintains that public administrators must act "in the public interest." That is, they must follow the ethical standards held for generations by the majority of Americans. In defining what the "public interest" is, administrators use values contained in the U.S. Constitution and U.S. Supreme Court decisions.

The core of a public administrator's responsibility is preserving constitutional values that seek to serve the needs of citizens (Terry, 1995). In balancing political and social requirements, bureaucrats "help form character of the citizenry as well as contribute to the continuous process of shaping a political way of life that is unique to the American regime" (Terry, 1995, p. 24).

NORMATIVE AND NONNORMATIVE ETHICS

NORMATIVE ETHICS

Normative ethics derive from the norms or standards that people develop and use. These norms are implicit, or taken for granted as standards for conduct. They reflect social values that people use to judge circumstances and relationships. Because social conditions change, however, norms also vary. Sometimes norms become outdated or so abstract that they lose all practical meaning. To act ethically in ambiguous situations, leaders must question the basic assumptions and validity of norms. Public leaders must consider several conditions, such as legal obligations, professional and moral responsibilities, and the expectations of clientele (Jos, 1990).

NONNORMATIVE ETHICS

Nonnormative ethics are principles based on legal and/or administrative authority. They dictate how to conduct business and make decisions. They often appear in formal prohibitions, charters, regulations, and policies. Whereas normative ethics rely on socially defined behaviors, nonnormative ethics are *formalized;* that is, they are codified in written form. Nonnormative ethics specify how people should act in certain situations, limiting personal discretion. This often poses problems because one must use *normative* ethics to interpret *nonnormative* documents, such as vaguely written or abstract policies. Because of this, various ethical dilemmas can result.

CONDITIONS AFFECTING ETHICAL BEHAVIOR

To fully understand how conditions can influence ethics, we describe three broad factors: individual qualities, organizational characteristics, and cultural effects.

INDIVIDUAL QUALITIES

Several phenomena contribute to individually developed ethics. The most prominent are explained by theories of moral development. Two in particular are Kohlberg's (1969) stages of moral development and Gilligan's (1982) feminist perspective.

KOHLBERG'S STAGES OF MORAL DEVELOPMENT In developing a model for the development of morality, Kohlberg bases much of his research on the works of Jean Piaget (1932, cited in Trevino, 1992). Piaget, who studied the ethical evolution of children, viewed morality as cognitive and developmental. In extending Piaget's work to young adults, Kohlberg finds that changes in moral reasoning result from cognitive instability. This occurs as adults find their ethical reasoning inadequate or contradictory. They then search for deeper explanations of an experience. Kohlberg maintains that there were three levels of moral development: preconventional, conventional, and postconventional. Each of these levels is further broken down into two stages of development.

Level 1: Preconventional

Stage 1—*A person is exposed to imposed and external rules. Morality consists of following the rules to obtain rewards and avoid punishments.*

Stage 2—*People adopt the moral norms of society or a version of it, such as family, school, or church. Obeying these adopted norms and fulfilling expectations is of central importance.*

Level 2: Conventional

Stage 3—*People assume the roles that are defined by specific personal relationships. They gain the trust and approval of others.*

Stage 4—*People perform fixed duties shaped by their membership in a specific group, institution, or society. Morality consists of performing activities to promote the common good.*

Level 3: Postconventional

Stage 5—*People develop a utilitarian method of evaluating ethics and observe how they affect actual stakeholders.*

Stage 6—*Having realized the shortcomings of widely accepted ethical behaviors, people fashion their own standards. They seek to find creative solutions to ethical dilemmas that serve the common good while respecting the individual rights of all involved.*

Carol Gilligan (1982) challenges Kohlberg's claim that these stages apply to all humankind. She observes that Kohlberg's model is based on reciprocity and equal respect; the greatest moral infraction is treating people unfairly. Gilligan contends that this view is biased toward a masculine perspective. From a feminist point of view, morality is concerned with a commitment to care; the greatest harm occurs when individuals abandon someone in need. Another feminist ethicist, Walker (1992) rejects Kohlberg's emphasis on rigid stages of moral development. She maintains that morality is based on "mutual adjustment," a process of examining alternatives and ambiguities.

PERSONAL ATTRIBUTES Moral development stages and individual traits are linked. For instance, Trevino (1986) found parallels between Kohlberg's stages and several personality traits, such as ego and locus of control. The higher a person's maturity level, the more that person has internalized social norms. As people mature—especially with increasing education and experience—they are more likely to develop greater morality.

SELF-MASTERY With increasing maturity, people acquire a greater capacity to fulfill promises, obey laws, and follow directives (Dobel, 1998). Knowles (1978) states that as people mature, they also develop self-control. This enables people to reflect on actions and adapt those actions to each situation, rather than reacting on impulse. Self-reflection enables people to become aware of their commitment to others. Accordingly, people take personal responsibility for their actions (Harmon, 1995).

Knouse and Giacalone (1992) describe several individual traits that help increase self-mastery. People who are pragmatic, persuasive, and manipulative have great control over their own behavior and the outcome of their efforts. These persons have a Machiavellian outlook; that is, they do whatever is necessary to achieve a goal. Further, individuals who have an external locus of control—or a belief that outside factors control their choices—take little responsibility for changing their situation. This inhibits them from progressing to higher stages of morality. Lastly, persons may mask an unethical situation by rationalizing their actions or twisting definitions to make unsavory situations seem beneficial.

ORGANIZATIONAL CHARACTERISTICS

Conditions affecting ethical development include: (1) organizational structure; (2) organizational climate; (3) job characteristics (reward systems, scope of responsibility, degree of risk-taking, personal discretion); and (4) supervisory style.

ORGANIZATIONAL STRUCTURES An organization with a clearly defined mission increases the opportunity for ethical behavior among its members. However, Behn (1998, p. 209) describes several conditions in the public sector that hinder ethical behavior:

- The inability of public agencies to gain support
- The short terms of elected leaders
- Legislation that offers vague guidance or fails to grant sufficient resources for projects to succeed
- Narrow interests that control public agency, recasting government programs for their own gain
- Citizens who lack the knowledge to carry out responsibilities
- A judiciary that focuses on narrow legalities rather than broader concerns of serving the public's needs

In large bureaucratic organizations, Jos (1990) notes it is difficult for a person to develop morality. He observed a tendency to suppress one's "awareness of moral concerns or to engage in tradeoffs between values or questions of whether objectionable means justified by noble ends" (p. 240). Further, ambiguous circumstances can produce conformity and timidity. In this climate, workers succumb to "groupthink," and cease to make independent judgments.

The complexity of an organization influences its ethics (Sridhar & Cambrun, 1993). For instance, in organizations with a simple structure and a dynamic interaction with clients, ethics are based on an exchange of goods or services. Organizations with more complex structures orchestrate many interests and coordinate workers to achieve a mutual goal. Knouse and Giacalone (1992), and MacIngan (1996) categorize organizational complexity according to Kohlberg's stages of moral development. At Level 1, for instance, organizations operate on an egoistic plane and focus on profitability. At Level 2, organizations are more aware of customers' needs and seek to contribute to social welfare. Level 3 is a principle-driven organization that grants personal responsibility and operates according to codes of ethical conduct.

CULTURAL NORMS The culture of an organization can inhibit the ethical development of its members. Snell (1993, p. 65) notes that when a "moral ethos" or social climate intimidates workers, individual growth suffers. A hostile work culture includes such practices as "pulling rank," demanding complete loyalty, intolerance of criticism, and formalization of rules. In other words, organizations that impose an autocratic style stifle individual development. This produces an "oral muteness" that condones unethical behavior (Bird, 1996).

THE JOB ITSELF In addition to the way organizations are fashioned, the structure of the job itself affects ethical development. Important factors are job responsibility, risk-taking potential, level of personal discretion, and level of accountability.

Responsibility. Jobs that allow people to establish roles not proscribed by regulation encourage people to take responsibility for their work. This gives individuals more control over their work as well as greater flexibility to meet unexpected demands (Higgins, Power, & Kohlberg, 1984). Role-taking, in this sense, also encourages persons to resolve moral conflicts by seeing a situation through the eyes of others (Trevino, 1986). However, when responsibility is diffused throughout an organization, moral thinking declines. Because there are no focal points for resolving conflicts, people are less likely to take personal responsibility for doing so.

Risk-Taking Potential. Jobs that encourage calculated risk-taking to reach legitimate goals foster ethical behavior. In a survey of 365 managers in public and private organizations, Bozeman and Kingsley (1998) identify several factors that influence the amount of risk workers are willing to take. Factors that reduce risk-taking are: (1) the oversight of elected officials; (2) a large number of internal controls; (3) excessive red tape and formal policy; (4) lack of goal clarity; and (5) the expectation that efforts will achieve desired goals, and the satisfaction when they do.

Bozeman and Kingsley (1998) note that the latter condition, in particular, gives employees a utilitarian approach to taking risks. That is, if a risk has a high probability of success and reward, individuals will act. Certain conditions in public agencies, however, decrease the likelihood that efforts will yield profitable results. These conditions include the rigid setting of pay rates by legislators (rather than basing it on performance) and slow promotion rates.

Discretion. Organizations that allow workers to use discretion in making decisions also encourage ethical behavior (Rubin & Miller, 1989). Lipsky's (1980) accounts of "street-level bureaucrats" highlight the need for employees to have day-to-day contact with clients of governmental services. Employees also need to have the ability to apply rules to these daily interactions. Discretion enables "street-level bureaucrats" to clarify technical jargon and to develop role-taking, or understanding how clients feel. This permits the bureaucrats to have empathy for clients' needs and base decisions on those conditions.

Based on Lipsky's analysis, Vinzant and Crothers (1996) identify four levels of discretion used by "street-level bureaucrats."

- **Level 1:** Employees exercise little discretion. Usually, they make routine decisions based on regulations.

- **Level 2:** Employees use some discretion in how to resolve a situation, but their judgment is guided by specifically outlined objectives.

- **Level 3:** Employees have discretion over the decision's outcome, but little over the process used. For example, police who stop a suspected drunk driver must assess the possible impact on the police, the community, and the driver if he or she is not drunk.

- **Level 4:** Bureaucrats make choices about process *and* outcomes. For example, whether to remove a child from an abusive home or attempt to rehabilitate a family is a critical decision a social worker must make.

Accountability. Harmon (1995, p. 25) defines *accountability* as being answerable to "a higher, usually institutional, authority for...actions." *Accountability* refers to a relationship where a person with authority is entitled to demand that another account for his or her actions.

Recent pressures to reform government have increased the importance of accountability. Yet, these pressures have also created additional stresses. As governments shrink their programs and personnel, employees are asked to take on more responsibilities (Vinzant & Crothers, 1996). In addition, relentless media scrutiny of the decisions bureaucrats make has caused what Thompson (1992, p. 257) calls an "appearance standard." That is, bureaucrats avoid the mere *appearance* of wrongdoing because "appearances are often the only window that citizens have on official conduct." People have higher expectations of public employees and evaluate appearances as well as behaviors on this basis.

CULTURAL EFFECTS

Belief systems that are developed in wider social contexts also affect ethical behavior in public employees. These beliefs grow out of family upbringing, school socialization, religious groups, and national values. For instance, cultures oriented toward individualistic values will place utilitarian, self-improving values over those that would benefit the common good (Hofstede, 1982; McDonough, 1982).

An important way to create common values is by discussing them in groups. Graham (1995) examined group dynamics and finds that leadership styles and ethical motivations contribute to shared values. Leadership that appeals to followers' self-interest is associated with preconventional moral development. However, leadership that focuses on communication and social networks is linked to conventional moral development. Leaders with the inclination to transform the group inspire postconventional moral development and participation among followers.

Similarly, Kohlberg and colleagues (1974) state that participation in "just communities" influences higher moral development. In this context, people participate in morality discussions and assimilate different points of view. In an atmosphere of trust, fairness, and personal security, individuals learn to take responsibility for making and enforcing rules. Trevino (1992) adds that these programs allow people to explore moral controversies using hypothetical dilemmas. Ethical reasoning improves if these discussions encourage the questioning of each person's rationale in exploring a scenario. Leaders must also encourage reasoning on successively higher levels as the group discusses these dilemmas.

QUALITIES OF ETHICAL PUBLIC LEADERSHIP

To meet many of the ethical demands outlined in this chapter, public leaders need to cultivate several qualities. Because the development of ethics is a two-way process, leaders must not only encourage growth in themselves, but also in organizations and society. Some essential characteristics, already discussed in detail, are summarized below.

DEMOCRATIC PHILOSOPHY

Denhardt (1988) argues that using a moral philosophy will help clarify reasoning and point to significant issues. She maintains that enacting democratic ideals is important to marrying official goals with a greater moral order in society. These official or governmental ideals include discretion to make decisions, encourage worker participation, and assume personal responsibility.

COSMOPOLITAN FOCUS

Public leaders must develop skills for meeting the increasing demands of diverse clientele. This requires leaders to find methods of sharing visions and values. They must also encourage followers to act on these visions.

Gilman and Lewis (1996), in describing the International Conference on Ethics in Government, note that panel discussions emphasized the importance of using shared values as the basis for ethics training. With such training, leaders can exert the moral leadership necessary for guiding follower decisions. Gilman and Lewis (1996) conclude that public administrators must remain intellectually open to a global dialogue on ethics.

COMMITMENT TO CONTINUOUS LEARNING AND CHANGE

Along with adapting to a diversity of value systems, public leaders require the skill of orchestrating continuous learning and change. Kiel (1994) notes that rapid change in an increasingly global public arena demands that leaders embrace change and teach others how to deal with it. He points out that because the public and private sectors worldwide are interdependent, a leader's seemingly minor decisions can have serious consequences. These changes force leaders to abandon old models. They must create new tools with which to understand the complexity of their environment. To this knowledge, leaders must add a higher system of values that foster a personal responsibility for outcomes.

STEWARDSHIP OF RESOURCES

Because public leaders are the trustees of the public's resources, they must be loyal to constitutional values in their professional ethics.

Behn (1998) argues that by exercising constitutional values, the resources of the organization become available for future use. "Active, intelligent, enterprising leadership," he says, "[is necessary to enable] astute initiatives designed to help the agency not only to achieve its purposes today, but also to create new capacity to achieve its objectives tomorrow" (Behn, 1998, p. 220).

CIVISM RESPONSIBILITY

The idea that leaders can stimulate the moral growth of followers suggests that it is necessary to build a "just community." Frederickson (1982, p. 505) reveals that without a strong sense of community, public administration will "continue to constitute a threat for the citizens and a scapegoat for elected officials." However, by infusing citizens with an ethical purpose, leaders can inspire a sense of care for one's neighbors, which is at the heart of constitutional values.

PRUDENCE

The administration role that public leaders must play places them in a neutral position within government. Because of this role, they must be careful to ensure that their actions do not serve to benefit elected officials or special interest groups (Vinzant & Crothers, 1996).

Dobel (1998) maintains that political prudence is the central moral re-source for public leaders. Prudence is a virtue derived from the require-ments of political achievement and the standards of administrative actions. Political prudence entails several important concepts:

- the leader's openness to experience, disciplined reason, and foresight
- the leader's timing and momentum, the deployment of power, and a proper balance between the means and the ends
- political outcomes must be legitimate and must benefit the community in the present and future.

CRITICAL AND SELF-REFLECTIVE THINKING

Because values are the keystone of action, public leaders must continually examine their beliefs and how they influence followers (Harmon, 1995). Rohr (1978, p. 25) says that leaders should not dictate their followers' be-havior, but rather should "provide them a method for discovering these val-ues themselves and putting them into practice as they see fit." Denhardt (1988) refers to these as "process ethics" because they allow followers to ex-amine, question, and deliberate. Process values also guard against overre-liance on customs. They allow for the honest scrutiny of conflicting values.

MORAL SENSITIVITY, UNDERSTANDING, AND COURAGE

The pressures confronting public leaders are often intense. These pressures include a relentless media, a hostile public, competing interest groups, un-clear or conflicting regulations, and the democratic environment that pre-cludes personal discretion. Jos (1988, p. 342) affirms that a public leader can cope with these demands by cultivating a "firm and unchangeable charac-ter." This type of character must have strength in three areas.

1. **Moral Sensitivity**—the ability to see the moral implications of even ambiguous situations.
2. **Moral Understanding**—the ability to reason in considering these im-plications.
3. **Moral Courage**—the willingness to act morally even when there is substantial pressure to the contrary.

Jos concludes that unless administrators can overcome both internal im-pediments—such as selfishness or greed—and external influences, a re-sponsible assessment of morality is impossible.

SUMMARY

A public leader who examines the validity of social norms and solicits feed-back takes responsibility for personal actions. Taking responsibility requires a continuous commitment to serve "the public interest" according to democratic principles. It calls for reflection on values and acting on those values. It also involves being sensitive to the need for changing old thought patterns. Responsibility demands incorporating the views of all affected by the leader's decision. When people understand the perspective of others and take responsibility for acting on their beliefs, they act with integrity.

As public leaders become more sensitive to the moral responsibility they hold as trustees of constitutional ideals, they develop what Covey (1991, p. 54) calls a "spirit of service." He says that until people have the spirit of service, they might say they love a companion, company, or cause, but they often despise the demands these make on their lives. Double-mindedness— having two conflicting motives or interests—inevitably sets us at war with ourselves, and an internal civil war often breaks out into war with others. The opposite of double-mindedness is self-unity or integrity. We achieve integrity through the dedication of ourselves to selfless service of others.

QUESTIONS FOR THOUGHT AND DISCUSSION

1. To what extent, in your opinion, are personal ethics important to public leadership ethical decisions and actions? If public leaders hold ethical values apart from mainstream or prevailing ethics, should those leaders be held accountable for their actions?

2. How much responsibility do public leaders bear for their decisions and actions? Does this differ from that of private sector leaders? Explain why or why not.

3. In your view, how can public organizations be made more conducive to ethical actions? What role should the leader play in this?

4. Public leaders represent large numbers and varieties of constituents. If a leader does not support a popular sentiment, but chooses to be a "maverick," is the leader fulfilling his or her leadership responsibility as a public "servant"?

ETHICAL VIGNETTES

TIME: APPROXIMATELY 30 MINUTES

DIRECTIONS

Read the following short descriptions of ethical problems that public leaders may encounter. Decide how you would respond. Then, divide into groups of three to five members and discuss your responses with others. You may appoint a spokesperson to summarize responses and report them to the larger groups.

VIGNETTE 1

Pat, a clerk in a large public service agency, provides information about agency programs, regulations, services, and eligibility requirements to the public. A man speaking only Spanish approaches and asks for information. Pat neither speaks nor understands Spanish. After a few exasperated attempts to tell the man he isn't communicating, Pat says, "You need to learn English." Evaluate Pat's response in light of practical needs and ethical responsibilities as a public employee.

VIGNETTE 2

Dusty is responsible for keeping track of travel expenses. A few weeks ago, Dusty's supervisor took a trip to Dallas and charged the expenses to a project the department had been assigned. The supervisor, however, revealed to Dusty the trip included a side trip to visit a friend who lives in that city. Should Dusty report this?

VIGNETTE 3

Recently, in Louisiana, several Cuban detainees in a state prison seized control of operations, took hostages, and demanded to be returned to Cuba. The detainees had all been illegal aliens arrested by the Immigration and Naturalization Service (INS) for a variety of crimes and imprisoned. Several had been in U.S. prisons for nearly 20 years before the INS decided to act on

their cases. Prisons agreeing to accept the detainees received federal funds. In Louisiana, this was $24 per day. After the detainees were returned to Cuba and the crisis ended, a local newspaper cited the state's underfunding of prisons as a prime contributor to the incident. If funding had been adequate, the newspaper maintained, the prison would not have had to accept the federal funds and endanger prison staff. Assuming the governor would like to address the newspaper allegation, what would be an ethical response?

VIGNETTE 4

You are a fourth-grade teacher in a public school. Many of your students have inadequate basic skills, such as in reading, writing, and speaking as well as computing. You realize that many of these students were "socially promoted"; that is, they were "passed" by previous teachers who, for one reason or another, did not give them adequate remedial help. You are now faced with the choice of doing the same as the other teachers. What do you do?

REFERENCES

Adams, S. (1992). Vietnam cover-up: Playing war with numbers. In R.J. Stillman (Ed.), *Public administration: Concepts and cases* (6th ed., pp. 261–270). Boston: Houghton Mifflin.

Altschuler, A.A., & Behn, R. (Eds.). (1997). *Innovation in American government: Challenges, opportunities, and dilemmas.* Washington, DC: Brookings Institution.

Anonymous. (1998, September). Team re-engineers city's water department. *The American City and County, 113*(10), 84–88.

Archer, M. (1988). *Culture and agency: The place of culture in social theory.* London: Cambridge University Press.

Argyris, C. (1993). *Knowledge for action: A guide to overcoming barriers to organizational change.* San Francisco: Jossey-Bass.

Argyris, C., & Schon, D.A. (1978). *Organization learning: A theory of action perspective.* Reading, MA: Addison-Wesley.

Bacharach, S.B., Bamberger, P., & Conley, S.C. (1990, May). Work processes, role conflict, and role overload: The case of nurses and engineers in the public sector. *Work and Occupations, 17*(2), 199–228.

Baden, D. (1994, September). Are symbolic racism and traditional prejudice part of a contemporary authoritarian attitude syndrome? *Political Behavior, 16*(3), 365–384.

Banovitz, J.M. (1994, Summer). City managers: Will they reject policy leadership? *Public Productivity and Management Review, 17*(4), 313–324.

Barnard, C.I. (1938/1996). The economy of incentives. In J.M. Shafritz & J.S. Ott (Eds.), *Classics of organization theory* (4th ed., pp. 101–111). Belmont, CA: Wadsworth.

Bass, B.M. (1985). *Leadership and performance beyond expectations.* New York: The Free Press.

Bass, B.M. (1990). *Bass & Stogdill's handbook of leadership: Theory, research, and managerial applications* (3rd ed.). New York: The Free Press.

Bass, B.M., & Avolio, B.J. (Eds.). (1994). *Improving organizational effectiveness through transformational leadership.* Thousand Oaks, CA: Sage Publications.

Battalino, J., Beutler, L., & Shani, A.B. (1996, September). Large-system change initiative: Transformation in progress at the California Department of Corrections. *Public Productivity and Management Review, 20*(1), 24–44.

Bazerman, M.H., Tenbrunsel, A.E., & Wade-Benzoni, K. (1998, April). Negotiating with yourself and losing: Making decisions with competing internal preferences. *Academy of Management Review, 23*(2), 225–241.

Behling, O., & McFillen, J.M. (1996, June). A syncretical model of charismatic/transformational leadership. *Group and Organization Management, 21*(2), 163–191.

Behn, R.D. (1998, May/June). What right do public managers have to lead? *Public Administration Review, 58*(3), 209–221.

Berman, E.M., & West, J.P. (1995, January/February). Municipal commitment to Total Quality Management: A survey of recent progress. *Public Administration Review, 55*(1), 57–66.

Berry, F.S., & Wechsler, B. (1995, March/April). State agencies' experience with strategic planning: Findings from a national survey. *Public Administration Review, 55*(2), 159–168.

Bingham, R.D. (1976). *The adoption of innovation by local government.* London: D.C. Heath and Co.

Bird, F.B. (1996). *The muted conscience: Moral silence and the practice of ethics in business.* Westport, CT: Quorum Books.

Blanchard, K., & Nelson, B. (1997, April). Recognition and reward. *Executive Excellence, 14*(4), 15–18.

Bounds, G., Yorks, L., Adams, M., & Ramsey, G. (1994). *Beyond Total Quality Management.* New York: McGraw-Hill.

Bozeman, B. (1987). *All organizations are public: Bridging public and private organizational theories.* San Francisco: Jossey-Bass.

Bozeman, B., & Kingsley, G. (1998, March/April). Risk culture in public and private organizations. *Public Administration Review, 58*(2), 109–118.

Brann, P., & Foddy, M. (1987, December). Trust and the consumption of a deteriorating common resource. *Journal of Conflict Resolution, 31*(4), 615–630.

Brass, D.J., & Burkhardt, M.E. (1992). Centrality and power in organizations. In N. Nohria & R.G. Eccles (Eds.), *Networks and organizations: Structure, form, and action* (pp. 191–215). Cambridge, MA: Harvard Business School.

Brass, D.J., & Krackhardt, D. (1999). The social capital of twenty-first century leaders. In J.G. Hunt & G.E. Dodge (Eds.), *Out-of-the-box leadership: Transforming the twenty-first century army and other top performing organizations.* Monographs in leadership and management: Vol. 1 (pp. 179–194). Stamford, CT: JAI Press.

Bryson, J.M., & Crosby, B.C. (1992). *Leadership for the common good: Tackling public problems in a shared power world.* San Francisco: Jossey-Bass.

Buessing, A., & Broome, D. (1999). Trust under telework. *Zeitschrift-fuer-Arbeits-und-Organisations psychologie, 43*(3), 122–133.

Burke, W.W. (1994). *Organization development: A process of learning and changing.* (2nd ed.). Reading, MA: Addison-Wesley.

Burt, R. (1992). *Structural holes: The social structure of competition.* Boston: Harvard University Press.

Butler, J.R., Cantrell, R.S., & Flick, R.J. (1999, Spring). Transformational leadership behaviors, upward trust, and satisfaction in self-managed work teams. *Organization Development Journal, 17*(1), 13–28.

Callahan, K., & Holzer, M. (1994, Spring). Rethinking governmental change: New ideas, new partnerships. *Public Productivity and Management Review, 17*(3), 201–221.

Campbell, D.J., Campbell, K.M., & Chia, H.B. (1998, Summer). Merit pay, performance appraisal, and individual motivation: An analysis and alternative. *Human Resource Management, 37*(2), 131–146.

Carnevale, D.G., & Wechsler, B. (1992, February). Trust in the public sector. *Administration and Society, 23*(4), 471–494.

Caro, R. (1982). *The years of Lyndon Johnson: The path to power.* New York: Alfred A. Knopf.

Caudle, S.L. (1994, Winter). Reengineering strategies and issues. *Public Productivity and Management Review, 18*(2), 149–154.

Chemers, M.M. (1997). *An integrated theory of leadership.* Mahwah, NJ: Lawrence Erlbaum Associates.

Clegg, S.R. (1990). *Modern organizations: Organization studies in the postmodern world.* Thousand Oaks, CA: Sage Publications.

Clegg, S.R. (1992). *Frameworks of power.* Thousand Oaks, CA: Sage Publications.

Clement, R.W. (1993). Teaching leadership theory: Reconsidering the situational view. *Management Research News, 16*(2), 12–19.

Coe, B.A. (1997, March/April). How structural conflicts stymie reinvention. *Public Administration Review, 57*(2), 168–173.

Cohen, S.G., & Bailey, D.E. (1997). What makes teams work: Group effectiveness research from the shop floor to the executive suite. *Journal of Management, 23*(3), 239–290.

Conger, J.A., & Kanungo, R.N. (1988). The empowerment process: Integrating theory and practice. *Academy of Management Review, 13*(3), 471–482.

Cook, B.J. (1998, May/June). Politics, political leadership, and public management. *Public Administration Review, 58*(1), 225–230.

Cooper, T.L. (1982). *The responsible administrator.* San Francisco: Jossey-Bass.

Corcoran, K.J. (1988, March). The relationship of interpersonal trust to self-disclosure when confidentiality is assured. *The Journal of Psychology, 122*(2), 193–195.

Covey, S.R. (1991). *Principle-centered leadership.* New York: Simon & Schuster.

Coyne, R.K. (1998, September). Personal experience and meaning in group work leadership: The views of experts. *Journal for Specialists in Group Work, 23*(3), 245–256.

Cox, T. (1993). *Cultural diversity in organizations: Theory, research, and practice.* San Francisco: Berrett-Kohler.

Creed, W. E. D., & Miles, R. E. (1996). Trust in organizations: A conceptual framework linking organizational forms, managerial philosophies, and the opportunity costs of controls. In R. M. Kramer & T. R. Tyler (Eds.), *Trust in organizations: Frontiers of theory and research* (pp. 261–287). Thousand Oaks, CA: Sage Publications.

Czarniawska, B. (1997). *Narrating the organization: Dramas of institutional identity.* Chicago: University of Chicago Press.

Delbecq, A. L., & Mills, P. K. (1985, Summer). Managerial practices that enhance innovation. *Organizational Dynamics, 14,* 24–34.

Delbecq, A. L., Van de Ven, A. H., & Gustafson, D. H. (1975). *Group techniques for program planning.* Glenview, IL: Scott, Foresman.

Denhardt, K. G. (1988). *Ethics of public service.* Westport, CT: Greenwood Press.

Denhardt, R. B. (1994). *The pursuit of significance.* Belmont, CA: Wadsworth.

Deutsch, M. (1973). *The resolution of conflict: Constructive and destructive processes.* New Haven, CT: Yale University Press.

Deutsch, M. (1994). Constructive conflict resolution: Principles, training, and research. *Journal of Social Issues, 50*(1), 13–32.

Devine, P. G., Tauer, J. M., Barron, K. E., Elliot, A. J., & Vance, K. M. (1999). Moving beyond attitudes: A change in the study of dissonance-related processes. In E. Harmon-Jones & J. Mills (Eds.), *Cognitive dissonance: Progress on a pivotal theory* (pp. 297–323). Washington, DC: American Psychological Association.

DeVries, R. E., Roe, R. A., & Taillieu, T. C. B. (1998, December). Need for supervision: Its impact on leadership effectiveness. *Journal of Applied Behavioral Science, 34*(4), 486–501.

Dion, K. L., & Dion, K. K. (1997). Belief in a just world and physical attractiveness stereotyping. *Journal of Personality and Social Psychology, 52*(4), 775–780.

Dobel, J. P. (1998, January/February). Political prudence and the ethics of leadership. *Public Administration Review, 58*(1), 74–81.

Dow, S. K., Markham, S. E., & Vest, M. J. (1996, Spring). The influence of a merit pay guide chart on employee attitudes toward pay at a transit authority. *Public Personnel Management, 25*(1), 103–118.

Drake, L. E., & Donohue, W. A. (1996). Communicative framing theory in conflict resolution. *Communicative Research, 23*(3), 297–322.

Drexler, A. B., Sibbet, D., & Forrester, R. H. (1990). The team performance model. In W. B. Reddy & K. Jamison (Eds.), *Team building blueprints for productivity* (pp. 45–63). San Diego: National Training Laboratory.

Elangovan, A. R. (1995, October). Managerial third party dispute intervention: A prescriptive model of strategy intervention. *Academy of Management Review, 20*(4), 800–830.

Elden, M., & Sanders, S. L. (1996, September). Vision-based diagnosis: Change in a public organization. *Public Productivity and Management Review, 20*(1), 11–23.

Emery, M., & Purser, R. E. (1996). *The search conference: A powerful method for planning organizational change and community action.* San Francisco: Jossey-Bass.

Epstein, J., & Olsen, R. T. (1996, Fall). Managing for outcomes: Lessons learned from state and local governments. *Public Manager,* 41–44.

Etzioni, A. (1961). *The comparative analysis of complex organizations* (2nd ed.). New York: The Free Press.

Etzioni, A. (1986). Mixed scanning revisited. *Public Administration Review, 46*(1), 8–14.

Farace, R. V., Monge, P. R., & Russell, H. M. (1977). *Communicating and organizing.* Reading, MA: Addison-Wesley.

Federal Quality Institute (1991). *Introduction to Total Quality Management in the federal government.* Washington, D.C.: Office of Personnel Management.

Fennel, M. L. & Alexander, J. A. (1987). Organizational boundary spanning in institutionalized environments. *Academy of Management Journal, 30*(3), 456–475.

Ferlie, E., Pettigrew, A., Ashburner, L., & Fitzgerald, L. (1996). *The new public management in action.* New York: Oxford University Press.

Fiedler, F. E. (1967). A theory of leadership effectiveness. New York: McGraw-Hill.

Fiorino, D. J. (1990, January/February). Can problems shape priorities? The case of risk-based environmental planning. *Public Administration Review, 50*(1), 82–90.

Fisher, R., & Ury, W. (1991). *Getting to yes: Negotiating conflict without giving in* (2nd ed.). New York: Penguin Books.

Fondas, N., & Stewart, R. (1995, January). Enactment in managerial jobs: A role analysis. *Journal of Management Studies, 31*(1), 83–103.

Frederickson, H. G. (1982). The recovery of civism in public administration. *Public Administration Review, 42*(4), 501–508.

Frederickson, H. G. (1996, May/June). Comparing the reinventing government movement with the new public administration. *Public Administration Review, 56*(3), 263–269.

French, J. R. P. , & Raven, B. (1959). The bases of social power. In D. P. Cartwright (Ed.) *Studies in social power* (pp. 150-167), Ann Arbor: The Institute for Social Research, The University of Michigan.

French, W. L., & Bell, C. H., Jr. (1999). *Organization development: Behavioral science interventions for organization improvement* (6th ed.). Englewood Cliffs, NJ: Prentice-Hall.

French, W. L., Bell, C. H., Jr., & Zawacki, R. A. (1994). *Organization development and transformation: Managing effective change* (4th ed.). Burr Ridge, IL: Irwin.

Freyerheim, A. E. (1994). Leadership in collaboration: A longitudinal study of two interorganizational rule-making groups. *Leadership Quarterly, 5*(3), 251–270.

Frost, P. J. (1987). Power, politics, and influence. In F. M. Jablin, L. L. Putnam, K. H. Roberts, & L. W. Porter (Eds.), *Handbook of organizational communication: An interdisciplinary perspective* (pp. 503–548). Newbury Park, CA: Sage Publications.

Gage, R. W. (1993, Winter). Leadership and regional councils: A mismatch between leadership styles today and future roles. *State and Local Government Review, 25*(1), 9–18.

Gardner, J. (1991). *Building community.* Washington, D.C.: Independent Sector.

Gergen, K. J., & Gergen, M. M. (1991). Toward reflexive methodologies. In F. Steier (Ed.), *Research and reflexivity* (pp. 76–95). Newbury Park, CA: Sage Publications.

Gibb, J. (1978). *Trust: A new view of personal and organizational development.* Los Angeles: Guild Press.

Gilligan, C. (1982). *In a different voice.* Cambridge, MA: Harvard University Press.

Gilman, S. C., & Lewis, C. W. (1996, November/December). Public service ethics: A global dialogue. *Public Administration Review, 56*(6), 517–524.

Goliembiewski, R. T. (1995). *Approaches to planned change.* New Brunswick, NJ: Transaction Publishers.

Goss, T., Pascale, R., & Athos, A. (1993). The reinvention roller coaster: Risking the present for a powerful future. *Harvard Business Review, 71*(6), 97–108.

Grint, K. (1997). Leadership: Classical, contemporary, and critical approaches. NY: Oxford University Press.

Graham, J. W. (1995). Leadership, moral development, and citizenship behavior. *Business Ethics Quarterly, 5*(1), 43–54.

Hackman, J. R., & Oldham, G. R. (1980). *Work redesign.* Reading, MA: Addison-Wesley.

Hammer, M., & Champy, J. (1993). *Reengineering the corporation.* New York: HarperCollins.

Hampton, D. R., Summer, C. E., & Webber, R. A. (1987). *Organization behavior and the practice of management* (5th ed.). Glenview, IL: Scott, Foresman.

Hardy, C., & Clegg, S. R. (1996). Some dare call it power. In S. R. Clegg, C. Hardy, & W. R. Nord (Eds.), *Handbook of organization studies* (pp. 622–641). Thousand Oaks, CA: Sage Publications.

Harmon, M. M. (1995). *Responsibility as paradox.* Thousand Oaks, CA: Sage Publications.

Harvey, J. B. (1996). *The Abilene paradox and other meditations on management.* San Francisco: Jossey-Bass.

Heider, F. (1994). Social perception and phenomenal reality. *Psychological Review, 51*(3), 358–374.

Heifetz, R. A. (1994). *Leadership without easy answers.* Cambridge, MA: The Belknap Press/Harvard University Press.

Henderson-Loney, J. (1996, May). Tuckman and tears: Developing teams during profound organizational change. *Supervision, 57*(5), 3–6.

Hendrick, R. (1994, Fall). A heuristic approach to policy analysis and the use of sensi. *Public Productivity and Management Review, 18*(1), 37–56.

Hersey, P., & Blanchard, K.H. (1969). Life-cycle theory of leadership. *Training and Development Journal, 23*, 26–34.

Herzberg, F. (1966). *Work and the nature of man.* New York: Crowell.

Herzlinger, R.E. (1996, March/April). Can public trust in nonprofits and governments be restored? *Harvard Business Review, 74*(2), 97–108.

Higgins, A., Power, C., & Kohlberg, L. (1984). The relationship of moral atmosphere to judgments of responsibility. In W.M. Kurtines and J.L. Gewirtz (Eds.), *Morality, moral behavior, and moral development* (pp. 74–106). New York: John Wiley & Sons.

Hofstede, G. (1982). *Culture's consequences.* Newbury Park, CA: Sage Publications.

Hofstede, G. (1991). *Cultures and organizations: Software of the mind.* London: McGraw-Hill.

Hollander, E.P. (1997, July). How and why active followers matter in leadership. In Kellogg Leadership Studies Project (Ed.), *The balance of leadership and followership* (pp. 11–28), Battle Creek, MI: W.K. Kellogg Foundation.

House, R.J. (1971). A path–goal theory of leader effectiveness. *Administrative Science Quarterly, 16*(3), 321–339.

House, R.J. (1974). Path-goal theory of leadership. *Journal of Contemporary Business, 3,* 81–97.

House, R.J. (1988). Power and personality in complex organizations. In B.M. Staw & L.L. Cummings (Eds.), *Research in organizational behavior. Vol. 10* (pp. 305–357). Greenwich, CT: JAI Press.

Howard, J.A., & Pike, K.C. (1986, June). Ideological investment in cognitive processing: The influence of social statuses on attribution. *Social Psychology Quarterly, 49*(2), 154–167.

Hult, K.M., & Walcott, C. (1992). *Governing public organizations: Politics, structures, and institutional design.* Pacific Grove, CA: Brooks/Cole.

Hunt, R.G., & Magenau, J.M. (1984). A task analysis strategy for research on decision making in organizations. In L.M. Nigro (Ed.), *Decision making in the public sector* (pp. 117–150). New York: Marcel Dekker.

Janis, I.L. (1989). *Crucial decisions: Leadership in policymaking and crisis management.* New York: The Free Press.

Janis, I.L & Mann, L. (1977). *Decision making: A psychological analysis of conflict, choice, and commitment.* NY: The Free Press.

Johnson, A.L., Luthans, F., & Hennessey, H. (1984, Spring). The role of locus of control in leader influence behavior. *Personnel Psychology, 37*(1), 61–75.

Johnston, J.M. (1998, Winter). Changing state–local fiscal relations and school finance in Kansas: Pursuing "equity." *State and Local Government Review, 30*(1), 26–41.

Jos, P. (1988). Moral autonomy and the modern organization. *Polity, 21*(3), 321–343.

Jos, P. (1990, August). Administrative responsibility revisited: Moral consensus and moral autonomy. *Administration and Society, 22*(2), 228–248.

Juran, J.M. (1995). *Managerial breakthrough: The classic book on improving management performance.* New York: McGraw-Hill.

Jurkiewicz, C.E., Massey, T.K., & Brown, R.G. (1998, March). Motivation in public and private organizations: A comparative study. *Public Personnel Management Review, 21*(3), 230–250.

Kanter, R.M. (1977). *Men and women of the corporation.* New York: Basic Books.

Kanter, R.M. (1988). When a thousand flowers bloom. In B.M. Staw & L.L. Cummings (Eds.), *Research in organizations. Vol. 10* (pp. 169–211). Greenwich, CT: JAI Press.

Kassing, J.W. (1998, November). Development and validation of the organizational dissent scale. *Management Communication Quarterly, 12*(2), 183-229.

Katzenbach, J.R., & Smith, D.K. (1993). *The discipline of teams.* New York: Harper-Business.

Kaufman, S. (1991). Decision making and conflict management processes in local government. In R.D. Bingham, W.M. Bowen, M.O. Chandler, T.L. Cornwell, J.P. DeSario, P.R. Donmel, K.L. Ender, C.L. Felbinger, E.W. Hill, S. Kaufman, W.D. Keating, L.F. Keller, N. Krumholz, D.A. Kuemmel, B.M. Murphy, D.C. Perry, K.P. Rasey, R.J. Rose, H.J. Rubin, J.D. Stack, N.F. Speltz, M.W. Spicer, P.D. Star, C.A. Washington, A.C. Weinstein, & R.R. Whitehead (Eds.), *Managing local government: Public administration in practice* (pp. 115–134). Newbury Park, CA: Sage Publications.

Kelley, R. E. (1998). In praise of followers. In W. E. Rosenbach & R. L. Taylor (Eds.), *Contemporary issues in leadership* (4th ed., pp. 96–106). Boulder, CO: Westview Press.

Kellough, J. E., & Seldon, S. C. (1997, Winter). Pay-for-performance systems in state government. *Review of Public Personnel Administration, 17*(1), 3–21.

Kerr, S., & Jermier, J. M. (1978). Substitutes for leadership: Their meaning and measurement. *Organizational Behavior and Human Performance, 22*, 375–403.

Kiel, L. D. (1994). *Managing chaos and complexity in government.* San Francisco: Jossey-Bass.

King, C. S., & Stivers, C. (1998). *Government is us: Public administration in an antigovernment era.* Thousand Oaks, CA: Sage Publications.

Kingdon, J. W. (1995). *Agendas, alternatives, and public policies* (2nd ed.). New York: HarperCollins College Publishers.

Knouse, S. B., & Giacalone, R. A. (1992, May). Ethical decision making in business: Behavioral issues and concerns. *Journal of Business Ethics, 11*(5), 369–381.

Knowles, M. (1978). *The adult learner: A neglected species.* Houston, TX: Gulf Publishing.

Koberg, C. S. (1987). Resource scarcity, environmental uncertainty, and adaptive organizational behavior. *Academy of Management Journal, 30*(4), 798–807.

Kofman, P., & Senge, P. (1994). Communities of commitment: The heart of learning organizations. In The American Management Association (Eds.), *The learning organization in action* (pp. 7–26). New York: AMACOM.

Kohlberg, L. (1969). Stage and sequence: The cognitive developmental approach to socialization. In D. A. Goslin (Ed.), *Handbook of socialization theory and research* (pp. 387–480). Chicago: Rand McNally.

Kohlberg, L., Kaufmann, K., Schaef, P., & Hickey, J. (1974). *The just community approach to corrections: A manual. Part 1.* Cambridge, MA: Moral Education Research Foundation.

Kopczynski, M. & Lombardo, M. (1999, March/April). Comparative performance measurement: Insights and lessons learned from a consortium effort. *Public Administration Review, 59*(2), 124–134.

Kram, K. E. (1983, December). Phases of a mentoring relationship. *Academy of Management Journal, 26*(4), 608–625.

Kramer, R. M., & Neale, M. A. (Eds.). (1998). *Power and influence in organizations.* Thousand Oaks, CA: Sage Publications.

Kravchuk, R. S., & Schack, R. W. (1996, July/August). Designing effective performance-measurement systems under the Government Performance and Results Act of 1993. *Public Administration Review, 56*(4), 348–359.

Krone, K. J., Jablin, F. M., & Putnam, L. L. (1987). Communication theory and organizational communication: Multiple perspectives. In F. M. Jablin, L. L. Putnam, K. H. Roberts, & L. W. Porter (Eds.), *Handbook of organizational communication: An interdisciplinary perspective* (pp. 11–40). Newbury Park, CA: Sage Publications.

Kruglanski, A. M., & Webster, D. M. (1995, April). Motivated closing of the mind: Seizing and freezing. *Psychological Review, 103*(2), 263–283.

Kumar, P., & Ghadially, R. (1989, April). Organizational politics and its effects on members of organizations. *Human Relations, 42*(4), 305–314.

Lau, A. W., Newman, A. R., & Broedling, L. A. (1980, September/October). The nature of managerial work in the public sector. *Public Administration Review, 40*(5), 513–520.

Lawler, E. E. (1986). *High involvement management.* San Francisco: Jossey-Bass.

Lawson, J. S. (1994). Success and failure among senior public administrators. *The International Journal of Career Management, 6*(4), 10–14.

Lewin, K. (1947). Frontiers in group dynamics: Concept, method, and reality in social science, social equilibria, and social change. *Human Relations, 1*, 5–41.

Lewis, G. B., & Durst, S. L. (1995, July/August). Will locality pay solve recruitment and retention problems in the federal civil service? *Public Administration Review, 55*(4), 371–379.

Light, P. (1994). Surviving reinvention. *Government Executive, 26*(6), 55–56.

Lindblom, C. (1959). The science of "muddling through." *Public Administration Review, 19*(1), 79–99.

Lipsky, M. (1980). *Street-level bureaucrat: Dilemmas of the individual in public service.* New York: Russell Sage Publications.

Luft, J. (1984). *Group processes: An introduction to group dynamics* (3rd ed.). Mountainview, CA: Mayfield Publishing.

MacIngan, P. (1996, June). The organization context for moral development: Questions of power and access. *Journal of Business Ethics, 15*(6), 645–656.

MacKay, D. (1992). Errors, ambiguity, and awareness in language perception and production. In B.J. Baars (Ed.), *Experimental slips and human error: Exploring the architecture of volition, cognition, and language* (pp. 39–69). New York: Plenum Press.

March, J.G., & Olsen, J.P. (1994). *A primer on decision making: How decisions happen.* New York: The Free Press.

Maslow, A. (1943). A theory of human motivation. *Psychology Review,* 370–396.

Maslow, A. (1954). *Motivation and personality.* New York: Harper.

Massey, D.S., & Denton, N.A. (1993). *American apartheid: Segregation and the making of the underclass.* Cambridge, MA: Harvard University Press.

May, L. (1996). *The socially responsible self: Social theory and professional ethics.* Chicago: University of Chicago Press.

Mayo, E. (1933). *The human problems of an industrial civilization.* New York: The Macmillan Co.

McAllister, D.J. (1995). Affective and cognition-based trust as foundations for interpersonal cooperation in organizations. *Academy of Management Journal, 8*(1), 24–58.

McDonough, E.L. (1982, August). Social exchange and moral development: Dimensions of self, self-image, and identity. *Human Relations, 35*(8), 659–675.

McGregor, D. (1960). *The human side of enterprise.* New York: McGraw-Hill.

Merton, R.K. (1957/1995). Bureaucratic structure and personality. In W.R. Scott (Ed.), *Institutions and organizations* (pp. 16–18). Thousand Oaks, CA: Sage Publications.

Millikin, F.J., & Martins, L.L. (1996). Searching for common threads: Understanding the multiple effects of diversity in organizational groups. *Academy of Management Review, 21*(2), 402–433.

Mintzberg, H. (1997). How is a manager also a leader? As answered by Henry Mintzerg in the (seductive) nature of managerial work. In K. Grint (Ed.), *Leadership: Classical, contemporary, and critical approaches* (pp. 356–359). New York: Oxford University Press.

Mintzberg, H., Raisin-ghani, D., & Theoret, A. (1976, June). The structure of "unstructured" decision processes. *Administrative Science Quarterly, 21*(2), 246–275.

Mishra, A.K. (1996). Organizational responses to crises: The centrality of trust. In R.M. Kramer & T.R. Tyler (Eds.), *Trust in organizations: Frontiers of theory and research* (pp. 261–287). Thousand Oaks, CA: Sage Publications.

Moe, R.C. (1994, March/April). The "reinventing government" exercise: Misinterpreting the problem, misjudging the consequences. *Public Administration Review, 54*(2), 111–122.

Moore, M.H. (1995). *Creating public value: Strategic management in government.* Cambridge, MA: Harvard University Press.

Morgan, D., Bacon, K.G., Bunch, R., Cameron, D.C., & Deis, R. (1996, July/August). What middle managers do in local government: Stewardship of the public trust and the limits of reinventing government. *Public Administration Review, 56*(4), 359–366.

Nachmias, D. (1985). Determinants of trust in the federal government. In D. Rosenbloom (Ed.), *Public personnel policy: Politics of civil service* (pp. 133–143). Port Washington, NY: Associated Faculty Press.

Neuse, S.M. (1983, November/December). TVA at age fifty—Reflections and retrospect. *Public Administration Review, 43*(6), 491–498.

Newsweek. (May 29, 1995). *Anita Septimus: She makes us feel wonderful.* New York: Newsweek, Inc. (Online at www.ncl.org/anr/stories/news2.htm)

Newton, T.J., & Keenan, A. (1987). Role stress reexamined: An investigation of role stress predictors. *Organizational Behavior and Human Decision Processes, 40*(3), 346–368.

O'Neill, O. (1996). *Towards justice and virtue.* London: Cambridge University Press.

Osborne, D., & Gaebler, T. (1992). *Reinventing government: How the entrepreneurial spirit* is transforming the public sector. Reading, MA: Addison-Wesley.

O'Toole, L. J., Jr. (1997, January/February). Treating networks seriously: Practical and research-based agendas in public administration. *Public Administration Review, 57*(1), 45–52.

Ott, J. (1997, August 18). FAA: Users attack political minds that pull agency apart. *Aviation Week and Space Technology, 147*(7), 38–43.

Parks, C. D., & Hulbert, L. G. (1995, December). High and low trusters' responses to fear in a payoff matrix. *Journal of Conflict Resolution, 39*(4), 718–730.

Patton, K. R., & Daley, D. M. (1998, Spring). Gainsharing in Zebulon: What do workers want? *Public Personnel Management, 27*(1), 117–131.

Perlmutter, F. D., & Cnaan, R. (1995, January/February). Entrepreneurship in the public sector: The horns of a dilemma. *Public Administration Review, 55*(1), 29–36.

Perry, J. L., & Wise, L. P. (1990). The motivational bases of public service. *Public Administration Review, 50*(3), 367–373.

Peters, B. G., & Savoie, D. J. (1996, May/June). Managing incoherence: The coordination and empowerment conundrum. *Public Administration Review, 56*(2), 281–289.

Pfeiffer, J. (1996). Understanding the role of power in decision making. In J. M. Shafritz and J. S. Ott (Eds.), *Classics of organization theory* (4th ed., pp. 359–374). Belmont, CA: Wadsworth Publishing.

Piaget, J. (1932). *The moral judgment of the child*. NY: The Free Press.

Poister, T. H., & Streib, G. D. (1999, March). Strategic management in the public sector: Concepts, models, and processes. *Public Productivity and Management Review, 22*(3), 308–325.

Porter, L. W., Allen, R. W., & Anglo, H. L. (1990). The politics of upward influence. In B. M. Staw & L. L. Cummings (Eds.), *Personality and organizational influence* (pp. 139–179). Greenwich, CT: JAI Press.

Quinn, R. E., Faerman, S. R., Thompson, M. P., & McGrath, M. R. (1996). *Becoming a master manager: A competency framework* (2nd ed.). New York: John Wiley & Sons.

Rago, W. V. (1996, May/June). Struggles in transformation: A study in TQM, leadership, and culture in a government agency. *Public Administration Review, 56*(3), 227–234.

Rahim, M. A. (1997). Styles of managing organizational conflict: A critical review of synthesis of theory and research. In M. A. Rahim & R. T. Golembiewski (Eds.), *Current topics in management. Vol. 2* (pp. 61–77). Greenwich, CT: JAI Press.

Rainey, H. G. (1997). *Understanding and managing public organizations* (2nd ed.). San Francisco: Jossey-Bass.

Riccucci, N. M. (1995, May/June). "Execucrats," politics, and public policy: What are the ingredients for successful performance in the federal government? *Public Administration Review, 55*(3), 219–230.

Rizzo, J. R., House, R. J., & Lirtzman, S. I. (1970). Role conflict and ambiguity in complex organizations. *Administrative Science Quarterly, 15*, 150–163.

Roberts, N. (1997, March/April). Public deliberation: An alternative approach to crafting policy and setting direction. *Public Administration Review, 57*(2), 124–132.

Roberts, N., & King, P. J. (1992, Winter). An investigation into the personality profile of public entrepreneurs. *Public Productivity and Management Review, 16*(2), 173–189.

Roessner, J. D. (1977). Incentives to innovate in public organizations. *Administration and Society, 9*(4), 341–365.

Roethlisberger, F. J., & Dickson, W. J. (1939). Management and the worker. Cambridge, MA: Harvard University Press.

Rogers, D. L., & Molnar, J. (1976, December). Organizational antecedents of role conflict and ambiguity in top level administrators. *Administrative Science Quarterly, 21*(4), 598–610.

Rogers, E. M. (1985). The diffusion of innovations in public organizations. In R. L. Merritt & A. Merritt (Eds.), *Innovations in the public sector*. Newbury Park, CA: Sage Publications.

Rohr, J. A. (1978). *Ethics for bureaucrats: An essay on law and values*. New York: Marcel Dekker.

Rohr, J. A. (1986). *To run a constitution: The legitimacy of the administrative state*. Lawrence: University of Kansas Press.

Rubin, J., & Miller, G. J. (1989, Summer). Moral code, compliance with authority, and productivity. *Public Productivity and Management Review, 12*(4), 423–438.

Rubin, I.S., & Stein, L. (1990, July/August). Budget reform in St. Louis: Why does budgeting change? *Public Administration Review, 50*(4), 420–426.

Rusaw, A.C. (1995). Role overload as a predictor of organizational stress. In E.C. Houck (Ed.), *Proceedings of Decision Sciences International* (pp. 391–393). Boston.

Rusaw, A.C. (1997, Winter). Reinventing local government: A case study of organizational change through community learning. *Public Administration Quarterly, 20*(4), 419–432.

Rusaw, A.C. (1998). *Transforming the character of public organizations: Techniques for change agents.* Westport, CT: Quorum Books.

Sabatelli, R.M., Buck, R., & Dreyer, A. (1983, February). Locus of control, interpersonal trust, and nonverbal communication accuracy. *Journal of Personality and Social Psychology, 44*(2) 399–609.

Savage, G.T., Blair, J.D., & Sorensen, R.L. (1989, February). Consider both relationships and substance when negotiating strategically. *The Executive, 3*(1), 37–47.

Schachter, H.L. (1995). Reinventing government or reinventing ourselves? Two models of improving government performance. *Public Administration Review, 55*(6), 530–537.

Schein, E.H. (1997). *Organizational culture and leadership* (2nd ed.). San Francisco: Jossey-Bass.

Schindler, P.L., & Thomas, C.C. (1993, October). The structure of interpersonal trust in the workplace. *Psychological Reports, 73*(2), 563–573.

Schneider, M., Teske, P., & Mintrom, M. (1995). *Public entrepreneurs: Agents for change in American government.* Princeton, NJ: Princeton University Press.

Schneider, S.K., Jacoby, W.G., & Coggburn, J.D. (1997, May/June). The structure of bureaucratic decisions in the American states. *Public Administration Review, 57*(3), 240–249.

Schwenk, C.R. (1990). Conflict in organizational decision making: An exploratory study of its effects for profit and not-for-profit organizations. *Management Science, 36*, 493–511.

Scott, K.D., Markham, S.E., & Vost, M.J. (1996, Spring). The influence of a merit pay guide chart on employee attitudes toward pay at a transit authority. *Public Personnel Management, 25*(1), 103–118.

Scott, W.R. (1992). *Organizations: Rational, natural, and open systems* (3rd ed.). Englewood Cliffs, NJ: Prentice-Hall.

Senge, P. (1990). *The fifth discipline: The art and practice of the learning organization.* New York: Doubleday.

Shafritz, J.M., & Hyde, A.C. (Eds.). (1987). *Classics of public administration* (2nd ed.). Chicago: Dorsey Press.

Shafritz, J.M., & Ott, J.S. (1996). *Classics of organization theory* (4th ed.). Belmont, CA: Wadsworth Publishing Co.

Shamir, B., Zakey, E., Breinin, E., & Popper, M. (1998, August). Correlates of charismatic leader behavior in military units: Subordinates' attitudes, unit characteristics, and superiors' appraisals of leader performance. *Academy of Management Journal, 41*(4), 387–409.

Shrum, W. (1990, August). Status incongruence among boundary spanners: Structure, exchange, and conflict. *American Sociological Review, 55*(4), 496–511.

Simon, H.A. (1976). *Administrative behavior: A study of decision-making processes in administrative organization* (3rd ed.). New York: The Free Press.

Sitkin, S.B., & Roth, N.L. (1993, August). Legalistic "remedies" for trust and distrust. *Organizational Science, 4*(3), 367–392.

Smith, A. (1961). *An enquiry into the nature and causes of the wealth of nations.* Indianapolis, IN: Bobbs-Merrill.

Snell, R.S. (1993). *Developing skill for ethical management.* London: Chapman & Hall.

Sridhar, B.S., & Cambrun, A. (1993, September). Stages of moral development of corporations. *Journal of Business Ethics, 12*(9), 729–743.

Steel, J.L. (1991, June). Interpersonal correlates of trust and self-disclosure. *Psychological Reports, 63*(3), Part 2, 1319–1320.

Stephan, W.C., & Beame, W.E. (1978). The effects of belief similarity and ethnicity on liking and attributions for performance. *Interamerican Journal of Psychology, 12*, 153–159.

Stephan, W.C., Ageyev, V., Coates-Shrider, L. & Stephan, C. (1994, June). On the relationship between stereotypes and prejudice and personality: An international study. *Personality and Social Psychology Bulletin, 20*(3), 277–284.

Stewart, J., & Ranson, S. (1988, Spring/ Summer). Management in the public domain. *Public Money and Management, 6*(2), 13–18.

Stogdill, R.M. (1974). *Handbook of leadership* (1st ed.). New York: The Free Press

Stubbart, C. (1987, Spring). Improving the quality of crisis thinking. *Columbia Journal of World Business, 22*(1), 88–99.

Sundstrom, E., DeMeuse, K.P., & Futrell, D. (1990). Work teams: Applications and effectiveness. *American Psychologist, 45*(1), 121–133.

Swift, M. (1991, November 17). A quarter century of Ilg. Hartford, CT: *The Hartford Courant.*

Tarrant, D. (1995, March 5). The "we" decade: Rebirth of community. *The Dallas Morning News,* 1-F.

Taylor, F.W. (1911). *Principles of scientific management.* New York: Harper and Brothers.

Teasley, C.E., III. (1999, Spring). The perpetual pursuit of purpose: PA—state of the discipline II. *Public Administrative Quarterly, 23*(1), 65–76.

Terry, L.D. (1995). *Leadership of public bureaucracies: The administrator as conservator.* Thousand Oaks, CA: Sage Publications.

Thomas, K.W. (1992). Conflict and negotiation processes in organizations. In M.D. Dunnette & L.M. Hough (Eds.), *Handbook of industrial and organizational psychology. Vol. 3* (2nd ed., pp. 651–717). Palo Alto, CA: Consulting Psychologists Press.

Thomas, K.W. & Velthouse, B.A. (1990). Cognitive elements of empowerment: An interpretive model of intrinsic task motivation. *Academy of Management Review, 15*(4), 666–681.

Thompson, D.F. (1992, May/June). Paradoxes of government ethics. *Public Administration Review, 52*(3), 254–259.

Thompson, J.R., & Ingraham, P.W. (1996, May/June). The reinvention game. *Public Administration Review, 56*(3), 291–298.

Tichy, N., & Devanna, M.A. (1986). *The transformational leader.* New York: John Wiley & Sons.

Trevino, L.K. (1986). Ethical decision making in organizations: A person–situation interactionist model. *Academy of Management Review, 11*(3), 601–618.

Trevino, L.K. (1992, May). Moral reasoning and business ethics: Implications for research, education, and management. *Journal of Business Ethics, 11*(5), 445–464.

Triandis, H.C. (1995). A theoretical framework for the study of diversity. In M.M. Chemers, S. Oskamp, & M.A. Costanzo (Eds.), *Diversity in organizations* (pp. 11–36). Thousand Oaks, CA: Sage Publications.

Trice, H.M., & Beyer, J.M. (1993). *The cultures of work organizations.* Englewood Cliffs, NJ: Prentice-Hall.

Van Wart, M. (1996, November/December). The sources of ethical decision making for individuals in the public sector. *Public Administration Review, 56*(6), 525–533.

Victor, B., & Cullen, J.B. (1988). The organizational bases of ethical work climates. *Administrative Science Quarterly, 33*(1), 101–125.

Vinzant, J., & Crothers, L. (1996, December). Street-level leadership: Rethinking the role of public servants in contemporary governance. *American Review of Public Administration, 26*(4), 457–476.

Vinzant, J.C., & Vinzant, D.H. (1996, Summer). Strategic management and total qualilty management: Challenges and choices. *Public Administration Quarterly, 20*(2), 201-219.

Vizzard, W.J. (1995, July/August). The impact of agenda conflict on policy formulation and implementation: The case of gun control. *Public Administration Review, 55*(4), 341–347.

von Cranach, M., Doise, W., & Mugny, G. (Eds.). (1992). *Social representations and the social bases of knowledge.* Lewiston, NY: Hogrefe & Huber.

Vroom, V.H., & Yetton, P.W. (1973). *Leadership and decision making.* Pittsburgh: University of Pittsburgh Press.

Wagner, J.A., III. (1995, February). Studies of individualism–collectivism on cooperation in groups. *Academy of Management Journal, 38*(1), 152–172.

Waldman, D.A., Bass, B.M., & Yammarino, F.J. (1990, December). Adding to contingent-reward behavior: The augmenting effect of charismatic leadership. *Group and Organization Studies, 15*(4), 381–304.

Walker, M.U. (1992, Summer). Feminism, ethics, and the question of theory. *Hypatia, 7*(3), 23–38.

Walmsley, G.L. (1990). The agency perspective: Public administrators as agential leaders. In G. L. Walmsley, R. N. Bacher, C. T. Goodsell, P. S. Kronenberg, J. A. Rohr, C. M. Stivers, O. White, & J. F. Wolf (Eds.), *Refounding public administration* (pp. 114–162). Newbury Park, CA: Sage Publications.

Walton, R. E. (1985). From control to commitment in the workplace. *Harvard Business Review, 63*, 77–84.

Wayne, S. J., & Green, S. A. (1993, December). The effects of leader–member exchange on employee citizenship and impression management behavior. *Human Relations, 46*(12), 1431–1440.

Weber, C. M. (1997, Summer). A case study in U.S. government financial management in cross-disciplinary teams. *Public Budgeting and Finance, 17*(2), 80–88.

Weber, E. P., & Khademian, A. M. (1997, September/October). From agitation to collaboration: Clearing the air through negotiation. *Public Administration Review, 57*(5), 396–410.

Weber, M. (1987). Bureaucracy. In J.M. Shafritz & A.C. Hyde (Eds.). *Classics of public administration* (2nd ed.) (pp. 50–55). Chicago: Dorsey Press.

Weber, M. (1915/1996, June). The social psychology of world religions. Cited In O. Behling & J. M. McFillen, J. M. A syncretical model of charismatic/transforma-

tional leadership. *Group and Organization Management, 21*(2), pp. 168–169.

Weick, K. E. (1984, January). Small wins: Redefining the scale of social problems. *American Psychologist, 39*(1), 40–49.

West, J. P., & Berman, E. M. (1997, June). Administrative creativity in local government. *Public Productivity and Management Review, 20*(4), 446–458.

Whitener, E. M., Brodt, S. E., Korsgaard, M. A., & Werner, J. (1998, July). Managers as initiators of trust: An exchange relationship framework for understanding managerial trustworthy behavior. *Academy of Management Review, 23*(3), 513–530.

Wilson, P. A. (1995, Spring). The effects of politics and power on the organizational commitment of federal executives. *Journal of Management, 21*(1), 101–119.

Yank, G. R., Barber, J. W., & Spradlin, W. W. (1994, October). Mental health treatment teams and leadership: A systems model. *Behavioral Science, 39*(2), 293–310.

Yukl, G. A. (1994). *Leadership in organizations* (3rd ed.). Englewood Cliffs, NJ: Prentice-Hall.

Zand, D. E. (1997). *The leadership triad: Knowledge, trust, and power.* New York: Oxford University Press.

Zanna, M. P. (1994). On the nature of prejudice. *Canadian Psychology, 35*(1), 11–23.

CREDITS

INDEX

significance, 62
structure, 19, 72, 73, 82, 140
Taylor, Frederic, 14
Teams
Cognitive Style Inventory, 154–160
conflict types, 147–151
developmental stages, 144–146
exercise, 152–153
innovation, 213
and innovation, 205
introduction, 139–140
public sector accountability, 140–141
skills, 142–147
Technical consultation, 17
Teleological ethics, 221
Telling style, 74
Tennessee Valley Authority (TVA), 109
The Economy of Incentives, 15
Theory X and Theory Y, 58–59, 62
Tit-for-tat, 91
Top-down bureaucracies, 111
Total Quality Management (TQM), 17,
    51–53, 140, 210–211
Transactional leadership, 14–15, 29, 30, 33,
    203
Transformation processes, 110
Transformational leadership
charisma, 37, 39, 203, 204
and innovation, 130, 203–204, 210
and SLI, 29–30
Trust
in bias reduction, 130
and charismatic leadership, 204
in commitment, 23, 43
components, 91
and confidentiality, 93
in conflict resolution, 169
as essential to leaders' success, 73, 91
ethical issues, 95, 220, 224, 228
exercise, 101–102
in government, 99–100
levels of, 90, 92, 93
in motivation, 144
in organizations, 91, 94, 143, 165
participation dilemmas, 116
power sharing, 132

and prejudice, 128
promotion of, 94–95
self-disclosure and feedback, 93, 96–99
situational theories, 84
stakeholder inclusion, 117
synopsis, 89
Turning on the Tax Department, 64–67
TVA (Tennessee Valley Authority), 109
Tyranny, 22
Tyranny of agreement, 116

Undifferentiated style, 157, 160
Upward influence, 41
Upward mobility, 56
Ury, W., 167
U.S. Congress, 43, 57

Value, development of, 51
Values (*see* Ethical issues)
Venting and negotiation, 168
Visibility, 21
Vision
corporate, 109
and empowerment, 212
and ethical public leadership, 229
and innovation skills, 205, 209, 212
leaders as catalysts for, 130
as leadership skill, 143
process of developing, 206–207
shared, 116
and SLI, 30
strategic planning, 184
and transformational leadership, 203
Vroom-Yetton Normative Decision-Making
    model, 70, 76–79, 84
Vulnerability and interdependence, 94

When Tornadoes Hit: Shared Leadership
    Roles, 24–25
'Wicked' problems, 165
Work modules, 62–63
Worker anxiety, 80

Zero-sum power games, 43